Handbook of Pragmatics
26th Annual Installment

Handbook of Pragmatics

ISSN 1877-9611

Founding Editors
Jan-Ola Östman and Jef Verschueren (University of Antwerp)

Prepared under the scientific auspices of the **International Pragmatics Association (IPrA;** https://pragmatics.international).

IPrA Presidents

1987–1990: John Gumperz (Berkeley)
1991–1994: Sandra Thompson (Santa Barbara)
1995–1999: Ferenc Kiefer (Budapest)
2000–2005: Susan Ervin-Tripp (Berkeley)
2006–2011: Sachiko Ide (Tokyo)
2012–2017: Jan-Ola Östman (Helsinki)
2018–2023: Stephen Levinson (Nijmegen)

IPrA Secretary General
Jef Verschueren (Antwerp)

IPrA Consultation Board (acting as Editorial Board for the Handbook 2018–2023):

Nana Aba Appiah Amfo (Accra)
Charles Antaki (Loughborough)
Rukmini Bhaya Nair (Delhi)
Barbara Bokus (Warsaw)
Diana Boxer (Gainesvillle)
Charles Briggs (Berkeley)
Frank Brisard (Antwerp)
Winnie Cheng (Hong Kong)
Jenny Cook-Gumperz (Santa Barbara)
Pilar Garcés-Conejos Blitvich (Charlotte)
Anita Fetzer (Augsburg)
Helmut Gruber (Vienna)
Yueguo Gu (Beijing)
Susanne Günthner (Münster)
Hartmut Haberland (Roskilde)
Michael Haugh (Brisbane)
Janet Holmes (Wellington)
Sachiko Ide (Tokyo)
Cornelia Ilie (Malmö)
Shoichi Iwasaki (Los Angeles)
Helga Kotthoff (Freiburg)
Dennis Kurzon (Haifa)
Sophia Marmaridou (Athens)
Rosina Márquez-Reiter (Surrey)
Yael Maschler (Haifa)
Yoshiko Matsumoto (Stanford)
Michael Meeuwis (Gent)
Jacob Mey (Odense)
Maj-Britt Mosegaard Hansen (Manchester)
Melissa Moyer (Barcelona)
Neal Norrick (Saarbrücken)
Tsuyoshi Ono (Edmonton)
Jan-Ola Östman (Helsinki)
Salvador Pons Bordería (Valencia)
Marina Sbisà (Trieste)
Gunter Senft (Nijmegen)
Tuija Virtanen (Åbo)
John Wilson (Belfast)

Handbook of Pragmatics

26th Annual Installment

Edited by

Sigurd D'hondt
University of Jyväskylä

Pedro Gras
University of Antwerp

Mieke Vandenbroucke
University of Antwerp

Frank Brisard
University of Antwerp

John Benjamins Publishing Company

Amsterdam / Philadelphia

The paper used in this publication meets the minimum requirements of the American National Standard for Information Sciences – Permanence of Paper for Printed Library Materials, ANSI z39.48-1984.

DOI 10.1075/hop.26

ISBN 978 90 272 1439 3 (HB)
ISBN 978 90 272 4923 4 (E-BOOK)

© 2023 – John Benjamins B.V.
No part of this book may be reproduced in any form, by print, photoprint, microfilm, or any other means, without written permission from the publisher.

John Benjamins Publishing Co. · www.benjamins.com

Table of contents

Editors' note	VII
User's guide	XI

Handbook A–Z

Activity types and pragmatic acts *Jacob L. Mey*	3
Crossing *Jürgen Jaspers*	21
Dell Hymes and communicative competence *Paul V. Kroskrity*	47
Directives (with a special emphasis on requests) *Nicolas Ruytenbeek*	67
Heteroglossia *Martina Björklund*	95
Michael Alexander Kirkwood (M.A.K.) Halliday *Jonathan James Webster*	111
Wakimae *Yoko Yonezawa*	127
Cumulative index	155

Editors' note

This year's Annual Installment of the *Handbook of Pragmatics*, the 26th edition, contains two articles about scholars who made a lasting impact on the field: the first charts the legacy of Dell Hymes, with a specific focus on communicative competence (Paul V. Kroskrity), the second is dedicated to M.A.K. Halliday, the pioneer of what is now known as Systemic Functional Linguistics (Jonathan James Webster). In the other articles, a variety of pragmatic topics is dealt with. First, the late Jacob Mey looks back at how he arrived at the concept of "pragmatic act" and examines how it relates to "activity type". Related to the same topic, another article looks at directive speech acts and requests (Nicolas Ruytenbeek). Two articles are concerned with linguistic diversity and address the question of how multilingualism influences speech practices. One addresses the sociolinguistic concept of crossing (Jürgen Jaspers), while the other traces the origins of Bakhtin's notion of heteroglossia and examines how it is reshaped in current research on (multilingual) discourse (Martina Björklund). The volume concludes with an article on the Japanese concept of *wakimae* or "discernment" (Yoko Yonezawa).

This installment of the *Handbook of Pragmatics* is the second one prepared by the new editorial team, which took over after Jan-Ola Östman and Jef Verschueren handed over this task in 2022. For those less familiar with the Handbook, a few words about its history and development may be useful here.

When Jan-Ola Östman and Jef Verschueren launched the idea of a **Handbook of Pragmatics** under the auspices of the **International Pragmatics Association** (IPrA; https://pragmatics.international) in the early 1990s, they wanted to create a format that would be endlessly moldable for and by the readership. The very essence of scientific research is that scientific insights are dynamic, guided by uncertainty. In a field like pragmatics, with the functioning and use of constantly changing styles and registers of language as its focus of research, they did not want to produce a single book as the ultimate 'handbook of pragmatics'. Since they saw this venture as a task that would take decades, if they wanted to do it properly, what they did not want either was to start with categories and traditions beginning with "A" and after a couple of decades finally reaching "Z".

At that time, Jan-Ola and Jef settled for a loose-leaf publication format, relatively unorthodox in the humanities and social sciences. The idea was that this would enable the editors to gradually build up a changeable and expandable knowledge base for the users of the Handbook. Moreover, each individual reader would be able to group and re-group the entries according to their own preferences and particular interests, which no doubt would themselves be changing over time. So, with every three or four annual installments of the Handbook, the subscriber received a new ring binder in which to collect and order the new entries. The series of loose-leaf installments was preceded in 1995 by a hardback bound **Manual**, which provided background information on a wide range of traditions and research methods underlying much of the pragmatic research described in the more topical entries of the annual installments. Needless to say, this background information has evolved as well and has necessitated numerous new entries on traditions and methods in the loose-leaf installments. So far, 23 installments of the Handbook of some 300 pages each have been published, in addition to the 658-page Manual. Subscribers to the printed version of the *Handbook of Pragmatics* should have a bookshelf filled with the Manual plus 7 ring binders.

Meanwhile, the world has gradually become more and more digital. In the early 1990s hardly anyone could have foreseen the radical changes that have come to take place on the publishing scene. The *Handbook of Pragmatics* quickly followed suit, went online, and is available for readers as, precisely, the *Handbook of Pragmatics Online* (https://benjamins.com/online/hop/). The online version has been continuously updated with new materials whenever and as soon as a new installment of the Handbook was published; and in cases where an entry has been totally rewritten, the older version has been retained in the Archive – all in the interest of giving readers a feeling of how the discipline itself has changed and evolved over the decades.

Meanwhile, the online version has become the most often used version of the Handbook, both by individual scholars (especially by members of the International Pragmatics Association) and by many of the institutions and universities they are affiliated with. The loose-leaf version on paper was seldom subscribed to by individuals, but we are happy to say that it did attract the interest of university libraries and research groups. It is, however, challenging for libraries to make loose-leaf versions of books available for the general readership in a shape where all leaves/pages are physically "a-loose".

Faced with this situation, Jan-Ola and Jef decided in close concertation with John Benjamins Publishing Company to produce further installments of the *Handbook of Pragmatics*, from the 21st onwards, in the form of bound volumes, of which the one you are now holding in your hands is the sixth. We are convinced that this makes the Handbook easier to handle and more attractive not only for libraries, but also for individual scholars who cherish the sensation and satisfaction of perusing a physical book. Meanwhile, the online version continues to integrate all additions and changes.

The gist of the User's Guide for the *Handbook of Pragmatics* and its online version largely remains the same as before – see below. As in the loose-leaf version, we have a cumulative index (at the end of each volume), covering not only the present installment, but linking it to the entire *Handbook of Pragmatics*.

Acknowledgments

A project of this type cannot be successfully started, let alone completed, without the help of dozens, or even hundreds, of scholars. First of all, there are the authors themselves, who have sometimes had to work under harsh conditions of time pressure. Further, members of the IPrA Consultation Board have occasionally, and some repeatedly, been called upon to review contributions. Countless other colleagues, too many to list, have provided essential input as well by reviewing manuscripts.

The former editors (as well as the present ones) want to make sure that the contribution made by the co-editors of the Manual and the first eight annual installments of the Handbook is not forgotten: Jan Blommaert[†] and Chris Bulcaen were central to the realization of this project. Similarly, Eline Versluys acted as editorial assistant for a five-year period ending in 2009. Our sincerest thanks to all of them.

Last but not least, the new editorial team wants to express its deepest appreciation for the people who started it all and who are responsible for carrying on the Handbook project for almost 30 years: Jan-Ola Östman and Jef Verschueren. They are an inspiration for all of us to remain honest and rigorous in our academic work.

Meanwhile, we hope the 26th installment of the Handbook will continue to serve your needs and inspire your future work.

Jyväskylä & Antwerp, September 2023.
Sigurd D'hondt, Pedro Gras, Mieke Vandenbroucke and Frank Brisard, editors

User's guide

Introduction

For the purpose of this publication, *pragmatics* can be briefly defined as *the cognitive, social, and cultural study of language and communication*. What this means exactly, and what it entails for the scientific status of linguistic pragmatics, was explained in detail in the introductory chapter, 'The pragmatic perspective' by Jef Verschueren, of the **Manual** (*Handbook of Pragmatics: Manual*, edited by Jef Verschueren, Jan-Ola Östman & Jan Blommaert, 1995).

The overall purpose of the **Handbook of Pragmatics** is that it should function as a tool in the search for *coherence*, in the sense of cross-disciplinary intelligibility, in this necessarily interdisciplinary field of scholarship. The background of the Handbook and its historical link with the International Pragmatics Association (IPrA), as well as its basic options, were described in the preface to the Manual. The Handbook format, although described in the same preface, will here be presented anew in this **User's Guide** for the sake of clarity.

The **Handbook of Pragmatics** will continue to be available *online* (see https://benjamins.com/online/hop). The printed version will continue to be expanded with *new articles* and will also incorporate *revised versions* of older entries. *Updates* that require minimal changes will be published only in the annual online releases. In addition, *Highlights* from the Handbook have been published in ten thematically organized paperbacks (in 2009, 2010, and 2011; cf. https://benjamins.com/catalog/hoph), making the contents accessible in an affordable way for use as practical teaching tools and reading materials for a wide range of pragmatics-related linguistics courses focusing specifically on general pragmatic, philosophical, cognitive, grammatical, social, cultural, variational, interactive, applied, or discursive aspects, respectively.

The Handbook format

In addition to the main body of the Handbook (including the topics listed under *Handbook A-Z* in this volume), the **Handbook of Pragmatics** contains three distinct types of articles:

i. *Traditions*: Major traditions or approaches in, relevant to, or underlying pragmatics, either as a specific linguistic enterprise or as a scientific endeavor in general. Collectively, the articles in this section give an overview of the traditions and approaches in question, with historical background information and a description of present and potential interactions with other traditions or approaches and the field of pragmatics as a whole.
ii. *Methods*: Major methods of research used or usable in pragmatics or pragmatics-related traditions.
iii. *Notational systems*: Different kinds of notational systems, including the most widespread transcription systems.

The main body of the *Handbook* (represented in this volume by the section *Handbook A-Z*) consists of articles of various sizes, organized around entry-like keywords, alphabetically organized. They range in generality: some provide a general overview of a particular field (which cannot be captured under the label of a 'tradition'; see above), others discuss a specific topic in quite some detail. They present a state-of-the-art overview of what has been done on the topic. Where necessary, they also mention what has not been dealt with extensively (e.g. acquisitional and diachronic aspects), thus suggesting topics for further research. Important research in progress is mentioned where appropriate. In addition, some references to major works are given.

A different type of article in the body of the Handbook (listed separately as 'Linguistic scholars' in the online version) is devoted to the contributions made by an individual influential scholar and may contain interesting biographical information as well.

The Handbook attempts to document pragmatics dynamically. Consequently, a *loose-leaf* publication format was initially chosen for maximum flexibility and expandability (see the Editors' Note above) – properties that are even more characteristic of the **Handbook of Pragmatics Online**, which has therefore taken over that specific functionality to the point of rendering the loose-leaf printed format superfluous and replaceable by bound annual installments. By definition, there is no point in time when it is possible to say that the Handbook will be complete, though a reasonably comprehensive overview could be said to have been obtained after the eighth annual installment published in 2002, so that from then onwards, in addition to further *expansion*, there have been regular *revisions* and (in the online version) *updates* of older contributions. In the case of articles that are being replaced completely, the older versions are kept in the Archive section of the online version.

Even though we have given up paper publication in loose-leaf format, the very idea of continuous flexibility and expandability is retained. Being a vibrant field, pragmatics sees new openings and coherent subfields emerging constantly. Thus, most annual installment of the **Handbook of Pragmatics** will naturally also contain entries on such new directions of research.

About the cumulative index

At the end of each printed annual installment of the *Handbook of Pragmatics*, you will find a complete index, with all necessary cross-references to ensure easy access to the available information (which continuously accumulates over the years). The index thus does not only contain references to concepts and matters to be found in the annual installment at hand, but cross-references to all Handbook entries that have appeared in the *Handbook of Pragmatics*. Needless to say, this cumulative index is also continuously updated in the online version of the Handbook, under the heading 'Subjects,' where it also contains direct links to relevant articles.

In addition to references to specific Handbook entries, the index also contains lists of terms which are not used as entry headings but which do occur as alternative labels in the literature, with an indication of where exactly the topics in question are treated in the Handbook.

Handbook A–Z

Activity types and pragmatic acts

Jacob L. Mey

Editors' note: In this Handbook entry, the late Jacob Mey addresses a central, if not the most central, issue in pragmatics: how, and on what basis, do language users come to regard certain utterances as actions? It documents a personal journey through the field that eventually resulted in the formulation of key notions such as pragmatic act *and* pragmeme. *The entry opens by revisiting Levinson's notion of* activity type *(1979), drawing attention to the role that the social situation plays in this process; because of this, action can never be explained exclusively in terms of a limited number of pre-existing categories, as is the case in classical speech act theory. From there, the text moves on to pointing out how certain types of actions may be specific to a particular social situation, and how actions may in turn be implicated in dynamically bringing about and defining situations. Next, this structuring role of the situation is elaborated in a discussion of indirect speech acts, and of the impossibility of imposing a priori constraints on the range of context-dependent meanings that can be inferred from them. Eventually, this leads to the formulation of a* pragmatic concept of speech act, *or* pragmatic act *for short. Intersubjectivity, then, is guaranteed by the* pragmeme *that these pragmatic acts instantiate (see also Allan 2019). The latter stands for a form of "generalized pragmatic act" (Mey 2001: 221) inspired by Trubetzkoy's notion of phoneme, which is defined here as "[a mapping of] situations onto individual activities" (ibid.) that sets out the interactional affordances available in a particular situation and that allows the interactants to mutually adapt to that situation.*

We received this manuscript in October 2022. Jacob passed away on February 10, 2023, before the process of refereeing and submitting revisions had been completed. The reader will quickly notice that it is far from a finalized paper. Hence, it still contains occasional omissions that would need fixing, there remain minor ambiguities to be resolved, and overall, the tone is more playful and more personal than some would expect from a Handbook entry. However, given the circumstances we have decided to publish this first draft without much polishing, or as Oliver Cromwell put it, "warts and all". We made this decision, first, because the text gives an introduction to the notion of pragmatic act that will be of great value to students and those who are new to the topic. Equally important, however, is the fact that it offers a fascinating insight into the thinking of one of the key scholars who helped to shape the field of pragmatics.

https://doi.org/10.1075/hop.26.act2
© 2023 John Benjamins Publishing Company

1. A bit of history

Back in the early seventies of the past century, linguists and philosophers seriously had begun to consider the emergent field of pragmatics as an independent field of scientific interest, and the term *pragmatic* was no longer considered an iconoclastic tool, allowing young hotspurs to "break down the walls" of historically validated and valued divisions between the individual humanistic disciplines.

So, when I was about to deliver a pragmatically-oriented paper at the XIth International Congress of Linguists in Bologna, 1972, I had (in an attempt to ward off prima-facie objections and terminological remonstrations) chosen to call my contribution "Some Practical Aspects of a Theory of Performance", choosing the innocuous term *practical*, rather than the (actually more appropriate) *pragmatic*, and using the Chomskyan buzzword *performance* to put some of the theoretically oriented linguists' minds at rest (published as Mey 1974; see also Mey 1979).

As for pragmatics itself, on returning to Denmark from Texas in the early seventies, I finally announced a course in "Pragmatics", to be delivered at my new place of work, the University of Southern Denmark (then still called Odense University). In my very first semester of teaching there, I had offered a course in "Syntax", basically regurgitating the well-known and by then somewhat trite Standard Theory developed by Noam Chomsky and his followers in the sixties and seventies; the students seemed happy, and the faculty clearly presumed there was something in it for them too, as I had a fair number of colleagues from the language departments among my hearers listening to my lectures while smoking their cigarettes (and even the odd cigar...).

At that time, the only way I could teach pragmatics properly was by making it a cross-departmental elective, which could be taken for credit if a department was willing to include it in its curriculum. But even with the departments of Nordic Languages and that of Linguistics supporting my initiative, I still had to look for a proper text to teach from, and since no such text was available (both Levinson's *Pragmatics* and Leech's *Principles of Pragmatics* didn't appear until 1983), I had to forge ahead on my own, making up the course as I went.

Among the results of these initial efforts was my production of a more practical (not to say pragmatic) manuscript, called *Whose language?* – a work that ended up as a manuscript of its own (Odense University 1976, mimeographed and bound, 1979), and finally published in book form by John Benjamins as Mey 1985).

In addition, I started to work on a condensed Danish version of Levinson's 1983 *Pragmatics*, when this finally became available; I was going to use my hand-written and partially typed-up notes for my own pragmatics course. In the end, the notes coalesced into a preliminary version of what I hoped would be a useful book for teachers of the newfangled discipline. However, the work's initial title, *Out of the Waste-Basket*, given in homage to the Grand Old Man of pragmatic studies, Yehoshua Bar-Hillel, and his early and influential article (1971) would have to go – given that, as a potential publisher remarked, "nobody was going to buy a book out of a wastebasket!"

During a summer study stay in Japan, 1983, while my project was still in its advanced planning phase, I had mentioned its "proto-existence" to my colleague and friend Harumi Sawada, of Shizuoka University. Harumi asked me to collect my notes and translate them into English, so he could use them in his own teaching. This I did – however the allusion to Bar-Hillel's humorous characterization of the extant work in pragmatics as a collection of odds and ends left over from real linguistic research, was abandoned – what I had thought was a pretty smart title could have turned into a built-in suicide device, as my publisher-in-spe had warned me earlier.

Then, in the fall of 1985, out of the blue, I received a phone call from Peter Trudgill, who (in fluent, accent-free Eastern Norwegian) had informed me of the interest that the publisher Basil Blackwell had shown in a book like the one I was working on – which Peter then generously offered to shepherd through the production process. The result, my *Pragmatics: An Introduction* (1993), proved to be a useful tool for the kind of teaching that both Harumi Sawada and myself had in mind (Harumi arranged for it to be translated into Japanese, where it went through several editions at Hitsuji Publishers in Tokyo). The book also served as the vehicle, especially in its second (2001) edition, for some of the concepts I had started to formulate in the first printed version and had used in my own teaching and writing, and whose subsequent corrections, reflections, and adjustments are included in the 2001 version.

Nevertheless, one small mystery remains. While I was working on what was going to be this first edition of *Pragmatics*, it had occurred to me that Stephen Levinson, one of my primordial sources of inspiration, perhaps would have some more to say on the topic of *activity types* – the subject of his earlier (1979) article in Mouton's soon to be defunct journal *Linguistics*. I was astonished not to find a single reference to the subject in the index to Levinson's 1983 book; I did manage to locate the place, where he (without naming his earlier work explicitly) briefly discusses the concept of activity type in the context of Dell Hymes' notion of *speech event* and Wittgenstein's *language game*; Levinson 1983: 278–281).

Possibly, at the time of writing his *Pragmatics*, Levinson did not put too much weight on the concept he had mentioned a few years earlier, but it would not be until 1992 that the work finally got its due attention by being included in Paul Drew and John Heritage's (1992) edited collection *Talk at Work: Interaction in Institutional Settings* – a title that well reflects the ideas presented in Levinson's article, by both confirming the validity of Searle's original distinction between *speech acts* and *speech activities*, and illustrating Levinson's own, corresponding insight that speech activities, such as the "questioning" in the quoted examples cannot be captured by simple notions such as speech acts *per se* (Levinson 1979: 393–394).

A complementary insight from the same author confirms that "Wittgenstein's failure to distinguish between speech acts and speech activities was not just an oversight: the two are connected in such fundamental ways that only a thorough-going pragmatic theory will be adequate to describe both phenomena" (Levinson 1979: 366) – except that describing alone won't do either: we have to be offered an explanation into the purchase.[1]

On a final note, it may be illuminating to compare Levinson's somewhat restrictive wording in his 1983 *Pragmatics* (pp. 279ff) with his original 1979 text, quoted here in full:

> A systematic set of constraints on language use are examined, namely those governing the roles and functions that language is expected to play within specific kinds of social activity. These constraints are the source of inferences that are activity specific. This level of pragmatic organization is then shown to have important repercussions for the concepts of speech act and conversational implicature. Both the nature of *speech acts* and the application of Grice's maxims are dependent on the nature of the *activity* in which talk is conducted.   (Levinson 1979: 365; italics mine)

Notice that the expression in Levinson's 1979 text, "based on the nature of the activity", now appears as "based on the social situation that the talk is conducted within" (Levinson 1983: 279) – maybe "things they have been a-changin'"?

2. From speech activity to social situation

A distinction such as the one between *speech* acts and *pragmatic* acts may not be the final word on the matter; still, it may serve to both affirm the "interconnection" and mark the "distinction" – the latter is not always observed in the ways we speak about activities and acts. In addition, many languages do not have specific terms for 'speech acts' as items realized in the lexicon. Some of the relevant terms are ambiguous between 'word' and 'act', as in the Latin *verbum*, or the Hebrew *dabar*, in contrast to the English term 'verb', used for a particular class of words; other languages have developed (or defined by linguistic *fiat*) a special lexical term for the verbal act as such, denoting the 'activity' that in other languages is expressed by earmarked terms. Thus, just as Dutch has *werkwoord* (lit. 'work word') to denote a 'verb' (in contrast to the Dutch lexeme *woord*, for 'word' *simpliciter*), Czech uses *sloveso* for 'verb', in contrast to *slovo*, 'word'; the term *sloveso* is explicitly defined in the Czech grammatical literature as 'denoting an activity', not as expressing a simple *act*; cf. *slovesa vyjadrují dej* ('verbs express [the/an] activity'; Niederle et al. 1956: 225).

---

[1]. In addition, neither is there any mention of the concept in Levinson's next major work (2000); though one might argue that the subject might be less suitable in a context determined by mostly linguistically-based discussions about generalized vs. particular conversational implicatures.

A further terminologically relevant (and not merely historically interesting) issue arose when my colleague Istvan Kecskes, thinking along similar lines, developed the important concept of *situation-bound utterances* (SBU), which he defined as being somewhat different from that embodied in my "pragmatic acts" (Kecskes 2010). Correct as his observation may be, still, given that there is a difference, it behooves us to examine it, and see if it does "make a difference". The fact that an SBU refers to the situation in which the utterance is performed is certainly a point in its favor, as the SBU explicitly connects us to the social context. Utterances need this context in order to make proper sense: "utterances are assigned their functions on the basis of the social situation that the talk is conducted within" (Levinson 1983: 279; cf. 1979: 366). But there is more.

In his 1979 article, Levinson also refers to a transcript from a Manchester, UK police interrogation, in which the officer tries to establish that the claimant in a rape case is actually responsible for the incident, given that she "confesses" to not being a virgin, having "had two men", while being "seventeen and a half" (Levinson 1979: 381). The point here is that the elicited statements and the police reformulations in fact *frame* the utterances as part of a scenario in which the claimant is portrayed as a woman of low moral standing. The police officer's utterance, "And you are seventeen and a half?", emphasizes the situational character of the utterance: from stating or questioning an innocent fact, it starts conjuring up a picture of irresponsible teenage lasciviousness. While stating a seemingly neutral fact, and asking a simple question (to which he already had the answer), the questioner appeals to a familiar, pre-existing picture, which not just is *statically* "bound to the situation", but in effect, *dynamically* interprets and *defines* it. In other words, it is an SDU, a *situation-defining utterance*, not just an SBU, a *situation-bound utterance*. In Levinson's 1983 terminology, the undefined "activity" is now replaced by the actual, "social situation", conform with the commonly established fact that all speech activity, basically and in principle, is *social* activity.

3. "Indirect" speech acts: Existential problems?

Imagine that you are living on the streets of Oslo, Norway, having been evicted from your apartment for non-payment of rent. It's 6:31 am on a regular weekday, and you have finally managed to find a bench to stretch out on and catch some sleep. The bench is located on Oslo's main thoroughfare, Karl Johan Street, some distance down from the National Theatre, in a small public park named *Studenterlunden* (lit. 'The Students' Grove'). Also, since you consider yourself (perhaps non-active, but still) a student, you may even feel a certain allegiance-cum-ownership to the park and its benches.

Next thing you know, you are rudely awakened by a park police officer shining a flashlight in your face and proclaiming that *klokka er seks tretti-en* (Norwegian for 'it's 6:31 a.m.'). Being a student and a competent user of Norwegian, who knows his pragmatics and perhaps even remembers Grice and his Maxims, still, although you may feel tempted to point out to the policeman that you have a watch on you and know what time it is, you realize that such a move would be extremely counterproductive in the situation at hand. You understand that the policeman's "naked" quoting of the time of day is nothing less than an *indirect speech act*: rather than being simply an informative, albeit a trifle solemn announcement of the time of day, the "social situation" (here: police officer addressing a presumed homeless vagrant) indicates that something else is being communicated. The indirect speech act at play actually represents a *warning*, or even something more serious (a fairly common sequel to the "informative act" in question could be the police uttering *og du er arrestert* ('and you are under arrest'): in Norway, as in many other countries, the activity [sic] of sleeping on a park bench embodies a misdemeanor that may lead to a citation or even an arrest.

4. From indirect speech acts to pragmatic acts

Indirect speech acts do not tell us what they are; they represent "acts that do not speak their name." The officer, in the extract above, made no reference in his first, indirect utterance to either police ordinances, city bylaws, park usage rules, normal civil behavior, and so on; by contrast, the second utterance is a "real" speech act, fitting into one of the so-called "canonic" slots for such acts (Searle 1975: 66 et passim). In the same work, however, Searle alludes to a potential infinity of understandings, by stating that:

> an utterance in context can indicate the satisfaction of an essential condition [on the act in question] without the use of the explicit illocutionary force indicating device [IFID] making it clear that the condition is satisfied.... Thus, for example, the sentence 'Could you do this for me?' is not characteristically uttered as a question concerning your abilities; it is characteristically uttered as a request   (Searle 1969: 68)

In fact, *Could you do this for me? is* essentially an *indirect* act of requesting a favor, masquerading as a tentative question about a possibility.

Taking the matter one level up, Levinson (1983) remarks that theoretically, there is no limit to the number of activities an indirect speech act may refer to. Having stated that "one could construct an indefinitely long list of ways of requesting an addressee to shut the door" (1983: 264), the author then comes up with an admittedly not "indefinitely long", but still impressive list of the numerous ways that are available at first sight: each of the seven options on the list contains from two to five variants on this fascinating theme (Levinson 1983: 264– 265). Likewise, the Israeli linguist Dennis Kurzon, writing on the speech act of *incitement*, observes that "any utterance may constitute an act of incitement if the circumstances are appropriate for such an interpretation" (1998: 28).

Traditionally, in classical speech act theory, an act of speaking that does not fall into one of the pre-established categories and/or "crosses over" into another act's domain, is dubbed "indirect". For instance, if I want somebody to close the window, I could say *Shut the window*, using a "bald" imperative (which is considered impolite in English); however, as Anna Wierzbicka has observed, the Polish literal equivalent, *zamknij okna*, is not felt to be impolite at all (1985: 156–157). Even so, normal English speakers would prefer to use a "circumlocution" (to borrow Charles Dickens' expression)[2] such as *Would you mind closing the window* (a question of a kind), or even using locally standardized formulas like *A window is either open or closed* (a statement), or *Some people never learn* [viz., to close windows] (an observation) – or other *passe-partout* expressions, applicable indiscriminately to a number of situations. As Levinson remarks, "we seldom use the imperative to express a request" (1983: 254); instead, in English (and many other languages), we use an *indirect* expression. And indeed "most usages [of requesting, etc.] are *indirect speech acts*" (Levinson *ibid.*; italics original).

On another note, it does not help, as has sometimes been suggested, to consider this kind of indirect speech as based on mere "idiomatic" uses of language. The idea that SDUs, SBUs and their likes are simply unrecognized "idioms" (a notion that was current in the early seventies) has been roundly gainsaid by Levinson, who points out that it would lead to an unnecessary multiplication of entities (such as adding a *please* every time an "indirect" force has been detected (1983: 269) – a clear violation of Occam's time-honored razor principle).

We may take this line of thought a bit further by considering a well-known objection. If pragmatics is primarily about how people use language, then the door would be wide open for all sorts of interpretations of all kinds of utterances; and where do we stop? Here is an example I have been using elsewhere (Mey 2001: 207ff.).

Imagine that in your local alternative weekly (such as the *Chicago Reader*, or the *Austin Chronicle*), you come across an advertisement for a particular restaurant, called "Sweet Alice". The ad contains a happy customer's remark, saying: "I brought home some sushi and cooked it; it wasn't bad" (Mey 2001: 207; actually from the *Chicago Reader*, August 21, 1992). The owners of the restaurant clearly were using this (actually found, not imagined) customer recommendation to promote their business; however, at first sight, this makes no sense at all. Obviously, sushi can be taken home, provided the restaurant in question has a sushi bar and lets you wrap up your purchase and possible leftovers; but that's not the point of the text. An obvious clash of meaning is involved here: sushi is not supposed to be cooked, so any reference to "cooking" is either misplaced, misleading, or plain ridiculous, when read against the backdrop of "normal" speech act practice. In Searle's terminology, this speech act of advertising fails ("misfires", Austin would have

---

2. Cf. Dickens' "Office of Circumlocution" (from his *Little Dorrit* (1855–1857), a work in which he (not too "indirectly") mocks the rampant bureaucracy of 19th century England).

said), and the perlocutionary effect could at best be a shrug, at worst a modicum of irritation at the hearer's end.

Consider now an alternative way of looking at this piece of text, by invoking its particular *context*. Given that the phrase above occurs in an advertisement for what probably is a popular cocktail bar (observe the indirect reference to Arlo Guthrie's classic, then ubiquitous hit, *Alice's restaurant*), we have to imagine this special context as a venue where things are said and done that normally might not be accepted elsewhere. An utterance like the one quoted here could be emblematic for precisely such an untraditional venue, by implication evoking the environment in question as a place where certain norms are relaxed, and the customary constraints on behavior and speech are significantly loosened. In addition, the ad text would imply this kind of environment as being suited for people with a need to relax from the strictures of normal city life; such readers would feel that "Sweet Alice's restaurant" was just their kind of place – and consider themselves invited to join the madding crowd.

In this way, the quoted sentence helps *define*, even mentally construe, Arlo Guthrie's original *Alice's Restaurant*, the virtual "location" to which the reader is being implicitly invited (the song has "we're just around the bend", implying 'we're your close by, uninhibited kind of people'). The special, contextually construed *pragmatic* act of "inviting" is specific for this bar environment; one could perhaps call the implicit reference in Guthrie's song an "alternative SBU", to remain in Kecskes' terminology, or even an "alternative SDU", in mine.

The advertisement speaks clearly to its readers, no matter how ridiculous it may appear to the general grammarians or semioticists, with their need for stringent rules and watertight classifications. Most importantly, the clash of meaning, embodied in the merger of the *sushi* and its alleged *cooking*, is not to be explained away by appealing to some established linguistic or philosophical practice of argumentation. Quite the contrary: the very silliness of the ad duly invokes the relaxed "silliness" of the bar scene in general (where you don't "proclaim" or preconize, or expound your proprietary theory on subatomic particle like the boson, unless you already are on your way to a Nobel prize). Normal people using everyday language, will simply identify with the context, and take the "silly" phrase at face value – not as given or uttered in a truth-conditional or truth-conditioning environment, but as an invitation to join the fun, relax, and be silly: an emergency hatch providing an escape away from the humdrum of normal life.

Precisely in this sense, the quoted phrase's wording can function as a particular, *pragmatic act* of advertising – not your usual canonic speech act (Mey 2001: 207 ff.) But if this is true of our bar case, then it potentially applies to all use of language – not in words alone or by acts of "Yes" or "No",[3] but by acting pragmatically. Rather than restricting

---

3. "Let your communication be, Yea, yea; Nay, nay: for whatsoever is more than these cometh of evil" (Matthew 5:37).

ourselves to speech acts and their classification, we should boldly move on to pragmatics and talk about *pragmatic* acts.

As the Berkeley anthropologist Bill Hanks once remarked, "meaning arises out of the interaction between language and circumstances, rather than being encapsulated in the language itself" (1996: 266). What is being *done* by the words is more important than what the words by themselves *say* – which may vary endlessly: compare the many ways we have of inviting someone to "sit down", "close the window", and so on, as we saw earlier. But this interaction can only result in successful communication if the situation and its participants are on the same page, that is, if the participants are willing to "grasp" the situation, even before they try to express themselves and react appropriately to what is coming from the other participants.

Here, one might suggest that "jumping to conclusions" is not always a bad idea, provided of course that the "jump" is *affordable*. Since "we only can (and do) understand what we can afford to hear" (Mey 2001: 221), indirect, pragmatic speech acting is typically an instance of situational *affordability*, to use a term created by the psychologist James J. Gibson (1979). And, as far as explanation goes, pragmatics does not try to explain speech activity from the inside out – "from words having their origin a sovereign speaker, and going out to an equally sovereign hearer" (Mey 2001: 221). A pragmatic explanation is *inductive* in the original sense, that is, it works from the outside in: the focus is on the environment, the situation, where both speakers and hearers find their affordances. In this sense, all speech acts have of necessity to be treated as *pragmatic acts*.

5. Practs and IPRAs

Individual pragmatics acts (sometimes called IPRAs; Mey 2002: 221) are realized as instantiations of what, using an analogy from phonology, I have called a *pragmeme*. They build on what is "existing between speakers" (Voloshinov 1973; quoted in Capone 2010: 2974), rather than on conditions and rules valid for individual speech acts. But also, inasmuch as they exist "between speakers", they embody the communicators' individual and social backgrounds, which may be different for the actual instantiations of a particular pragmeme, called *allopracts* (Mey 2001: 220–221), however without diminishing their common reference and understanding. This is in explicit analogy to phonemes, which may be realized via multifarious phonetic avatars, dressed up in rather different phonetic garb without losing their intelligibility, as in the case of the Portuguese Brazilian /r/, discussed frequently in the literature as an example of a phoneme with a considerable divergence on its phonetic baseline, ranging all the way from a velar or guttural fricative [h], to a palatal fricative [x], to an apical trill [r].

Voloshinov's idea that pragmatic acts are something "existing between speakers" should be extended to encompass not just the vocal aspect of our communicative behavior. What traditionally is missing in many scientific accounts of the interactivity in human communication is the *bodily* aspect. In effect, *body language* is a powerful tool in communication; I venture to say that in the theory of pragmatic acting, the corporeal aspect serves not only as an illustration of, or a "handmaid" to, the data of conversation analysis; it is an integral part of the interaction, in the shape of a *bodily pragmeme*. In other words, the concept of the pragmeme should be understood as wide-ranging – in fact, wide enough to encompass all the bodily aspects of the interaction, including those that traditionally are called "gestures", and not excluding a proper understanding of various gaits and garbs as potential ways of pragmatic acting.

As a popular Norwegian proverb has it, *en kjenner lusa på gangen* ('one knows the louse by its moving'), just as we recognize the human bodies moving in the frenzy of the mosh pit as expressing an authentic "metal" or other "hard rock" identity and attitude. We do not want to restrict these options to the transmission of a certain *verbal* communication (like gestures often have been interpreted as mainly serving or complementing oral messaging). The conversation analysts have early been aware of this, but due to their restrictive methodology, their approach has not been universally accepted or even tolerated, given that conversation analysts in principle (though not always in practice) reject the introduction of non-conversationally documented social features or facts.

Going back to the original source of the term *phoneme* (see, for example, Trubetzkoy 1939: 7), it seems natural to follow the Prince's lead of looking at the phoneme as an overarching *functional* unit of expression, encapsulating under its label all of the various realizations (*allophones*) that function in the same way and with the same meaning. But also, if the pragmeme is considered as a *function*, rather than as another isolated descriptive unit of, or even a slightly superfluous addition to, the already overcrowded linguistic terminological vocabulary, it behooves us to ask what the term *function* really stands for, and how it applies to the pragmeme and its functional allopracts.

Generally, as in mathematics or in business, a function relates one set of items to another set, as in the case of two independently defined national currencies (this particular function usually goes by the name of "exchange rate"). As for pragmatics, the pragmeme maps situations onto individual human activities; for instance, in the extensively studied and often quoted example of the *promise*, the pragmeme in question maps the static conditions and dynamic potential of the environment onto the act of the person issuing a promise. These conditions refer not just to what can be, or is actually said; they map out the actual affordabilities of the user *vis-à-vis* the environment, thereby creating an interactivity-based way of operating.[4]

Actually, this way of looking at promises, and by extension, at pragmatics and pragmemes, involves a mutual *adaptation* to the environment. Through the pragmeme of

---

4. Perhaps one should speak of an *operation* rather than of a *function*, if one wants to be in tune with received formal terminology.

promising, promiser and promisee are adapting to one another by using the functionally appropriate allopracts under the conditions of their shared situation. Seen in this light, the pragmeme, as an adapting function, becomes an *ecological* activity; the pragmeme, by its functional character of two-way adaptability, is the expression of a pragmatic view on sustainability, and as such, a major potential actor in the ecological debates current in our real, not only our verbal, world.

By adopting the mutual adaptability feature as its main defining function, the concept of the pragmeme as both "adapting" and "adaptable" (Mey 2006) seems eminently suitable to serve as a framework for the often conflicting views presented by environmental debaters focusing on isolated aspects of the current ecological crisis; here, the choice of words seems often more important than their pragmatic functions as parts of a given pragmeme. Far from being an "ivory tower"-bound, more or less abstract set of speculations, the theory of pragmatic acts points to a better understandable and more manageable way of dealing with existential problems of which the purely linguistic debates are no more than symptomatic reverberations – something which is aptly illustrated by the pragmatic acts and activities occurring in a well-known historical intermezzo, with its pragmatic activity of negotiation, to be recounted in the following.[5]

6. Negotiation in Hebron A.D. 3000: A pragmeme at work

Negotiating often takes the form of what is called *hedging*, understood as a way of indirect speaking that on the surface seems neutral, but is used to conceal, or set aside for further treatment, any undecided or controversial (but negotiable) matter. Hedging techniques of this kind (such as about the price to be paid for a piece of land) are timeless and near-universal, as seen from a negotiation that occurred about 3,000 years ago. in the plains of Mamre, in biblical Palestine.

It is often said (and certainly more frequently thought) that in business interaction, "anything goes", provided the goals of the partners to the interaction are met. For this reason, it is important to know exactly what kind of speech and other pragmatic activities facilitate this "going" and make for a felicitous outcome of the interaction. The following illustration of the time-honored *pragmeme of negotiation* may help clarify matters.

The scene is probably familiar to many, and not only in the Eastern or Western world. The Old Testament patriarch Abraham, a nomadic chief from Chaldaea, who had temporarily settled in Canaan with his "house", meaning his wives, offspring, servants, animals, and other livestock, just lost his favorite wife of many years, the "hundred and

---

5. For a schematic illustration of the pragmeme/allopract operation, see the schema on p. 222 of Mey (2001).

seven and twenty years old" Sarah (Genesis 23:1) in a place called *Kirjat-Arba*, 'the town of the Four',[6] today better known as Hebron, in the part of Palestine that currently (for political reasons) is referred to as the "West Bank" of the river Jordan.

The entire episode is recounted in chapter 23 of the Judeo-Christian Bible's First Book of Moses (also referred to as *Genesis*), in which Abraham is negotiating with a local "son of Heth" (a "Hittite", as we too would call him today) named Ephron, the son of Zohar, who owns a piece of land that Abraham wishes to purchase as a "burying place" for his deceased wife, "out of my sight". To which "the children of Heth" (the Hittites) tell Abraham, in a very diplomatic and elaborate response "in the audience of the children of Heth", that for him, as a "mighty prince among us", "none of us shall withhold from thee his sepulchre", and: "in the choice of our sepulchres bury thy dead" (Genesis 23:6) – which of course is not exactly what Abraham had in mind.

After the obligatory acknowledgment in the next turn, Abraham feels the need to make his wishes clear by saying, while "[bowing] himself to the people of the land," even to the children of Heth", that if they really are serious about the matter, they should "hear me" and intreat for me to Ephron the son of Zohar" (Genesis 23:7–8).

In other words, having first been told that "no one of us shall withhold from thee this sepulchre" (note the vagueness of this diplomatic response: nothing definite is forthcoming, in this bland, impersonal general statement), Abraham now asks the "audience" to actually intervene and put some pressure on Ephron, a local chief and land-owner, to allow him, Abraham, to buy the land, rather than having to put away his wife in a "cloudily titled" piece of property with (as in the case of a foreign owner) uncertain legal status. And to make himself perfectly clear as to his honest intensions, Abraham calls up the elephant eternally present in any negotiation, money, by stating "that he may give me the cave of Machpelah, which he hath, which is in the end of his field; for as much money as it is worth he shall give it to me for a possession of a buryingplace amongst you" (Genesis 23:9; note the continued willful vagueness of the interchange).

Ephron then repeats his intention to let Abraham "have the land", but (again) using an ambiguous expression, *to give*, without mentioning any of the money involved in the gift. Instead, he actually seems to stress the actual "giving" by using a negative injunction, along with a solemn, threefold request to be taken seriously on the "giving", by uttering: "Nay, my lord, hear me: the field give I thee and the cave that is therein I give it thee; in the presence of the sons of my people give I it thee: bury thy dead" (Genesis 23:11).

Abraham, picking up on the ambiguity of Ephron's use of *give* in "the field give I thee" (especially, the uncertainty with regard to the financial aspect), wants to be clear about the money issue that is implicitly present in most negotiations. In a lengthy monologue, he launches into an explicit review and reframing of the process so far:

---

6. "The Four" were the mighty robber baron named *Arba* (a Hebrew word meaning '4') and his three "giant" sons (see Numbers 13:22).

"[Abraham] spoke unto Ephron in the audience of the people of the land, saying, But if thou wilt give it, I pray thee hear me: I will give thee money for the field; take it of me, and I will bury my dead there" (Genesis 23:13). The earlier financial uncertainty is now being replaced by a direct reference to *purchasing* the field, albeit with a repeated vagueness on Abraham's part with regard to the actual amount of money involved.

It is only at this point that the Hittite can be certain that there *will* be a deal, and that he need not be afraid to lose out on it; yet he, too, is indirect in his reply by (casually, one might say) mentioning some essential monetary information: "the land is worth four hundred shekels of silver" – just in case you need to know, as it were. Ephron immediately "downgrades" the pecuniary part of the deal, including the actual amount quoted, by saying: "What is that betwixt me and thee?" – a typical rhetorical question, followed by the final accept of the offer and Ephron's concession to let Abraham "bury therefore thy dead" (Genesis 23:15).

Upon recognizing that Ephron had been purely ceremonial in his pretending that "money has got nothing to do with it," even Abraham is now clear with regard to the precise interpretation of the "giving". And since he no longer is in doubt as to the exact conditions of the agreement about to be concluded, Abraham fulfills his part of the deal by publicly counting out the exact amount specified by the Hittite: "and Abraham weighed to Ephron the silver, which he had named in the audience of the sons of Heth, four hundred shekels of silver, current money with the merchant" (Genesis 23:16).

In the concluding act, the personal contract between Abraham and Ephron is duly made official ("promulgated", as one might say, using a modern term; Mey 2001:126) "in the presence of the children of Heth, before all that went in at the gate of his [Ephron's] city" (Genesis 23:18). And finally, the text summarizes the course of events and their legal conclusion, by telling us that "Abraham buried Sarah his wife in the field of Machpelah before Mamre: the same as Hebron in the land of Canaan" (Genesis 23:19), and that this accord was "made sure unto Abraham for a possession of a burying place by the sons of Heth" (Genesis 23:20).[7]

7. Concluding remarks

Pragmatic thinking has historically moved between two poles: on the one hand, there was the linguistic-philosophical tradition, starting with figures such as Pierce and Frege, and continued through the classical works by Peirce, Saussure, Austin, Searle, Grice, Levinson, and Wilson, to name a few; this was followed by later developments taking off

---

[7] In the Appendix, I will list (by Genesis 23, chapter and verse) the various (allo-)practs coming successively into function in this negotiation.

on "practical" studies in "applied" fields such as anthropology, cultural studies, conversation analysis, discourse studies, technology, and a bevy of other practice-oriented works focusing on the use and misuse of language in society, both overall and in its various subsections: technical, medical, political, business, juridical, and so on.

Some of the workers in these fields have been known to have worn different "hats" from time to time; thus, Stephen Levinson trained and initially worked as an anthropologist, whereas researchers such as Asa Kasher, Jay Atlas, Kasia Jaszczolt, Alessandro Capone, François Recanati and many others have kept their links to philosophy and analytic thinking alive and well. What is most interesting in this development is the way several junior scholars, both in the West and in places like Africa and China, have picked up on the most recent developments, and have started to work with notions such as the pragmeme. Compare also the multiple forays into cultural and anthropologic linguistics undertaken in Anna Wierzbicka's school of *cross-cultural pragmatics* and *cultural scripts* (see, for example, Wierzbicka 1994, 2003), by researchers from various fields whom each have steered a proper, independent, and highly successful course outside of the traditions of learning mentioned above.

As to the pragmeme itself, it has proved to be a useful complementary theoretical tool, apt to gather and systematize various strands of early and current pragmatic thinking, witness the various contributions to volumes such as Allan et al. (2016); Capone and Mey (2016), and the various studies that have accumulated over the past decades in the usual venues (such as *Pragmatics and Society, Journal of Pragmatics, Pragmatics, Pragmatics and Beyond*, and elsewhere), and offered by researchers as far apart, geographically or by approach, as are Akin Odebunmi in Nigeria, Etsuko Oishi in Japan, Mary Bucholtz in the US, Yueguo Gu in China, Michael Haugh in Australia, Jonathan Culpeper in the UK, Yan Huang in New Zealand, Claudia Caffi in Italy, Dennis Kurzon in Israel and many others.

In this connection, it makes special sense to note that one of the above-mentioned scholars, Etsuko Oishi, in her clever analysis-cum-comparison of Searle's speech acts and my pragmemes (Oishi 2016), has observed that, when all is said and done, it is still the *situation* that characterizes, and actually defines, the discourse elements that appear in it. While this is certainly correct, it should be added (as Oishi herself does in the final part of her insightful article) that the speech situation could be better described as one of "discourse" – thereby underlining the participants' reciprocal generation of meaning. Oishi also remarks that when "Mey develops the theory of [pragmemes], it is the 'categorization' which constitutes the major stumbling block" (2016: 339). However, if one appeals to the *reciprocal* (sometimes called *dialectic*) character of the pragmeme, as different from the *speech activity types* that Levinson as early as 1979 wrote about, and if one abandons the idea of the situation as a stationary, one-of-a kind, photographically representable "snapshot" – the mirage that Ferdinand de Saussure was one of the first theoreticians to let himself be tempted by – the apparent "stumbling" block dissolves.

The concept of the pragmeme thus allows for a more comprehensive view on, and explanation of, human interaction, both verbal and otherwise – something that already was adumbrated by Stephen Levinson in his early, at the time not properly acknowledged study (1979) – a discussion of which was the starting point of the present work.

Concluding, then, let me again underline that the *subsumption* of various different allopracts under the same pragmeme allows us to include accessory levels of expression, containing the various features concomitant to the supposedly unique *real* thing: the speech activity, as produced by the rule-conforming speakers/hearers and described and enforced by the professional analysts. At the end of the day, in the *real* world (as Ludwig Wittgenstein has taught us in his very first written production), "language is a form of life" (Wittgenstein 1922: § 19).

References

Allan, Keith. 2019. "Pragmemes." In *Handbook of Pragmatics 22 Annual Installment*, ed. By Jan-Ola Östman & Jef Verschueren, 199–202. Amsterdam: John Benjamins Publishing Company.

Allan, Keith, Alessandro Capone and Istvan Kecskes (eds.) 2016. *Pragmemes and Theories of Language Use*. Cham: Springer.

Bar-Hillel, Yehoshua. 1971. "Out of the pragmatic waste-basket." *Linguistic Inquiry* 2: 401–407.

Capone, Alessandro. 2010. "Barack Obama's South Carolina victory speech." *Journal of Pragmatics* 42: 2964–2977.

Capone, Alessandro & Jacob L. Mey (eds.). 2016. *Interdisciplinary Studies in Pragmatics, Culture and Society*. Cham: Springer.

Drew, Paul & John Heritage (eds.) 1992. *Talk at Work: Interaction in Institutional Settings*. Cambridge: Cambridge University Press.

Gibson, James J. 1979. *The Ecological Approach to Visual Perception*. Boston, Mass.: Houghton Mifflin.

Hanks, William F. 1996. "Language form and communicative practice." In *Rethinking Linguistic Relativity*, ed. by John Gumperz and Stephen C. Levinson, 242–270. Cambridge: Cambridge University Press.

Kecskes, Istvan. 2010. "Situation bound utterances as pragmatic acts." *Journal of Pragmatics* 42: 2889–2897.

Kurzon, Dennis. 1998. "The speech act of incitement". *Journal of Pragmatics* 29 (5): 571–596.

Levinson, Stephen C. 1979. "Activity types and language." *Linguistics* 17: 365–399. [Reprinted as Levinson, Stephen C. 1992. "Activity types and language." In *Talk at Work*, ed. by P. Drew and J. Heritage, 66–100. Cambridge: Cambridge University Press.

Levinson, Stephen C. 1983. *Pragmatics*. Cambridge: Cambridge University Press.

Levinson, Stephen C. 2000. *Presumptive Meanings: The Theory of Generalized Conversational Implicature*. Cambridge, Mass.: The MIT Press.

Mey, Jacob L. 1974. "Some practical aspects of a theory of performance." In *Proceedings of the Eleventh International Congress of Linguists*, ed. by Luigi Heilmann, 111–125. Bologna: Il Mulino.

Mey, Jacob L. 1979. "Introduction' & 'Zur kritischen Sprachtheorie" [Towards a critical theory of language]. In *Pragmalinguistics: Theory and Practice*, ed. by Jacob L. Mey, 9–17 & 411–434. The Hague, Paris & New York: Mouton.
Mey, Jacob L. 1985. *'Whose Language?' A Study in Linguistic Pragmatics*. Amsterdam & Philadelphia: John Benjamins.
Mey, Jacob L. 2001 [1993]. *Pragmatics: An Introduction* (Second ed.). Oxford & Malden, Mass.: Blackwell.
Mey, Jacob L. 2006 [1998]. "Adaptability in Human-Computer Interaction." *Concise Encyclopedia of Pragmatics*. (Second ed.), ed. By Jacob L. Mey, 7–13. Oxford: Elsevier.
Niederle, Jindrich, Václav Niederle & Ladislav Varcl. 1956. *Mluvnice reckého jazyka*. Praha: Státní Pedagogické Nakladelství.
Oishi, Etsuko. 2016. "Austin's Speech Acts and Mey's Pragmemes." In *Pragmemes and Theories of Language Use*, ed. by Keith Allan et al., 2016: 335–350. Cham: Springer.
Searle, John R. 1969. *Speech Acts: An Essay in the Philosophy of Language*. Cambridge: Cambridge University Press.
Trubetzkoy, Nikolaj S. 1939. *Grundzüge der Phonologie* (Fundamentals of Phonology). Prague: Travaux du Cercle Linguistique de Prague, vol. 1.
Voloshinov, Valentin V. 1973. *Marxism and the Philosophy of Language*. Cambridge, Mass.: Harvard University Press.
Wierzbicka, Anna. 1985. "Different languages, different cultures, different speech acts." *Journal of Pragmatics* 9 (2/3): 145–178.
Wierzbicka, Anna. 1994. "Cultural scripts: A new approach to cultural analysis and cross-cultural communication.". In *Pragmatics and Language Learning Monographs*, ed. by Martin Pütz, 5: 1–14.
Wierzbicka, Anna. 2003 [1991]. *Cross-Cultural Pragmatics; The Semantics of Human Interaction* (Second ed.). Berlin: Mouton de Gruyter.
Wittgenstein, Ludwig. 1922 [1921]. *Tractatus Logico-Philosophicus*. London: Kegan Paul.

Appendix.   The pragmeme of negotiation in Genesis 23

The list below provides an overview of the agents and the successive allopracts of negotiation, as they occur in Genesis 23 (by chapter: verse) and naming them in the order in which they appear (along with their agents).

Agents

A: Abraham
H: Hitttite(s)
E: Ephron
N: Narrator

Allopracts (arranged by Chapter: Verse)

23: 1 (N) Narrative framing: Sarah's passing
21: 2 (N) Historic framing: Abraham in Kiryat-Arba
23: 3 (A) Announcing his errand & original Request
23: 4 (A) Pleading for Sarah's burying place
23: 5 (H) Replying formally
23: 6 (H) Evasive responding, wrong offer
        ('take your pick of our sepulchres')
23: 7 (A) Debasing himself strategically
23: 8 (A) Gainsaying &
        (repeated) Request to H, mediated by H to E
23: 9 (A) Specified request &
        Offer of money (unspecified)
23: 10 (E) Evasive response
23: 11 (E) Offer of "giving [Abraham] the burying place"
23: 12 (A) Renewed self-debasing
23: 13 (A) Offer to E of (unspecified) money for buying cave & Repeated pleading by A
23: 14 (H) Acknowledging A's pleading
23: 15 (H) Specifying exact value of land to A &
        Pretending money not important "betwixt us"'
23: 16 (A) Depositing exact amount of silver ("400 [old] *sheqalim*")
        [No haggling by A]
23: 17 (H) Confirming the deal: Naming land, trees, etc. that are included in deal
23: 18 (H) Adding legal weight by
        Promulgating the deal ("making sure unto Abraham in the presence of the children of Heth")
23: 19 (N) Report of A burying Sarah in cave (now "possessed by A in field before Mamre")
23: 20 (N) Legal recording of "making sure" by H of A's rights to Sarah's (and A's own future) "buryingplace"

Crossing

Jürgen Jaspers
Université Libre de Bruxelles

1. Introduction

Crossing is one of the sociolinguistic concepts that have been proposed since the 1990s to describe the multilingual practices of mostly young, multi-ethnic, working-class speakers in Western urban contexts. It draws specific attention to:

> code alternation by people who are not accepted members of the group associated with the second language that they are using (code switching into varieties that are not generally thought to belong to them). This kind of switching involves a distinct sense of movement across social or ethnic boundaries and it raises issues of legitimacy which, in one way or another, participants need to negotiate in the course of their encounter.
> (Rampton 1995b: 485)

By focusing on practices that raise questions of entitlement, crossing offers more than a sociolinguistic riff on the themes of hybridity, masquerade, and the carnivalesque that, inspired by Bakhtin's work (1981), made a furore across the social and cultural sciences since the 1980s. Indeed, crossing in its original conception certainly referred to the improvised, spectacular, and often jocular code alternation practices of multi-ethnic youth which occurred during moments when the restraints of ordinary life were temporarily relaxed. But the concept was also meant to underline the rather sharp ethnic and class-based restrictions on who could experiment with which varieties when, where, and in whose presence. The genuine sense of peer group belonging that crossers pursued in the study that first attended to their behaviour (Rampton 1995a) was equally difficult to reconcile with the scholarly interest in irony and pastiche at the time, inspired by postmodernist critiques of totalising narratives and universal ethical objectives. The notion of crossing, then, in its original sense but also in its later inflections, does not merely serve to highlight speakers' transgression of social and linguistic boundaries; it also emphasises a continued observance of these boundaries, an awareness of the wider social, ethnic, and class structures that keep these boundaries in place, and a sense of anomaly and precariousness when the transgression occurs. Crossing, in short, highlights how people weave a linguistic path between a sense of togetherness and a sensitivity to difference and conflict.

https://doi.org/10.1075/hop.26.cro1
© 2023 John Benjamins Publishing Company

Since its original study, inspired by the vibrant linguistic practices of young people in the UK (Rampton 1995a, 1995b), crossing has given a massive impetus to the study of multi-ethnic adolescent speech practices in a great many Western urban settings. It has, in addition, stimulated a great deal of research into how these speech practices are influenced by or contribute to public discourses, popular culture, and media representations of migrant neighbourhoods and/or ethnicity. To be sure, it is not overstated to claim that the emergence of crossing on the sociolinguistic scene caused quite a furore of its own. This was not just because of Rampton's innovative, wide-ranging, and impressively detailed focus on practices that were hitherto only sparingly attended to. His discussion of these practices also provided an exceptional meeting place for strands of research as diverse as variationist and interactional sociolinguistics, ethnography, second language acquisition research, conversation analysis, code-switching research, Goffmanian sociology, Bakhtinian heteroglossia studies, language ideology research, ethnic and racial studies, and language education policy. The study of crossing thus offered a multifaceted, conceptually luxurious, and empirically firmly rooted lens for exploring socially situated language use and learning processes, and for analysing how speakers negotiate race stratification, ethnic inheritance, and established language ideologies. In that light the study of crossing itself at that time transgressed existing disciplinary boundaries, integrating insights into sociolinguistics that were not generally thought to belong to it in order to destabilise established explanations for code alternation, language learning, and ethnicity. Yet, while one can scarcely overrate the pioneering character of this work and its impact on subsequent analyses of young people's language use, there is also a sense in which, like other scientific concepts, crossing has to be seen as the product of its time. Rampton's study was not the only indication of a growing scientific interest in ethnic and racial rather than class differentiation since the 1980s (see, e.g., Gillborn 1988; Gilroy 1987; Hewitt 1986; Mac an Ghaill 1988; Mirza 1992; Wright 1992), and it was published in the immediate, optimistic, post-Cold War years when cultural and national boundaries were opening up or were at least discussed in liberating terms. The question is therefore what relevance crossing has today, almost 40 years after the first data that motivated its conception were collected, in a world where the experience of ethnic and racial differences has become relatively more mundane, and where debate about national boundaries and cultural differences has acquired fairly different overtones. To address these issues, I will first go into the original study of crossing before explaining how crossing can be distinguished from similar phenomena. I will then address crossing's generality, applicability, and durability to indicate how Rampton and others have revised the concept so as to explain present-day experiences of (in)security as well as the formation of new urban vernaculars.

2. Crossing: The original study

Crossing, also code-crossing, emerged from Rampton's (1995a [2005]) study of the linguistic practices of ethnically mixed young people in the UK. It is based on ethnographic fieldwork carried out in 1984 and 1987 among nearly 60 11-to-16 year olds with diverse backgrounds (Caribbean, Pakistani, Anglo, Indian, and Bangladeshi), although most of these youngsters had been born in the UK. The fieldwork was carried out in Stoneford (a pseudonym, like other fieldwork-related names that follow), a town with a population of about 100,000 in the South Midlands of England which had experienced a considerable labour migration history after WWII, first from Europe and later, from 1958 onwards, from the West Indies, India, and Pakistan. This history had had a substantial impact on the population of Southleigh, the state middle school in the working-class neighbourhood (Ashmead) where the research was carried out: at the time of the fieldwork, the school counted 9% of pupils of African-Caribbean descent, 20% Anglo, 12% Bangladeshi, 28% Indian, and 28% Punjabi. There was a general tendency among pupils to socialise with peers of the same sex and ethnic descent, but school and peer recreation were also important places for ethnic mixing and male-female interaction compared to these youngsters' homes and the adult communities they were familiar with.

Ashmead's linguistic ecology included the use of Standard English at school and minority languages like Punjabi in adolescents' homes and community centres. But Rampton focuses on adolescents' use of varieties that are not really "theirs": uses of Punjabi by youngsters of Anglo and Caribbean descent, the use of English-based Creole by youngsters of Anglo and Asian descent, and the production of Stylised Asian English by all three groups. This focus was inspired by prevalent sociolinguistic assumptions at the time. To oppose leading ideas in twentieth-century linguistics that language variation was no more than a chaotic surface feature of an underlying, more fundamental, grammatical system, sociolinguists had been seeking to demonstrate the regularity of linguistic variation, the grammaticality of non-standard speech as well as the impact of linguistic variation on the linguistic system overall. Yet they adopted in the process from their opponents the view that this regularity and competence were the product of speakers' early socialisation in stable community networks of which they were the authentic, native, representatives. Consequently, inter-ethnic interaction tended to be understood as a site for intercultural communication where people expressed the distinctive speech styles they had inherited from their communities, potentially facing communicative breakdown if these styles diverged too much. Alternatively, such interaction was identified in a more agentive way as a site where interlocutors could downplay or accentuate their ethnolinguistic background, depending on situational needs and demands. Such a view still assumed, however, that ethnicity was the most significant feature of speakers' lives, it left no space for the possibility of adopting a different ethnicity, and it saw reflexivity about ethnicity as an analyst's privilege rather than a capacity of speakers themselves (Rampton 1995b: 486–487; cf. Cameron 1995: 15–17).

Such a *linguistics of community* (Pratt 1987) failed to do justice to what Rampton observed in his ethnographic data. He noticed that youngsters in their multi-ethnic peer group (1) espoused varieties that were not usually associated with their ethnic backgrounds and did so in improvised, imperfect, and self-conscious ways; that (2) these youngsters often did not seek to increase their expertise in these varieties but enjoyed the experience of "their own exclusion from groups that they actually like[d] and interact[ed] with daily" (Rampton 1995b: 489); and that (3) these youngsters were not merely (de)emphasising inherited ethnolinguistic identities but were using these *and* a range of institutional and interactional ones (joker, games player, pupil, learner, friend, attractive member of the opposite sex, etc.) as resources for the construction of innovative, temporary or more enduring, local allegiances. Analysing these phenomena requires what Pratt called a "linguistics of contact" (1987: 59ff.) which expands the study of language variation to across-group interaction; to impromptu, faulty, and quasi-uses of language; to language use which is marked by speakers' interaction with contexts outside the home (social and public media, local communities, other families, and so on); and to speakers' navigation of a whole range of local and less-local discourses of language and identity rather than merely ethnic ones (cf. Rampton & Charalambous 2012).

This linguistics of contact did not merely have analytical relevance, as a lens with which to address a set of linguistic phenomena that had unfortunately slipped through the disciplinary nets. By drawing attention to a greater variety of meanings around ethnicity and race than were commonly recognised in established discourses, and to how adolescents in their interactional practices recognised ethnolinguistic difference without suppressing it, Rampton argues that this approach also points up the political potential of crossing: without containing an explicit or coherent political message, crossing revealed "a sense of the historic emergence of new allegiances, cross-cutting kinship descent, reworking inherited memberships" (Rampton 1995b: 487) – what Hall (1988) referred to as "new ethnicities". Such emergent allegiances may, if they crystallise into more enduring practices, eventually reorganise macro-ideological trends and political structures. Rampton's study does not contain a full investigation of this political potential, though, and it is important to see that it also allows to draw conclusions that go in the opposite direction. Indeed, the scholarly value of his work is that the capacity of crossing to destabilise established discourses on language and ethnicity did not invite him to emphasise transgression at the expense of boundary maintenance. We shall see in the next section that his analysis rather insists on the continuing tension between cross-ethnic peer-group allegiances on the one hand, and, on the other, adolescents' keen observance of established ethnolinguistic groups.

3. Crossing in action

Let us turn to some examples of crossing – each reproduced from Rampton (1995a) – to see how partial linguistic skills can be a source of mutual enjoyment and contribute to the formation of a peer culture which remains internally fragmented and distinguished from other groups. The first example involves crossing into Punjabi (transcription conventions are available at the end of this chapter):

Example (1) Ray the cool
Participants: Raymond [13, mixed Anglo/Afro-Caribbean descent, male; wearing radio-mike], Ian [12, Anglo descent, male], Hanif [12, Bangladeshi descent, male], others. *Setting*: 1984. Coming out of lessons into the playground at break. Ian and Ray are best friends. Stevie Wonder is a singer whose song 'I just called to say I love you' was very famous. Ray has a bad foot, cf. line 17.   (reproduced from Rampton 1995a: 171–172)

```
1   Ray:     IA::N::
2   Hanif:   (                   )
3   Ian:     ((from afar)): RAY THE COO:L RAY THE COO:L
4   Hanif:   yeh Stevie Wonder YAAA ((laughs loudly))
5   Ray:                [it's worser than that
6   Ian:     ((singing))[I just called to say
7   Hanif:   ha (let's) sing (him) a song
8   Ian:     I hate you
9   Hanif:   ((loud laughs))
10  Anon:    ((coming up)):(      ) are you running for the school
                      (.)
11  Ray:     huh
12  Anon:    are [you running for the school=
13  Ray:         [no
14  Anon:    =[I am
15  Ian:     [he couldnt run for th-he couldnt [run for the school
16  Ray:                                       [SHUT UP=
17  Ray:     =I couldn- I don wan-[I can't run anyway
18  Hanif:                        [right we're wasting our [time=
19  Ian:                                                   [I did=
20  Hanif:   =[come on     (we're) wasting our time=
21  Ian:      [you come last (     )
22  Hanif:   =    [mʌmʌmʌ:]
23  Anon:         [I came second
24  Ian:     ((singing)):I just called to say [I got      [a big=
25  Ray:                                      [I hate you [
26  Ian:     =[lʊlɬɑ:] ((Panjabi for 'willy'))
27  Hanif &  ((loud laughter))
    others
28  Ray:     ((continuing Ian's song)): so's Ian Hinks (1.5)
29           ((Ray laughs)) no you haven't you got a tiny one (.)
30           you've only got (a big arse)
```

This example illustrates how Ian, with Anglo background, uses Punjabi, mixed with some Stevie Wonder song lines, to direct jocular abuse at his friend Ray. Although Ian in lines 6–8 seems to adopt the first person character in the song, lines 24–26 suggest he is now speaking as if he were Ray, which Ray appears to confirm in line 28 by pointing out that it is not just him who is well-endowed. We can also see that Ian's use of Punjabi in line 26, just when Ray anticipates Ian's completion of his phrase, is appreciated by his peers (line 27), and that Ray's own riposte in line 28–29 is somewhat less successful.

Rampton's point about such examples is that Ian was not a fluent speaker of Punjabi and neither sought to become one, and that this makes Ian's switch to Punjabi difficult to explain as a form of unobtrusive code-switching as is observable among fluent bilinguals. In fact the occurrence of Ian's Punjabi in the punchline of a piece of jocular abuse that was heartily received rather illustrated its conspicuous nature as well as its embeddedness in and contribution to a jesting-and-joking based friendship among male adolescents of different ethnic groups.

Ian's limited knowledge of Punjabi was itself a condition on being an effective and accepted crosser, Rampton argues. Becoming too good at speaking Punjabi went against the much-valued practice where youngsters of Anglo or Afro-Caribbean descent were invited to say things in Punjabi. Since these phrases often contained elements that those who were unfamiliar with Punjabi did not understand, temporary learners often incriminated themselves, which Punjabi speakers found very entertaining. Punjabi learners in their turn had the double opportunity of showing interest in their friends' linguistic background and proving that they could take a joke and treat this as a basis for mutual enjoyment rather than offense-taking. "The rudimentary Panjabi [sic] L2 learner was a significant and enjoyable local identity", Rampton underlines, taken up by adolescents who "didn't want to improve their proficiency in Panjabi, and who were evidently quite happy to remain permanently as pre-elementary language learners" (1995b: 505). Such findings are opposed to the idea in much L2 research that language learning generates anxiety or that learners eventually seek to increase their competence. Speakers' limited skill in other varieties and their orientation to non- or multi-ethnic identities equally contrasts with the overall focus in code-switching research, Rampton argues, where attention has mostly gone to competent code-switching in bilingual in-groups and to the role of such switching in speakers' downplaying or manifesting of a single ethnic identity.

A limited competence was equally evoked in switches to a Stylised Asian English (SAE): an English marked by deviant verb forms, the omission of auxiliaries, copulas, and articles, abrupt intrasentential pitch raises, diphthongs which are realised as monophthongs and by an often significant change in loudness, pitch, speed of delivery and voice quality, among others (Rampton 1995a: 68). Here is one short example:

Example (2) Outside with a drink
Participants and setting: Razia [15, female, Pakistani descent, wearing radio-microphone] and two friends [female, Pakistani descent] are walking around outside. They see a small Asian boy bringing a drink out of the canteen (this was explained retrospectively by the participants). Mr Cogan is the deputy head-teacher.   (reproduced from Rampton 1995a: 144ff.)

```
1   Raz:   you're not allowed outside with a drink
2   A:     ((high pitched)) OI COME INSIDE COME IN COME IN (HERE)
3   B:     ((high pitched)) (   )'MISTER ,CO ,GAN ,CATCH "YOU
                            [mistə   keʊgan   kætʃ   ju]
4   Raz:   see look at 'at (.)
5   A/B:   what (.) (      )
6   Raz:   he just dropped it oh my go:d (26.0)
```

In this example we can see Raz and her friends (A and B) orient to an impropriety (lines 1–3), at first in ordinary, vernacular English (lines 1–2), before a switch to exaggerated Asian English occurs in line 3. This critical SAE, in fact, occurred on various other occasions and Rampton suggests, based on Goffman's (1971) work on remedial interchanges, that adolescents' switches to a variety which stereotypically evokes limited linguistic and cultural competence helped account for the perceived offence as a symptom of someone's overall behaviour: by addressing the boy in SAE, a variety that flagged incompetence, Raz and her friends were treating him as if his behaviour stood for an overall ignorance of social norms and, thus, limited responsibility. This treatment has the effect of a sanction or, if the boy is slow to pick up on the hint or is out of earshot, symbolically compensates for the infraction and unites the offended in their joint recognition of proper behaviour.

Such examples may intimate that crossing was a form of uncomplicated linguistic mixing and borrowing, but Rampton draws attention to a range of constraints and avoidance strategies. Inheritors of Punjabi responded less positively than in Example (1) to crossing in that variety if crossers failed to distinguish between "safe" and "dangerous" crossing, and this also held for adolescents' use of SAE and Creole. First of all, crossing as a practice was off-limits for posh whites from other neighbourhoods as well as for youngsters who had recently migrated from Bangladesh and who were seen as socially inferior by the focal group. Those who were allowed to cross, second, generally avoided doing so in certain contexts: black and white adolescents did not target SAE to Punjabi-speaking friends, whereas most whites and youth of Asian descent avoided using Creole when among black peers or only did so in very restricted ways.

This avoidance was partially inspired by pejorative representations in public discourse of Asian people as inept and servile and of Blacks as virile and threatening: making free use of the varieties associated with each group raised the spectre of colour-blind appropriation or racist parody. So, thirdly, those who could and did cross, tended to produce their crossing in the margins of ordinary social behaviour, what Rampton, based on Turner's (1974) work, calls liminal moments:

> at the boundaries of interactional enclosure, in the vicinity of delicts and transgressions, in self-talk and response cries, in games, cross-sex interaction and in the context of performance art [...] in moments when the constraints of everyday life were relaxed.
> (Rampton 1995a: 281)

One implication of this is that, in those situations that youngsters treated as normal, relatively stable relations were imagined between language use and ethnic inheritance: "this counters any temptation to see young people's language crossing as a successful collective effort to eliminate wider patterns of ethnic stratification and division, at least within the protected boundaries of peer group recreation" (Rampton 1995a: 197). A second implication is that increasing one's expertise in or use of other-ethnic varieties was found fairly remarkable. This was not entirely off limits, but it required a display of genuine and long-term commitment, like close friendship or romance, besides the gradual embedding of other-ethnic variety features as ordinary elements of one's routine vernacular.

Crossing into Punjabi and SAE had a different symbolic resonance than crossing into Creole: Punjabi constituted a new linguistic territory which promised enjoyment and adventure for those moving into it, while SAE represented a migration history that adolescents wished to distance themselves from. So, crossing into Punjabi and SAE usually signalled that speakers were not speaking as themselves. This was different for Creole, which was found attractive, if not 'the future language', on account of its association with assertiveness, quick-wittedness, and opposition to authority. These different resonances also emerged when adolescents interacted with adults, as the next example shows:

Example (3) ATTENTION BENJAMIN
Participants: Asif [15, male, Pakistani descent), Kazim [15, male, Pakistani descent], Alan [15, male, Anglo descent], BR [the researcher, 30+, male, Anglo descent). *Setting:* 1987. An interview, in which Ben is struggling to elicit some retrospective participant commentary on extracts of recorded data, and is on the point of giving up.

(reproduced from Rampton 1995a: 115–117; cf. also Rampton 2011a; Harris and Rampton 2002: 39–44)

```
1   BR:       right shall I- shall we shall we stop there
2   Kazim:    no
3   Alan:     no come [on carry on
4   Asif:            [do another extract
5   BR:       le- lets have (.) [then you have to give me more=
6   Alan:                       [carry on
7   BR:       =attention gents
8   Asif:     ((quieter)): yeh [alright
9   Alan:     ((quieter)):          [alright
10  Asif:     ((quieter)):          [yeh
11  BR:       I need more attention
12  Kazim:    ((in SAE)): I AM VERY SORRY BEN JAAD
                          [aɪ æm veri sɒri ben dʒɑːd]
13  Asif:     ((In SAE)): ATTENTION BENJAMIN
                          [əthenʃɑːn bendʒəmɪn]
14                [((laughter))
15  BR:       [right well you can- we cn-
16  Alan:     [BENJAADEMIN
17  BR:       we can continue but we er must concentrate a bit
18            [more
19  Asif:     [yeh
20  Alan:     alright    [(go on) then
21  Asif:     ((in SAE)): [concentrating very hard
                          [kɒnsəstretɪŋ veri ɑr]
22  BR:       okay right
23            ((giggles dying down))
24  Kazim:    ((in SAE)): what a stupid (    )
                          [vʌd ə stupɪd     ]
25  BR:       ((returning the microphone to what he considers to be
              a better position to catch all the speakers)):
              concentrate a little bit-
26  Alan:     alright then
27  Kazim:    ((in Creole)): stop movin dat ting aroun
                             [dæt tɪŋ ərɑun]
```

```
28  BR:      WELL YOU stop moving it around and then I'll won't
29           need to (.)    r[ight
30  Kazim:  ((in Creole)): [stop moving dat ting aroun
                                        [dæʔ tɪŋ əraʊn]
31  BR:     right okay  [ right
32  Kazim:              [ BEN JAAD
33  Alan:   ((laughs))
34  BR:     what are you doing
35  Alan:   ben jaa[ad
36  BR:            [ well leave (    ) alone
37  Kazim:  IT'S HIM that ben jaad over there
38  BR:     right
            ((BR continues his efforts to reinstitute the
            listening activity))
```

Examples like these illustrate the overall reflexivity of Rampton's work: they present the fieldwork as a social practice which could entail tedium, mutual impatience, and mocking,[1] and they show that the activity of information retrieval itself can be turned into a pertinent object for analysing adult-adolescent interaction. By revealing that adolescents at times had the upper hand in the proceedings, such examples at least symbolically compensate for the asymmetry between adolescents and researchers. Rampton shows, moreover, that data which are marked by the *observer paradox* still offer valuable research opportunities: Example (3), and perhaps the preceding and subsequent parts of the interview, could not be seen as a reliable source for truthful commentary; but it revealed how adolescents experienced the interview and which linguistic resources they found appropriate to enact their response to it.

To be sure, we see in line 1 that BR proposes to stop the interview since it had not been going particularly well, but that his interviewees invite him to carry on (lines 3–4, 6) which he is willing to do if they pay more attention (lines 5–7, 11). After agreeing with this (lines 8–10), Asif and Kazim formulate mock apologies in SAE to BR's complaint (lines 12–13, 21, 24) which, as in Example (2), cast their former behaviour as a symptom of overall ineptitude. SAE here creates a gap between self and voice, what Bakhtin (1981) calls "vari-directional double-voicing" to refer to those moments when speakers or authors oppose their own voice with the one they are temporarily borrowing. By doing so, Asif and Kazim are suddenly highlighting a (caricatural) social identity rather than the personal/biographical one they had been developing with BR. This also happened on other occasions, and Rampton argues that, rather than seeing the evocation of Asian deference as a straightforward sign of resistance to white authorities, it often represented something like a coin toss, mobilising racist images to see how adults would respond to these. In the worst scenario, the interaction would deteriorate and confirm the evoked imagery. In the best, adult recipients of SAE would play along with the jocular frame at hand to overcome the interactional hitch, reassuring all participants that intergroup friction did not impede the development of convivial local relationships

---

1. Rampton (1995a: 116–117) explains that 'ben jaad' (lines 12, 16, 32, 35, 37) fell ambivalenty between [ben jɑr], 'Ben, friend', and [pɛn tʃɔd], 'sister fucker'.

(Rampton 1995a: 78ff.). In between these scenarios is the hesitant response that BR and other adults tended to produce (lines 15, 17–18, 22, 25) (Rampton 1995a: 80).

After BR's repeated call for more attention and adjusting of the microphone (lines 17–18, 25), Kazim switches to Creole (lines 27 and 30) to address not his own but BR's behaviour as a sanctionable act. Here, in contrast to the switch to SAE, Creole does not create a gap between Kazim's self and voice but rather reinforces his negative evaluation of BR's move. Such "uni-directional double-voicing" (Bakhtin 1981) was in line with a common trend in Rampton's data where adolescents with Anglo or Asian backgrounds switched into Creole when a potential conflict emerged and aligned with the assertive qualities Creole evoked (though vari-directional crossing into Creole equally occurred, Rampton 1995a: 208ff.). If the use of Creole was relatively uncomplicated in Example (3), it could be much more risky when Afro-Caribbean adolescents were in the vicinity. On those occasions, crossers had to be more circumspect, by avoiding crossing into Creole altogether or by presenting it as a part of their ordinary English. In such cases, uni-directional double voicing could be so subtle that it became difficult to distinguish it from crossers' routine language use.

These examples illustrate that adolescents were using language to engage in "everyday cultural politics" (Rampton 2005: 1): they negotiated established discourses of ethnicity by experimenting with other-ethnic varieties and creating cross-ethnic friendship; they evoked problematic racial images that addressees had to interpret as somehow relevant to what they were doing together; and they adopted other-ethnic varieties not to claim ethnic inheritance but to be a successful jester or to underscore their assertiveness and *ennui* in the face of adult control. Each time adolescents were merely alluding to the symbolic resonances of varieties, however, and since such resonances can be multiple or contrasting, close interactional analysis and ethnographic insight are vital to detail the use potential and limitations of these varieties. We have also seen that the lines between crossing and speakers' routine vernacular can sometimes become tenuous. It is worthwhile therefore to discuss how crossing can be differentiated from other linguistic phenomena.

4. Crossing versus other linguistic practices

Crossing can be distinguished from other linguistic contact phenomena in two respects, Rampton and Charalambous (2012: 484–485) argue: its non-routine character, and the potential controversy it raises (in speakers' view, not analysts'). So, crossing is not to be confused with the use of multi-ethnic vernaculars (local versions of majority languages that are grammatically, lexically, or phonologically marked by speakers' migration histories) given that the use of these vernaculars is, just like borrowing and interference phenomena, generally considered quite everyday, that is, it is seen as speakers' habitual style.

Neither is crossing to be seen as a type of code-mixing or code-switching. The first of these refers to a more pronounced mixture of linguistic codes than what can be found in multi-ethnic vernaculars (which are based primarily on the local vernacular). But the use of mixed codes is generally not considered exceptional by speakers who use them in their everyday lives. The second concept, code-switching, designates the meaningful (participant or discourse-related) switches fluent bilinguals produce in the sequence of conversational events (Auer 1998). But, like style-shifting from a formal to an informal variety within what is regarded as a single code, such switches tend not to be found remarkable *per se*: they fall within the range of expected moves people are known to produce and are not treated as notable or non-routine in themselves.

Such ordinary shifts and switches are different however from what have come to be called stylisations (Bakhtin 1981: 361; Coupland 2001, 2007; Jaspers & Van Hoof 2019; Rampton 1995a, 2006): sudden, momentary, and exaggerated productions of linguistic styles that lie beyond speakers' regular linguistic repertoires, or beyond what is usually expected in the situation at hand (say, a shift into a multi-ethnic vernacular during a highly formal and televised ceremony). Stylisations interrupt the routine flow of life and they turn others present into temporary observers who are subsequently invited to interpret the stylisation's link to the ongoing situation and their utterers' social positioning in it. Understood in this way, there are good reasons for seeing crossing as a type of stylisation. Rampton and Charalambous (2012) underline though that it is useful to distinguish between crossing and stylisation because of the legitimacy issues crossing entails. Such issues are virtually absent when, for example, adolescents at school stylise a foreign language (Jørgensen 2008; Madsen 2015; Rampton 2006) or when speakers of Asian descent stylise Asian English, because the stylisers run little risk of being held accountable by the owners of stylised varieties (who live in other countries, or, in the case of SAE, come from stylisers' own community and may not even recognise SAE as stylised). This is different for crossing, as we have seen, which could be precarious if crossers used the wrong variety at the wrong time.[2]

There are ambiguities and subtleties that complicate this distinction, though (Rampton & Charalambous 2012: 485). The more close friendship allows speakers of different ethnic groups freely to cross into each other's variety, the more such crossing must be seen, in the eyes of those friends, as mundane code-mixing or speakers' habitual style (Rampton 1995a: 215ff.). But should an outsider who claims inheritance of one of those varieties overhear such convivial code-mixing, this mundane usage may suddenly become a dangerous crossing act. Chun (2004) reports that an Asian-American stand-up comedian's use of Mock Asian evoked racialising discourses and raised the spectre of

---

2. This distinction between stylisation and crossing implies, however, that what was first called 'crossing into Asian English' in Rampton's original study later became 'stylising into Asian English' (cf. Rampton 2005: 9), and it invited the use of 'crossing and stylisation' in a number of post-1995 publications.

criticism, which the comedian avoided by presenting her revoicings as liminal (part of performance art) and legitimate (given her commitment to racial justice). In such cases, intra-ethnic stylisations may have to be called *crossing*. Foreign language stylisations can similarly become controversial once these are overheard offline by tourists or encountered online by those who see themselves as owners of that language.

Others indicate that what looks like downright mockery may also imply the opposite or something different altogether. Coupland (2001) argues that Welsh radio presenters' playful selections of Welsh dialect must be understood as a way to ironically evoke (and, so, potentially mock) *and* to self-identify (and align) with typically Welsh cultural styles ('gossiping over the garden fence') and stances (anti-heroism, pragmatism). Auer points out that white German adolescents' stylised rendition of a "migrants German" they have become familiar with through the media (cf. Mock Spanish and Mock Ebonics, Bennett 2012; Hill 1998) can, depending on the context, signal mocking or, instead, "inde[x] media competence and access to a code that is as fascinating as its primary owners are despised" (2006: 491). Chun (2009), in her turn, underlines that fluent English-speaking Asian students' accommodation practices (speaking in a simplified English) could sometimes transform into a mocking of less fluent Asian students because of the linguistic overlap between accommodation and mocking; the eventual meaning of simplified English was sometimes left to hover in between these two polar opposites. Entitlement issues are not always raised by the putative owners of varieties, moreover: Jaspers (2011b) shows that when adolescents of Moroccan descent used features of Antwerp dialect unidirectionally to mobilise the stance of assertiveness and verbal resourcefulness that is commonly associated with vernaculars, they risked criticism from co-ethnic adolescents that they were "acting white".

Uses of varieties that are not usually considered one's own cannot be divided unequivocally into two crossing and stylising piles, then. The same practices can be called acts of crossing, stylisation, routine vernacular use, or code-mixing, depending on how they are perceived by ratified participants and/or unratified overhearers. Contextualisation and interpretation are paramount (Chun 2009; Coupland 2007: 175–176): the more speakers present other voices as part of their authentic repertoire, the more this invites others to see such forms as an acceptable, habitual part of speakers' linguistic repertoire; conversely, the more speakers contextualise speech as "not their own", the more others are encouraged to interpret the disjunction between speaker and voice and its relation to the situation at hand. In each case, though, participants' speech, and the legitimacy of its production, will be read against the background of speakers' and hearers' usual linguistic repertoire, their position in the local community or their social trajectory across time: what is presented as "other" may not be recognised as such, while what is presented as "habitual" may be seen as hateful mockery (Auer 2006). Naturally, different, competing, readings are possible of the same speech forms and of people's linguistic repertoire and community membership.

Crossing can also be compared to concepts that have been much in vogue in recent years and with which it is often seen to be equivalent, like polylingualism (Jørgensen 2008), metrolingualism (Otsuji & Pennycook 2010), or translanguaging (García & Li 2014). Like crossing, these concepts have been proposed to address practices that are hard to explain as the result of speakers' orientation to separate linguistic codes (*code-switching, code-mixing, multi-lingualism*). So in principle, they could just as well be deployed to describe the practices Rampton identified as *crossing*. The relevances that have guided research on poly-metro-translanguaging would usually overstate or downplay specific aspects of crossing, however. To be sure, Rampton's analysis was motivated by a concern that the primacy attributed to inherited ethnicity and community-based linguistic differences had become absolute and that this needed to be offset by an appreciation of the importance of adopted ethnicity, across-group contact, and non-ethnic identity resources. The value-assumptions that underlie much research on poly-metro-translanguaging, however, are not just that ethnolinguistic boundaries are given too much primacy in research or policy, but that these must be opposed (as ideological, oppressive, and inauthentic) and ultimately rejected; as a logical consequence the practice of poly-metro-translanguaging is in this perspective presented as desirable (natural, authentic, liberating) while the idea is generally that it must also become routine or the new norm. Leaving the matter of the reasonableness of such value-assumptions aside (see Jaspers & Madsen 2019, for more elaborate discussion), it is clear that Rampton's account of crossing emphasises phenomena that research into poly-metro-translanguaging would only one-sidedly address: crossing highlights adolescents' transgressive experiences, but also their adherence to enduring ethnolinguistic boundaries; it underlines crossers' reworking of ethnic and linguistic boundaries, but also their implication in the construction of sharp boundaries within the peer group; and it insists that a great deal of the attractiveness and promise of crossing, for adolescents, resided in its conspicuous and improvised precarity than in its normalisation. Crossing thus highlights a tension field between fluid practices and established varieties, or describes a practice of "transgress[ing] ethnic boundaries in the act of observing them" (Woolard 2008: 319), whereas analyses of poly-metro-translanguaging basically prescribe the fluid practices they observe as desirable for all speakers, regardless of speakers' orientation to social and linguistic boundaries.

Concepts are not always used canonically though, neither are value-assumptions shared across the board. Others have had less qualms about equating crossing with poly-metro-translanguaging (see, e.g., Canagarajah & Liyanage 2012: 51; Coulmas 2018: 227; but see García & Li 2014: 36–37). It could be argued, too, that the emergence of concepts like poly-metro-translanguaging in fact reveals that multi-ethnic youth's *bricolage* of the different varieties they hear in their neighbourhoods has become a more mundane, less controversial, practice than it was 40 years ago (cf. Rampton et al. 2019). Such arguments raise the question what operability crossing has: must it be seen as an appropriate label for a local, historically situated, practice from which it is hard to draw any generalising conclusions?; or does it have a wider use-potential for the analysis of present-day sociolinguistic processes? In the latter case, how can we avoid emptying it of its meaning so that we can use it to do more specific work than just underlining any and all kinds of boundary transgression? Such questions enquire into the generality of Rampton's initial findings and to the applicability limits of crossing as a concept.

5. Generality and applicability

To the extent that putting on someone else's voice can be seen as an inevitable part of language learning and acquisition, there is a good case for calling stylisation or Bakhtinian double-voicing "probably as old as language itself" (Rampton & Charalambous 2012: 485). Crossing, however, emerged in an ethnographic study as a type of stylisation that raised issues of entitlement, mostly occurring in liminal situations to reduce the risk of criticism, for a whole range of quite local purposes. Here, the potential for generalisation seems less obvious. Ethnographic studies report on cases of human interaction which are inevitably unique, and they inevitably provide a partial description of their research object, inspired by what scholars find relevant to investigate (Hammersley 1992). Such insights do not fatally prevent generalising from particular findings, however, if at least this operation does not presume the exact similarity as much as the comparability of observed facts in one context to another (Hambye 2015: 90ff.): analysts can interpret whether observed facts belong to the same category of phenomena, which implies focusing on a finding's essential aspects and "shav[ing] off a lot of its nuanced particularity" (Rampton 2005: 8).

Such shaving can be relatively minimal. When the idea is retained of using varieties one is not seen to own and the legitimacy issues this involves, and if it is accepted that local peer groups, varieties' symbolic resonance, and the surrounding public discourses and media representations can vary a great deal and that crossing may not just be a "liminal" event, a wide variety of studies in Europe and beyond can be cited to demonstrate the generality of Rampton's original findings, at least in the Global North. Many of these studies have been carried out in working-class neighbourhoods and/or schools that are broadly comparable to the one that Rampton investigated in the 1980s (a.o., Auer & Dirim 2003; Birken-Silverman 2003; Bucholtz 1999; Doran 2004; Hambye & Siroux 2008; Hewitt 1986; Jaspers 2005; Lytra 2007; Madsen 2015; Nortier & Svendsen 2015; Pooley & Mostefai-Hamsphire 2012; Quist & Jørgensen 2009; Vaish & Roslan 2011; see also Rampton et al. 2019). Other studies have examined the link between local crossing practices and the representation of language and ethnicity in official discourse and popular culture: they have drawn attention to the entitlement issues that arise as young people's language use is adopted by the media, they have revealed that public media and popular music styles are major sources of inspiration for young people's stylisation and crossing practices, and they have demonstrated that music and public/social media provide important platforms for youthful destabilisations of established images and expectations (see, a.o., Androutsopoulos 2001, 2007; Auer 2006; Cutler 1999; Deppermann 2007; Hinnenkamp 2003; Madsen 2016; Stæhr 2015; Tetreault 2009; cf. also Rampton et al. 2019).

The number and widespread emergence of these studies provide strong evidence that the practices first described as crossing were not highly unique. Yet the predominant appearance of these studies in the first 10 to 15 years after Rampton's 1995 study may indicate that attestations of crossing elsewhere were, just like the original study, not only informed by the analytical relevance of addressing overlooked linguistic phenomena. They were also inspired by assumptions about what it was socio-politically relevant to investigate at that time. It is probably not a coincidence that many accounts of crossing and stylisation (including my own) addressed recreational contexts or moments where language use is convivial, jocular, inspired by popular culture, and often resistant to the values of schooling; neither is it surprising to discover a hint of hope in these accounts that young people's negotiation of established identities will contribute to the gradual erosion of these as they become older. Such interests resonate with the optimism of the post-Cold War era just as they illustrate a widespread postmodern criticism of the superiority, efficacy, or refinement of established social and linguistic standards. Analysing young people's recreational use of each other's varieties may today be considered increasingly trivial, however, in light of the growing concerns with national (in)security and boundary patrolling (Rampton & Charalambous 2020). Underlining the value of improvisation and linguistic incompetence in the construction of adolescent friendship may now equally seem inopportune if not naïve given the increasing influence of neoconservative and neoliberal discourses on superior, entrepreneurial, communicative skills (Martín-Rojo & Del Percio 2020). From this perspective crossing may well have been an exciting notion for explaining an interesting set of practices in the past which still merits respectful discussion in a pragmatics handbook; but its analytical purchase now seems to have become rather limited.

Rampton, Constadina Charalambous, and Panayiota Charalambous insist that this perception can be avoided if more extensive conceptual trimming is applied (Rampton et al. 2019; Rampton & Charalambous 2020). Thus, they propose to detach crossing from its frequent association with jocular/spectacular behaviour, multi-ethnic friendship, popular culture, and non-curricular orientation. Instead, they suggest that crossing's essential usefulness resides in its capacity to sensitise us to people's controversial and fragmented use of a language they are not usually seen to own in contexts where intergroup antagonism is more than a remote possibility. This capacity is critical today they argue, notably in contexts of language education where people learn languages that are imbued with histories of violent conflict.

One example is the teaching and learning of Turkish in Greek-Cypriot classes (Charalambous 2012, 2019; Charalambous et al. 2021; Rampton et al. 2019). Such lessons have been installed in secondary schools and adult institutes since 2003 as part of the reconciliation initiatives of the Greek-Cypriot authorities in the wake of Cyprus' integration into the EU. But these classes are far from self-evident given the history of enmity between the Greek-Cypriot and Turkish-Cypriot communities and because of the continuing emphasis on clear-cut ethnolinguistic boundaries in schools and public media. Based on their ethnographic research in both contexts, C. Charalambous, P. Charalambous, and Rampton noticed that these lessons were very differently received. Turkish lessons in adult institutes provided a platform for forging new connections with Turkish-Cypriot compatriots by learners who were generally sympathetic towards the other community and who also had regular contacts with them in and out of school – though learners still risked disapproval in their own networks for learning the former enemy's language. Here, we find practices that are not so different from the ones that Rampton initially observed.

Turkish language lessons were quite differently received in secondary schools, however. Students who opted for Turkish were often treated with hostility by peers and teachers, while Turkish teachers faced various kinds of institutional sabotage. Not all students of Turkish were sympathetic to the language or to Turkish-Cypriots, moreover, with about 25% of them indicating that they took these classes for security reasons (to learn the enemy's language) or out of convenience (an easier route to the necessary marks for admission into university). Faced with the potential for controversy, many Turkish teachers depoliticised their classes by avoiding materials that evoked the world outside school or by presenting Turkish as a neutral lexico-grammatical code. As platform events these lessons could hardly be called liminal. Yet they reduced the potential for controversy, Rampton et al. argue, referring to Goffman's notion of "technical redoings" (1974:59), because of their distinct rehearsal-like quality: by focusing learners' attention on grammatical correctness rather than meaning, these classes projected the idea of genuine communication with Turkish Cypriots as a mere future possibility.

Such hesitant language learning experiences in a politically arduous context cannot be adequately explained as a type of foreign language teaching, Rampton et al. (2019) argue. It is more revealing to understand them as institutionally supported crossing events: occasions where uses of "the Other's" language raise entitlement issues that interactants try to keep in check by turning lessons into inauthentic happenings (in the case of teachers), or by displaying a rather frosty commitment to and limited skill in the target language (in students' case). Clearly, though, crossing in this type of analysis does not draw attention to interactional practices like the ones we have seen in Examples (1) to (3). Indeed, C. Charalambous, P. Charalambous, and Rampton indicate that uses of Turkish at secondary school mostly occurred as an unspectacular aspect of foreign language teaching classes, and that it made little sense to speak of crossing in that context as an interactional phenomenon. Rather, crossing there highlights the institutional and ideological levels of language use that impacted on Turkish lessons, that is, it provided a lens for understanding an unspectacular but precarious event as "language learning in conflict riven settings" (Rampton et al. 2019). This conceptual redesign does not only enrich the descriptive potential of crossing, Rampton et al. point out. It also underlines the role that language plays in large-scale intergroup relations, and it allows to examine, in research on language education, political issues (national loyalty, transgression) which are latent, unstated, or taboo in class – issues which, consequently, only pop up in interviews outside class (Charalambous 2019) or highly implicitly and playfully within (Charalambous 2012).

It might be argued that this redesigned concept still provides a snapshot of linguistic practices, and that, like its precursor, it has little to say about what happens when young people become older. Crossing, in other words, mostly appears to accentuate adolescent, passing, experiences, and it may be wondered if its contribution to the larger sociolinguistic objective of explaining language variation in society is not, all in all, rather limited. It might be asked, too, if this revised crossing concept does not raise entitlement issues: if crossing does not describe linguistic forms, can we still place its application within sociolinguistics or must we see it as a type of educational sociology with a whiff of language? Put differently, what durability does crossing have beyond adolescence, and where should we place its analytic use in the broader sociolinguistic project?

6. Crossing's durability and significance

Although crossing and stylisation as interactional practices have not been exclusively associated with younger people (Androutsopoulos 2007; Bell 1999; Coupland 2007; De Fina 2007; Jaspers 2014; Kotthoff 2007; Woolard 2008; cf. the adults and teachers in Rampton et al. 2019), the bulk of studies into crossing and stylisation have concentrated on adolescents. Rampton in his first study already indicated, moreover, that Punjabi crossing in its playground form tended to "mellow" over time since adolescents stopped playing chasing games as they got older (1995a: 185ff., 260). Others have noticed comparable evolutions (Cutler 1999; Jaspers 2011a). Such observations lead to believe that crossing and stylisation are transitory phenomena which, like other forms of youth language, wear off as speakers grow up and increasingly dissociate themselves from language forms they find unsuitable for demonstrating adulthood (Eckert 2000).

Rampton (2011b) indicates that the predominant association of mixed language practices with youthful vitality, sociability, and a non-canonical allure can in be part be explained as the effect of how such practices have generally been characterised in public discourse. He finds similar connotations in interview reports from 2008 and 2009 by post-adolescent and adult speakers in London who were mainly of Punjabi descent.

But this association is complicated by (1) reports that Creole features, Stylised Asian English, and non-Asian uses of Punjabi, in combination with non-standard, slang, features, continued to be a part of informants' daily language practices; and by (2) recordings of a 40+ London-born businessman of Punjabi descent whose vernacular English was peppered with the Creole features and Punjabi phrases that Ashmead adolescents had been observed to produce 20 years earlier. Such findings indicate that at least for some speakers, crossing is not an adolescent fad. The major difference however was that this businessman's style was far from transgressive, ludic, or humorous. On the contrary, it was "adjusted to the concerns and constraints of adulthood" (Rampton 2011b: 287), appearing in daily business affairs as well as in advice giving to a close friend. It was also perceived as a routine part of the speaker's linguistic repertoire (which also contained more formal speech and more idiomatic Cockney English) rather than raising legitimacy issues. The durability of crossing thus seems to come at the cost of its banality: as crossers mature, their once conspicuous use of other-ethnic varieties sediments into a habitual style, "a dense, vernacular mix of Creole, Cockney and Punjabi forms [that] can still be a valued and quite flexible resource in the repertoire of successful middle-aged professionals" (Rampton 2011b: 288).

Taken together these findings suggest that crossing as a non-routine and controversial act is a typical symptom of the linguistic vivacity adolescents display before they stabilise their speech and retain a number of the innovative features they produced during adolescence in an habitual, routine, adult vernacular (Eckert 2000; Tagliamonte & D'Arcy 2009). Crossing then provides valuable indications of the possible development of routine vernacular language in the future, at least among a particular group of speakers. But rather than arguing that crossing thus earns its place in the larger sociolinguistic project as a potential source of information about larger-scale patterns of language variation and change, Rampton (2011b) moves in the opposite direction and proposes a revision of the notion of vernacular to argue that crossing and stylisation are fundamental, chronic, aspects of language, as basic to sociolinguistics as vernacular language is. This revised concept of vernacular not only allows analysts to transgress long-standing boundaries within sociolinguistics, where the study of unselfconscious, systematic, language use in dialectology and variationism is often separated from the attention to reflexive, expressive, language use in pragmatics and interactional sociolinguistics. It also places the use of crossing as a lens for highlighting other dimensions than linguistic form squarely within the purview of sociolinguistics.

To explain this, Rampton (2011b) draws on two notions, Agha's (2004) *enregisterment* and Silverstein's (1985) *total linguistic fact*. Agha's central insight is that the social existence and career of registers necessarily depends on enregistering activities, that is, a wide variety of "overt (publicly perceivable) evaluative behaviour" (2004: 27) like names, accounts of usage, prescriptions, non-verbal reactions to usage, acceptance of usage, and other typifying actions such as stylisations and crossing. We cannot recognise a register *qua* register, nor a vernacular *qua* vernacular, Agha argues, without such reflexive, metapragmatic behaviour and a trajectory of socialisation during which we become familiar with predominant social distinctions. Descriptions of a variety in terms of mere form and distribution are incomplete, therefore, since they fail to explain how speakers are able to differentiate varieties from each other and "how [a variety] come[s] to be associated with social practices at all" (Agha 2004: 25). If this view is accepted, the language forms routinely produced by speakers, local and non-local discourses about language, as well as crossing, stylisation, and other self-conscious uses of language, can all be seen as "integral facets of the same sociolinguistic process – different sides of the same (rather multi-dimensional) 'coin'" (Rampton 2011b: 290). A vernacular by this reasoning necessarily consists of systematic, routine, linguistic forms *and* non-routine enregistering activity that marks it off from neighbouring varieties, and this makes crossing an enduring aspect of language rather than a temporary symptom of adolescence. Indeed, no vernacular, slang, nor standard variety is ever fully and finally enregistered: such social evaluations can and often are re-evaluated, and several authors have drawn attention to the crucial role of meta-pragmatic activity on mainstream and social media to explain changing public perceptions of existing varieties (Agha 2015; Androutsopoulos 2014; Coupland 2010; Mortensen et al. 2016).

Rampton (2011b) connects Agha's reflexive perspective on registers to Silverstein's notion of the *total linguistic fact*, according to which "the datum for a science of language, is irreducibly dialectic in nature. It is an unstable interaction of meaningful sign forms, contextualised to situations of interested human use and mediated by the fact of cultural ideology" (1985: 220). If, as this view suggests, the occurrence of linguistic features must be understood in relation to their mediation by ideology and their contextualisation in specific interaction, then there is no objection in principle to using crossing as a concept that highlights other dimensions than linguistic form. Indeed, drawing attention to those dimensions must be considered as integral a part of the sociolinguistic project as its focus on linguistic form. Ultimately the adoption of this perspective may, as Rampton indicates (2011b: 290–292) bring coherence to a sociolinguistic research practice which has tended to focus on one of the abovementioned dimensions at the expense of the others.

7. Concluding remarks

This review chapter has discussed the evolution of the concept of crossing, from a notion that challenged existing explanations for code alternation (code-mixing, code-switching) in order to account for the risky use of other-ethnic varieties by which multi-ethnic youth negotiated ethnolinguistic boundaries and created cross-ethnic friendship; to a concept that can be deployed to reveal the precarity of language learning in conflict afflicted settings. We have seen in addition that whereas crossing in its original study mainly drew attention to rather spectacular forms of language in small-scale interaction, it was later deployed to highlight the institutional and ideological tensions that surround relatively unglamorous linguistic forms in a context of large-scale intergroup conflict. Not least, this chapter has insisted that although crossing is predominantly associated with youthful linguistic vivacity, there are good empirical grounds for associating it with adult life and official educational policy as well as convincing theoretical arguments for seeing crossing and other types of self-conscious language use as a fundamental aspect of linguistic variation and change.

Such conceptual flexibility may seem too much of a good thing, but it is intrinsic to social research: the singularity of contexts and analysts' specific, changing, research interests typically produce a variety of concepts, concept revisions, if not endless disagreement about definitions (Passeron 2006:35, in Hambye 2015:78–88). What can be verified though is the care, precision, and prudence behind a concept's application and revision, and here, it would seem that the efforts by Rampton, C. Charalambous, and P. Charalambous steer clear from a couple of unproductive strategies. Thus, rather than using the concept in summary fashion, these authors have consistently applied and revised crossing in connection to exhaustive ethnographic fieldwork, recruiting crossing in the analysis of specific empirical phenomena. This is crucial for any productive discussion over the suitability and accuracy of its application as much as it pushes such discussion to combine a focus on observable linguistic form with the other dimensions that mediate its production. Related to this empirical ambition has been the drive to deploy crossing "as a point of entry into the understanding of social process rather than as an autonomous topic in its own right" (Rampton & Charalambous 2012:493–494). Although formulating a new concept is always bound to draw attention to the concept itself and its author(s), Rampton and his collaborators' ambition has not been to demonstrate that "crossing occurs", using any data that come in handy, but each time to explore how the concept can serve the analysis of sociolinguistic processes the meaning and importance of which the existing conceptual apparatus has perhaps not yet quite managed to reveal. Given the academy's fondness for discoveries and original terms that attract funding (cf. Pavlenko 2019) such an ambition is less obvious than it seems. In an era where concerns with personal well-being or methods like auto-ethnography take up increasing discursive space, such a goal is also testament of a profound commitment to the explanation of the world that extends beyond the self.

Next to this, rather than progressively including more and more phenomena within the purview of crossing and increasing its fame, Rampton has not shied away from drawing relatively narrow boundaries around crossing nor from stripping a quite successful concept to its bare essentials. This has not entirely avoided the mis-use or inflation of the term by others. But it has contributed to diminishing its over-use and to maximising the chance that crossing retains its capacity to "generate the friction, force, and freshness [that is] needed to push arguments further and generate new insights" (Brubaker

2001: 15). Rampton and his collaborators have done a great deal of work to show how crossing can be deployed in other settings. Others will have to pick up the baton to explore how it can be usefully applied to throw a fresh light on precarious linguistic moves among adults; across gender, sexuality, class, or other identity boundaries than ethnolinguistic ones; in other than educational sites; and in relation to official policy. Analyses of such self-conscious behaviour will be of major importance for explaining the social existence and career of the ways of speaking we commonly identify as languages, codes, standards and vernaculars.

Transcription conventions

[ ]	overlapping turns
=	latching, turn continues below, at the next identical symbol
(.)	pause of less than a second
(1.5)	approximate interval in seconds
AAA	loud volume
a::	lengthening of preceding sound
(( ))	'stage directions'
( )	unclear or unintelligible speech
(text)	analyst guess
Bold	example of crossing under discussion

References

Agha, Asif. 2004. "Registers of language." In *A companion to linguistic anthropology*, ed. by Alessandro Duranti, 23–45. Malden: Blackwell.
Agha, Asif. 2015. "Tropes of Slang." *Signs and Society* 3: 306–330.
Androutsopoulos, Jannis. 2001. "From the Streets to the Screens and Back Again: On the Mediated Diffusion of Ethnolectal Patterns in Contemporary German." *LAUD Linguistic Agency*, paper 522, 1–24. Essen: University of Essen.
Androutsopoulos, Jannis. 2007. "Style Online: Doing Hip-Hop on the German-speaking Web." In *Style and Social Identities*, ed. by Peter Auer, 279–317. Berlin: Mouton de Gruyter.
Androutsopoulos, Jannis. 2014. "Mediatization and sociolinguistic change." In *Mediatization and Sociolinguistic Change*, ed. by Jannis Androutsopoulos, 3–48. Berlin: Mouton de Gruyter.
Auer, Peter. 1998 (Ed). *Code-Switching in Conversation*. London: Routledge.
Auer, Peter. 2006. "Sociolinguistic Crossing." In *Encyclopedia of Language and Linguistics*, 2nd edition, Vol. 11, ed. by Keith Brown, 490–492. Amsterdam: Amsterdam: Elsevier.

Auer, Peter, and Inci Dirim. 2003. "Socio-Cultural Orientation, Urban Youth Styles and the Spontaneous Acquisition of Turkish by non-Turkish Adolescents in Germany." In *Discourse Constructions of Youth Identities*, ed. by Jannis Androutsopolous and Alexandra Georgakopoulou, 223–246. Amsterdam-Philadelphia: John Benjamins.

Bakhtin, Mikhail. 1981. *The Dialogic Imagination: Four Essays*, ed. by Michael Holquist, translated by Caryl Emerson and Michael Holquist. Austin: University of Texas Press.

Bell, Allan. 1999. "Styling the Other to Define the Self: a Study in New Zealand Identity-Making." *Journal of Sociolinguistics* 3: 523–541.

Bennett, Joe. 2012. "And What Comes out May be a Kind of Screeching: the Stylization of *Chavspeak* in Contemporary Britain." *Journal of Sociolinguistics* 16: 5–27.

Birken-Silverman, Gabriele. 2003. "Language Crossing among Adolescents in a Multi-Ethnic City Area in Germany." In *Trilingualism in Family, School and Community*, ed. by Charlotte Hoffman and Jehannes Ytsma, 75–100. Berlin: Mouton de Gruyter.

Brubaker, Rogers. 2001. "Cognitive Perspectives." *Ethnicities* 1: 15–17.

Bucholtz, Mary. 1999. "You Da Man. Narrating the Racial Other in the Production of White Masculinity." *Journal of Sociolinguistics* 3: 443–460.

Cameron, Deborah. 1995. *Verbal Hygiene*. London: Routledge.

Canagarajah, Suresh, and Indika Liyanage. 2012. "Lessons from Pre-Colonial Multilingualism." In *The Routledge Handbook of Multilingualism*, ed. by Marilyn Martin-Jones, Adrian Blackledge, and Angela Creese, 49–65. London-New York: Routledge.

Charalambous, Constadina. 2012. "*Republica de Kubros*. Transgression and Collusion in Greek-Cypriot Adolescents' Classroom Silly Talk." *Linguistics and Education* 23: 334–349.

Charalambous, Constadina. 2019. "Language Education and 'Conflicted Heritage': Implications for Teaching and Learning." *The Modern Language Journal* 103: 874–891.

Charalambous, Constadina, Panayiota Charalambous, and Ben Rampton. 2021. "International relations, sociolinguistics and the 'everyday'." *Peacebuilding* 9: 1–22.

Chun, Elaine. 2004. "Ideologies of Legitimate Mockery: Margaret Cho's Revoicings of Mock Asian." *Pragmatics* 14: 263–89.

Chun, Elaine. 2009. "Speaking like Asian Immigrants: Intersections of Accommodation and Mocking at a US High School." *Pragmatics* 19:17–38

Coulmas, Florian. 2018. *An Introduction to Multilingualism. Language in a Changing World*. Oxford: Oxford University Press.

Coupland, Nik. 2001. "Dialect stylisation in radio talk." *Language in Society* 30: 345–375.

Coupland, Nik. 2007. *Style*. Cambridge: Cambridge University Press.

Coupland, Nik. 2010. "Language, Ideology, Media and Social Change." In *Performing the Self*, ed. by Karen Junod and Didier Maillat, 127–151. Tübingen: Gunter Narr.

Cutler, Celia. 1999. "Yorkville Crossing. White Teens, Hip Hop and African American English." *Journal of Sociolinguistics* 3: 428–442.

De Fina, Anna. 2007. "Style and Stylisation in the Construction of Identities in a Card-Playing Club." In *Style and Social Identities*, ed. by Peter Auer, 57–84. Berlin: Mouton de Gruyter.

Depperman, Arnulf. 2007. "Playing with the Voice of the Other: Stylised Kanaksprak in Conversations among German Adolescents." In *Style and Social Identities*, ed. by Peter Auer, 325–360. Berlin: Mouton de Gruyter.

Doran, Meredith. 2004. "Negotiating Between 'Bourge' and 'Racaille': Verlan as Youth Identity Practice in Suburban Paris." In *Negotiating Identity in Multilingual Contexts*, ed. by Aneta Pavlenko and Adrian Blackledge, 93–124. Clevedon: Multilingual Matters.

Eckert, Penelope. 2000. *Linguistic Variation as Social Practice*. Oxford: Blackwell.

García, Ofelia, and Li Wei. 2014. *Translanguaging*. Basingstoke: Palgrave Macmillan.

Gillborn, David A. 1988. "Ethnicity and Educational Opportunity: Case Studies of West Indian Male-White Teacher Relationships." *British Educational Research Journal* 16: 335–350.

Gilroy, Paul. 1987. *There Ain't No Black in the Union Jack*. London: Hutchinson.

Goffman, Erving. 1971. *Relations in Public*. London: Allen Lane.

Goffman, Erving. 1974. *Frame Analysis*. Boston: Northeastern University Press.

Hall, Stuart. 1988. "New Ethnicities." *ICA Documents* 7: 27–31.

Hambye, Philippe. 2015. "L'ethnographie Comme Méthode d'Enquête Sociolinguistique: 'Faire Preuve' à Partir d'un Cas Singulier?" *Langage et Société* 154: 83–97.

Hambye, Philippe, and Jean-Louis Siroux. 2008. "Langage et 'Culture de la Rue' en Milieu Scolaire." *Sociologie et Sociétés* 40: 217–237.

Hammersley, Martyn. 1992. *What's Wrong with Ethnography*. London: Routledge.

Harris, Roxy, and Ben Rampton. 2002. "Creole Metaphors in Cultural Analysis: On the Limits and Possibilities of (Socio-)linguistics." *Critique of Anthropology* 22: 31–51.

Hewitt, Roger. 1986. *White Talk, Black Talk*. Cambridge: Cambridge University Press.

Hill, Jane. 1998. "Language, Race, and White Public Space." *American Anthropologist* 100: 680–689.

Hinnenkamp, Volker. 2003. "Mixed Language Varieties of Migrant Adolescents and the Discourse of Hybridity." *Journal of Multilingual and Multicultural Development* 24: 12–41.

Jaspers, Jürgen. 2005. "Linguistic Sabotage in a Context of Monolingualism and Standardization." *Language and Communication* 25: 279–297.

Jaspers, Jürgen. 2011a. "Talking like a Zero-Lingual. Ambiguous Linguistic Caricatures at an Urban Secondary School." *Journal of Pragmatics* 43: 1264–1278.

Jaspers, Jürgen. 2011b. "Strange Bedfellows. Appropriations of a Tainted Urban Dialect." *Journal of Sociolinguistics* 15: 493–524.

Jaspers, Jürgen. 2014. "Stylisations as Teacher Practice." *Language in Society* 43: 373–391.

Jaspers, Jürgen, and Sarah Van Hoof. 2019. "Style and stylisation." In *The Routledge Handbook of Linguistic Ethnography*, ed. by Karen Tusting, 109–124. London: Routledge.

Jaspers, Jürgen, and Lian Malai Madsen (Eds). 2019. *Fixity and Fluidity in Sociolinguistic Theory and Practice*. London: Routledge.

Jørgensen, Jens Normann. 2008. "Polylingual Languaging around and among Children and Adolescents." *International Journal of Multilingualism* 5: 161–76.

Kotthoff, Helga. 2007. "The Humorous Stylisation of 'New' Women and Men and Conservative Others." In *Style and Social Identities*, ed. by Peter Auer, 445–476. Berlin: Mouton de Gruyter.

Lytra, Vally. 2007. *Play Frames and Social Identities*. Amsterdam-Philadelphia: John Benjamins.

Mac an Ghaill, Máirtín. 1988. *Young, Gifted and Black*. Milton Keynes: Open University Press.

Madsen, Lian Malai. 2015. *Fighters, Girls and Other Identities*. Bristol: Multilingual Matters.

Madsen, Lian Malai. 2016. "The Diva in the Room. Rap Music, Education, and Discourses on Migration." In *Everyday Languaging. Collaborative Research on the Language Use of Children and Youth*, ed. by Lian Malai Madsen, Martha Sif Karrebæk, and Janus Spindler Møller, 167–198. Berlin: Mouton de Gruyter.

Martín-Rojo, Luisa, and Alfonso Del Percio (Eds). 2020. *Language and Neoliberal Governmentality*. London: Routledge.

Mirza, Heidi Safia. 1992. *Young, Female and Black*. London: Routledge.

Mortensen, Janus, Nik Coupland, and Jacob Thøgersen. 2016. "Introduction." In *Style, Mediation and Change*, ed. by Janus Mortensen, Nik Coupland and Jacob Thøgersen, 1–24. Oxford: Oxford University Press.

Nortier, Jacomine, and Bente Ailin Svendsen (Eds). 2015. *Language, Youth and Identity in the 21st Century*. Cambridge: Cambridge University Press.

Otsuji, Emi, and Alastair Pennycook. 2010. "Metrolingualism. Fixity, Fluidity and Language in Flux." *International Journal of Multilingualism* 7: 240–254.

Passeron, Jean-Claude. 2006. *Le Raisonnement Sociologique*. Paris: Albin Michel.

Pavlenko, Aneta. 2019. "Superdiversity and Why it Isn't." In *Sloganizations in Language Education Discourse*, ed. by Barbara Schmenk, Stephan Breidbach and Lutz Küster, 142–168. Bristol: Multilingual Matters.

Pooley, Tim, and Zoubida Mostefai-Hampshire. 2012. "Code Crossing and Multilingualism among Adolescents in Lille." *Journal of French Language Studies* 22: 371–394.

Pratt, Mary Louise. 1987. "Linguistic Utopias." In *The Linguistics of Writing*, ed. by Nigel Fabb, Derek Attridge, Alan Durant and Colin MacCabe, 48–66. Manchester: Manchester University Press.

Quist, Pia, and Jens Normann Jørgensen. 2009. "Crossing. Negotiating Social Boundaries." In *Handbook of Multilingualism and Multilingual Communication*, ed. by Peter Auer and Li Wei, 371–389. Berlin: Mouton de Gruyter.

Rampton, Ben. 1995a. *Crossing. Language and Ethnicity among Adolescents*. London: Sage.

Rampton, Ben. 1995b. "Language Crossing and the Problematisation of Ethnicity and Socialisation." *Pragmatics* 5: 485–513.

Rampton, Ben. 2005. "Preface to the second edition." In *Crossing. Language and Ethnicity among Adolescents* (Second Edition), 1–17. Manchester: St. Jerome Publishing.

Rampton, Ben. 2006. *Language in Late Modernity*. Cambridge: Cambridge University Press.

Rampton, Ben. 2011a. "Style Contrasts, Migration and Social Class." *Journal of Pragmatics* 43: 1236–1250.

Rampton, Ben. 2011b. "From 'Multi-Ethnic Adolescent Heteroglossia' to 'Contemporary Urban Vernaculars'." *Language & Communication* 31: 276–294.

Rampton, Ben, and Constadina Charalambous. 2012. "Crossing." In *The Routledge Handbook of Multilingualism*, ed. by Marilyn Martin-Jones, Adrian Blackledge and Angela Creese, 482–498. London: Routledge.

Rampton, Ben, and Constadina Charalambous. 2020. "Sociolinguistics and Everyday (In)securitization." *Journal of Sociolinguistics* 24: 75–88.

Rampton, Ben, Constadina Charalambous, and Panayiota Charalambous. 2019. "Crossing of a Different Kind." *Language in Society* 48: 629–655.

Silverstein, Michael. 1985. "Language and the culture of gender." In *Semiotic Mediation*, ed. by Elizabeth Mertz & Richard J. Parmentier, 219–259. Academic Press: New York.

Stæhr, Andreas. 2015. "Reflexivity in Facebook interaction. Enregisterment across Written and Spoken Language Practices." *Discourse, Context & Media* 8: 3–45.

Tagliamonte, Sali A., and Alexandra D'Arcy. 2009. "Peaks beyond Adolescence." *Language* 85: 58–108.

Tetreault, Chantal. 2009. "*Cité* Teens Entextualizing French TV Host Register: Crossing, Voicing, and Participation Framework." *Language in Society* 38: 201–231.

Turner, Victor. 1974. "Liminal to Liminoid in Play, Flow and Ritual." *Rice University Studies* 60: 53–92.

Vaish, Viniti, and Mardiana Roslan. 2011. "'Crossing' in Singapore." *World Englishes* 30: 317–331.

Woolard, Kathryn A. 2008. "Language and Identity Choice in Catalonia: The Interplay of Contrasting Ideologies of Linguistic Authority." In *Lengua, nación e identidad. La regulación del plurilingüismo en España y América Latina*, ed. by Kirsten Süselbeck, Ulrike Mühlschlegel, Peter Masson, 303–323. Frankfurt am Main: Vervuert/Madrid: Iberoamericana.

Wright, Cecile. 1992. "Early Education: Multiracial Primary School Classrooms." In *Racism and Education. Structure and Strategies*, ed. by Dawn Gil, Barbara Mayor, Maud Blair, 5–41. London: Sage.

Dell Hymes and communicative competence

Paul V. Kroskrity
UCLA

1. Introduction

A linguistic anthropologist, folklorist, innovator in communication studies, educational theorist, and administrator, Dell H. Hymes (1927–2009) was a key figure in the historical development of linguistic anthropology and a major force in bringing ethnographic approaches to educational institutions and their applied research during the mid to late 20th century. This treatment will (1) outline his biography and professional career, (2) focus on his important concept of *communicative competence* as a critical effort in staking out an alternative to Chomskyan autonomous linguistics, (3) explore the range of his own research agenda, (4) and offer a concluding assessment about his continuing influence in such fields as pragmatics, communication studies, cultural anthropology, linguistic anthropology, ethnopoetics, and education.

2. Biography and career

Hymes was born in Portland, Oregon, in 1927 to a family that, like many during the period, endured the hardship of the Depression era. After attending public schools and graduating high school at the age of 17, Hymes attended Reed College. However, his studies were then interrupted after only one year for two years of military service in (South) Korea with the U.S. Army's Seventh Infantry Inspector General's office. When he returned in 1947, he resumed his studies while supported by the G.I. Bill and eventually earned his B.A. in 1950. His Reed experience provided a foundation for his later academic work since it allowed him to combine his emerging interests in Anthropology, Literature, and the Indigenous peoples of Oregon. Especially significant, he began a long association with his mentor, David H. French (1918–1994), an anthropologist – and student of Franz Boas – who introduced the young Hymes to the *Kiksht* – a Chinookan-speaking people who resided on the Warm Springs Reservation in Central Oregon (Moore 2008; Silverstein 2010: 933).

Hymes went to Indiana University in order to pursue a Ph.D. in anthropology and folklore. Indiana University was developing innovative and convergent programs in anthropology, linguistics, and folklore. During the 1950s the Department of Anthropology created the Archives of Languages of the World, the Summer Field Station in Anthropological Linguistics (Flagstaff, Arizona), and The Research Center for Anthropology, Folklore and Linguistics (under the direction of Thomas Sebeok). Though Hymes' academic interests – like those of his first mentor David French – were initially more cultural than linguistic, he moved toward linguistic anthropology under the influence of C. F. (Carl) Voegelin (Murray 1998: 100), a former student of Alfred Kroeber at the University of California, Berkeley, who had completed a dissertation on Tübatulabal, an Indigenous language of Central California. At this point in time, Indiana University had made Bloomington into a virtual Mecca for various innovative approaches in the study of language and communication well beyond the behaviorism of the linguist Leonard Bloomfield. Faculty appointments of C. F. Voegelin and Thomas Sebeok, Richard Dorson, and others helped to focus and generate academic interests in anthropological linguistics, folklore, psycholinguistics, sociolinguistics, and semiotics. Indiana University hosted major national and international conferences on psycholinguistics, sociolinguistics, and linguistic style, as well as several summer institutes of the Linguistic Society of America. The net effect of Hymes' participation was to immerse himself in the flow of many emerging currents in the study of language and to enrich these currents with the Boasian cultural emphasis he had acquired at Reed. At this time, he also met influential figures such as anthropologist Claude Levi-Strauss and the poet and literacy critic Kenneth Burke.

In 1954–1955 Hymes returned to Warm Springs, Oregon, to complete his dissertation, *The Language of the Kathlamet Chinook*, largely based on texts previously published by Franz Boas. He was soon hired as a Lecturer and later an Assistant Professor of Social Anthropology at Harvard where he worked closely with Roman Jakobson. Hymes was very much influenced by Jakobson's Prague Circle approach to language and his representation of a "functionalist" perspective on language that recognized many communicative functions, such as referential, emotive, conative, phatic, metalinguistic, and poetic (Jakobson 1960: 355–370). These functions greatly expanded the more narrow interests of formal taxonomic linguistics of linguists like Leonard Bloomfield (1933) in the U.S.A. This wider range of functions, including especially metalinguistic and poetic (Hymes 1975: 364; Murray 1998: 100; Caton 1987: 247) provided an alternative model of language and communication that influenced Hymes' thinking. He would amplify, develop, rework, and apply this functional approach to cultural anthropological concerns (Silverstein 2010: 936), which would significantly inform his later work on contextualized language use and poetic function.

After leaving Harvard, from 1960–1965, Hymes joined the Anthropology Department at UC-Berkeley as an Associate and later a full Professor. Berkeley provided an especially appropriate environment of language and communication scholars across departments including Erving Goffman, John Gumperz, Susan Ervin-Tripp, and John

Searle. His network of language scientists and concern for creating an approach to language that emphasized its sociocultural foundations prompted him to craft his first major editorial accomplishment, the volume *Language in Culture and Society: A Reader in Linguistics and Anthropology* (Hymes 1964). This massive tome (in excess of 750 pages) is often regarded as the first reader in the developing field of linguistic anthropology. Hymes' goal was to display the relevance of language and linguistic inquiry to various forms of social analysis and cultural interpretation. At a time when linguistic anthropology was still not even routinely represented in all Anthropology departments, Hymes attempted to demonstrate the many ways that the study of language "intersects almost every concern of the anthropologist, [...] and to show that the field has a noteworthy history, a lively present, and a future of promise" (Hymes 1964:xxii). Though many of the nearly 70 chapters were written by non-anthropologists, the volume was clearly a clarion call to linguists, as well as anthropologists, for a socioculturally centered view of language at a time when the influential linguist Noam Chomsky was constructing an asocial linguistics preoccupied not with actual speech communities, but with idealized, perfectly homogenous speech communities, and equally idealized, monolingual speakers whose capacity for decontextualized but grammatical form would become the focus of autonomous linguistic theory (see Section 3). But the volume was also directed at anthropologists and anthropology departments, many of which by the mid-1960s had lost the Boasian emphasis on language due to the influence of British social anthropology and its relative lack of linguistic emphasis. Hymes' edited volume, often affectionately called "the red book" was designed to restore a prominent place for language study in anthropology and to reimagine the role of linguistic anthropology as much more than a "service" subfield charged with teaching anthropologists their field languages. No one during this period was more influential than Hymes in transforming a field formerly known as anthropological linguistics and rebranding it into one that would come to be routinely called linguistic anthropology.

Hymes later found a more enduring academic home at the University of Pennsylvania in 1965 where he was a professor of folklore, linguistics, sociology, and education. This interdisciplinary array of scholars from both UC-Berkeley and the University of Pennsylvania provided the basis for the foundational symposium on the *Ethnography of Communication* at the American Anthropological Association Meetings in 1963 and many later publications such as "Toward Ethnographies of Communication" (Hymes 1964), "Two Types of Linguistic Relativity" (Hymes 1966), and "The Anthropology of Communication" (Hymes 1967). During this period, Hymes was a tireless author of many programmatic articles that promoted a sense of unity and organization in an emerging science of the study of language *usage*. In a manner both eloquent and ubiquitous, Hymes argued for the importance and the need for such inquiry at a time when Chomsky's emphasis on innate grammatical knowledge and formal universals seemed to restrict linguistic investigations to concerns about the nature of a speaker's innate grammatical *competence* – a Chomskyan concept that will be further explored in the next section.

During his 22-year career at the University of Pennsylvania, Hymes would eventually take on the role of Dean of the Graduate School of Education. While at Penn, his intellectual interests further developed in interaction with colleagues such as Erving Goffman, Ward Goodenough, John Szwed, and William Labov. During this period, Hymes' mentoring efforts helped develop a distinguished cohort of younger scholars who would further shape the ethnography of communication and other fields that he had so steadfastly promoted. During this period, Hymes' disciplinary influence was recognized in his election as President of four academic societies: the American Folklore Society (1973–1974), the Linguistic Society of America (1982), the American Anthropological Association (1983), and the Society for Applied Linguistics (1986–1987).

Completing his service as Dean, Hymes relocated to the University of Virginia in 1987 where he served as a Professor of Anthropology and English. There he renewed and fortified earlier interests in Native American verbal art, verse analysis of narrative discourse, and related interests in the area of a field of inquiry he variously called anthropological philology or ethnopoetics. These interests preoccupied him during this period and into retirement in 1998. He died in 2009 at the age of 83 as Commonwealth Professor Emeritus of Anthropology at the University of Virginia.

3. Communicative competence

More than any other concept, *communicative competence* summarizes Hymes' scholarly quest to transform linguistic anthropology into a theoretically alternative approach to language. This concept would not only oppose the asocial object constructed by Chomsky as linguistic competence; it would also organize a wide circle of social scientific language researchers into an alliance based on the need to study language in its social and cultural contexts. During the 1960s, linguistic theory in the U.S. was being transformed from a physicalist, taxonomic structuralism exemplified by Leonard Bloomfield's (1933) *Language*, to a mentalist, transformational-generative one identified with Noam Chomsky's (1965) *Aspects of a Theory of Syntax*. Though widely hailed as a superior theoretical breakthrough by its adherents, Chomsky's narrow scope in this autonomous linguistic approach was nearly exclusively focused on grammar. Many sociolinguists regarded this approach as dismissive to those researchers who understood language, and languages to be irreducibly social and cultural phenomena. The following widely cited passage from Chomsky was received by many as an inappropriate dismissal of such sociocultural approaches:

> Linguistic theory is concerned primarily with an ideal speaker-listener, in a completely homogenous speech community, who knows its language perfectly and is unaffected by such grammatically irrelevant conditions as memory limitations, distractions, shifts of attention and interest, and errors (random or characteristic) in applying his knowledge of the language in actual performance. (1965:3)

While this bracketing of the sociocultural world can be rationalized from the perspective of an autonomous linguistics, sociolinguistic theorists sought alternative approaches that gave sociocultural considerations more prominence. John Gumperz (1968) created an alternative focus on the complexity – the "organization of diversity" – within actual speech communities as an alternative to Chomsky's imagined homogenous ones. In a similar manner, Hymes confronted Chomsky's core concept of linguistic competence. Defined as "the speaker-hearer's knowledge of his [sic] language" (Chomsky 1965:3), this knowledge is purified by the theoretical assumptions stated above which erase a speaker's social and cultural worlds. Hymes (1972:272) responds to this dismissive decontextualization when he writes, "It takes the absence of a place for sociocultural factors and the linking of performance to imperfection, to disclose an ideological aspect to the theoretical standpoint." That ideology is a professional preference for not just perpetuating a focus on linguistic structure but also for completely dismissing speakers' systematic knowledge and patterned use. Orderly language use is lumped with performance miscues in a Chomskyan wastebasket of linguistic phenomena not worthy of scholarly attention. For Hymes, who was programmatically developing the *Ethnography of Speaking* (later *Ethnography of Communication*) approach at this time, this was an intolerable dismissal. Exclusively centered on linguistic structures amputated from the sociocultural worlds of speakers, Chomsky's theory erased the significance of such matters as cultural difference, social inequality, differences between passive understanding and active production, and linguistic styles. But Hymes argues for the insufficiency of linguistic competence, when he defines communicative competence as inclusive of not only grammatical knowledge but as also of the ability to use that knowledge in ways that are appropriate for a wide range of social contexts. Contrasting the acquisition of communicative competence to the innate knowledge of grammatical competence foregrounded by Chomsky, Hymes writes:

> We have then to account for the fact that a normal child acquires knowledge of sentences, not only as grammatical, but also as appropriate. He or she acquires competence as to when to speak, when not, and as to what to talk about with whom, when, where, and in what manner. In short, a child becomes able to accomplish a repertoire of speech acts, to take part in speech events, and to evaluate their accomplishment by others. (1972:277)

Having reformulated performance not as a waste bin of linguistic disorder but rather as including the knowledge of underlying rules and models for linguistic and communicative production, Hymes (1974:75) further describes communicative competence as the child's "ability to participate in society as not only a speaking, but also a communicating member." Like Chomsky, he is concerned with understanding speakers' "rule-governed creativity" and their relative "freedom" in producing new sentences they have never heard. But whereas Chomsky restricts linguistic competence to grammar, Hymes' communicative competence seeks to encompass the more inclusive capacity to communicate – including all the cultural, social, interactional and contextual "rules" used by the communicating speaker. Hymes identifies the task of discovering these rules with the Ethnography of Speaking in the following passage:

> An ethnography of speaking approach shares Chomsky's concern for creativity and freedom, but recognizes that a child, or person, master of only grammar is not yet free. Chomsky's attempt to discuss the "creative" aspect of language use (Chomsky 1966) suffers from the same difficulty as his treatment of competence. The main thrust is independence of situation. (1974: 93–94)

Whereas for Chomsky the social, cultural, and interactional contexts are theoretically erased because of their presumed irrelevance to a decontextualized grammatical creativity, for Hymes it is speakers' knowledge of context and their capacity to use that knowledge to improvise and engage in emergent communicative acts that represent the more inclusive creativity and freedom associated with his more encompassing concept of *communicative competence* (Hymes 1992: 57).

In further explicating the basis for the inclusion of something like grammatical competence within communicative competence, Hymes (1972, 1974: 95) repeatedly distinguishes four dimensions of competence. The first, *systemic potential*, he identifies with Chomsky's linguistic competence and a speaker's knowledge of the compositional rules of grammar (Hymes 1974: 95). The second is *appropriateness* – a term he associates with cultural anthropology (Hymes 1972: 285) and one which invokes speakers' knowledge of how to use sentences, and other communicative forms, in relevant cultural and social contexts. *Occurrence* is the label for the third competence and this is "whether and to what extent something is done" (Hymes 1974: 95). For Hymes this seems to include style, precedent, sequencing, and norms and these are opposed to grammatical potentialities (like infinite recursion) that may never or can never be realized in actual communication. Finally, there is *feasibility* – whether and to what extent something is possible given the means of implementation available" (Hymes 1974: 95). Hymes' understanding of means here takes the form of biological constraints such as psycholinguistic parameters of memory and attention or cultural constraints on the complexity of terminological systems (Hymes 1972: 285). We might also think of these as types of affordances – constraints and capacities built into the coding medium – not unlike those associated with contemporary mediated communication platforms like Twitter, YouTube, and Zoom.

In contrast to a Chomskyan dismissal of the social worlds of speakers, Hymes opts for an integrative approach toward linguistic competence, viewing grammatical knowledge as but one of multiple competences required for speakers. In doing so, he has engaged in a larger ideological debate (Blommaert 1999) about what language is and how it should be studied. Speaking against the marginalization of language use not only countered Chomskyan formal linguistic priorities but also contributed to the formation of alternative approaches that were deeply centered in the sociocultural worlds of their speakers. In the US with its long history of reductive linguistic structuralism, Chomsky's mentalism represented an improvement over the behaviorist models associated with Bloomfield's taxonomic structuralism but, as Hymes and others demonstrated, it was not up to the task of understanding speakers' ability to communicate in their socially saturated cultural lives.

The Ethnography of Speaking became the dominant approach in linguistic anthropology, setting a more ambitious agenda based much more on the Hymesian concept of communicative competence than on Chomsky's linguistic competence. While communicative competence, as a concept, successfully rationalized an alternative approach to language, it served a dual function of both resisting a narrowing of the scope of linguistic inquiry and fortifying the role of linguistic anthropology within Anthropology. Even though it enhanced linguistic anthropology's relevance to cultural Anthropology, it was more an inspirational guide than a well-defined academic agenda. Communicative competence was more explicitly a core concept for the more specialized interests associated with the ethnography of speaking (Gumperz and Hymes 1972; Bauman and Sherzer 1974), language socialization (for example, Bernstein 1964; Slobin 1967) and research in Ethnopoetics (for example, Hymes 1981; Briggs 1988) and though it was not as explicitly connected to future developments in anthropology, such as the language ideological turn (for example, Silverstein 1979; Schieffelin et al. 1998; Kroskrity 2000; Gal and Irvine 2019), and work on indexical orders (Silverstein 2003), enregisterment (Agha 2003, 2007) or raciolinguistics (Alim et al. 2016; Rosa 2019), these developments certainly follow in a path illuminated by it. These were indeed later elaborations of the complex sociocultural contextualization of language that Hymes exhorted socially minded researchers to pursue.

Like his esteemed forerunner Edward Sapir who had critiqued the failure of formal linguists "to look beyond the pretty patterns of their subject matter" (Sapir 1949:166), Hymes sought to firmly establish a socially relevant form of linguistic research. The import of communicative competence and its compelling appeal to socially engaged research mattered even more to applied fields where a theoretically purified language was clearly of little or no value. Communicative competence was arguably as important, if not more so, to fields like applied linguistics and education. In areas such as the teaching of foreign languages, communicative competence is one of the concepts on which several models have been constructed. These models include research by Michael Canale and Merrill Swain (1980; see also Canale 1983), by Marianne Celce-Murcia, Zoltan Dornyei, and Sarah Thurrell (1995), by Constant Leung (2005), and by Lyle Bachman and Adrian Palmer (2010). Like Hymes' communicative competence these theoretical orientations view linguistic competence as a part of a more encompassing ability of the speaker to communicate appropriately in a language. Some of these approaches distinguish other competences as part of communicative competence including strategic competence, sociocultural competence, and discourse competence, further extending the Hymesian concept into the applied goal of teaching learners the complex task of communicating appropriately in a foreign language. In the area of Education, Hymes' concept of communicative competence has been similarly influential and a welcome foundation for better approaches to learning and for pedagogical reform. Cazden (2011) begins an article that revisits the concept by noting that in the mid-1960s the most likely professional assessment for the cause of school failure for many Black children was presumably their nonstandard dialect. Hymes would provide conceptual tools for better appreciating the capabilities of individual students. As Cazden (2011: 365) observes: "A focus on individual knowledge – so useful in education – entails evidence about variation in the share of the systemic potential particular individuals actually command." Along with recognizing the internal diversity of communities (for example, class variation, gender, and ethnic difference, etc.) as part of the rejection of Chomsky's idealized homogenous speech communities, communicative competence conceptually encouraged developments leading to Gutierrez and Rogoff's (2003) *repertoires of practice* and its rejection of an essentialized community culture and a uniform individual style. Thus the concept of communicative competence and its professional uptake, especially when joined with Hymes' emphasis on the role of ethnography as a critical method, combine to form an influential legacy with extraordinary influence on educational practice and theory.

4. Communicative competence and pragmatics

But perhaps most relevant for HoP readers, is the impact of Hymes' communicative competence and his related concepts for the field of pragmatics itself. As Stephen Levinson has observed in his influential textbook, pragmatics is not easily defined (Levinson 1983: 5). Though varying ideological perspectives on pragmatics can agree on a basic definition of pragmatics as "the study of language usage" (Levinson 1983: 5), or "language in use" (Huang 2014: 1), they quickly diverge in what "use" means and how it should be analytically managed. Two basic approaches to pragmatics have emerged since the late twentieth century, and these differ in how much, and in what ways they incorporate sociocultural considerations. Representing what he calls the Anglo-American school (as opposed to the Continental), Yan Huang views pragmatics as a component within a more encompassing theory of language. In this view, "the central topics of inquiry of pragmatics include implicative, presupposition, speech act, deixis, and reference" (Huang 2014: 2), and pragmatics "excludes other 'hyphenated' branches of linguistics such as anthropological linguistics, educational linguistics, and sociolinguistics" (Huang 2014:5). This component view attempts to find an especially orderly and culture-independent view that keeps the analytical spotlight on language by not admitting social and cultural factors. While this may seem to produce an admirable analytical rigor it can be faulted for not properly confronting actual contextualized use.

Informed in part by Hymes' treatment of communicative competence and other work in sociolinguistics and conversational analysis, Stephen Levinson defined pragmatics in a more inclusive manner: "the term pragmatics covers both context-dependent aspects of linguistic structure and principles of language usage and understanding that have nothing or little to do with linguistic structure" (1983:9). This approach permits a more complete exploration of communicative contexts. While Levinson rejects appropriateness as *the* defining objective of pragmatics, he recognizes that some overlap with sociolinguistics is either necessary of inevitable: "[…] most definitions of Pragmatics will occasion [sic] overlap with the field of sociolinguistics, but this definition [centered on appropriateness] would have as a consequence exact identity with a sociolinguistics construed, in the manner of Hymes (1971), as the study of *communicative competence*" (Levinson 1983:25; emphasis original). Though Levinson recognizes the complexity of appropriateness and its attendant cultural diversity and sociolinguistic variation, he also envisions a goal of filling the gap between a semantic theory and a more "complete theory of linguistic communication" rather than merely providing a minimalist context of use for a semantic component of language structure (Levinson 1983:38).

Expanding on Levinson's more broadly defined scope of pragmatics, Jef Verschueren (1999:7–11) later writes, "pragmatics constitutes a 'general functional' (i.e., cognitive, social, and cultural) perspective on linguistic phenomena in relation to their usage in the form of behavior." Even though Huang decries the supposed lack of rigor associated with a pragmatics that he describes as "the study of everything" (2014:6), he also concedes that this approach is more faithful to the original views of pragmatics expressed by Charles Morris (1938) in his *Foundations of the Theory of Signs* and more representative of Eastern European views and to the Continental school of Pragmatics more generally. Influenced by a Jakobsonian emphasis on a functional analysis of speaking, Hymes worked to develop an ethnography of communication to explore the cultural aspects of context and how speakers chose appropriate ways of speaking to accord with the cultural context of speaking. He, in turn, promoted an approach to language use that would affirm and extend this influence on the more inclusive and more socially relevant school of pragmatics. In his 1964 "Toward Ethnographies of Communication", he specifically envisions a Morris-like tripartite model with Pragmatics as a bridge between language structure and socioculturally contexted use:

> Pragmatics, concerned with the use of signs by an interpreter, might be the bridge between the present area of concern [the ethnography of communication] and Linguistics proper, and stand as name for the cultivation of theory of the use of language (and other

> codes), alongside theory of their formal and semantic structure [Morris' syntagmatics and semantics]. (Hymes 1964: 6)

Though Hymes commented on what he regarded as the proper scope of pragmatics, his more lasting contributions were in his elaboration of the sociocultural contexts of language use, and especially in his creation of the S-P-E-A-K-I-N-G mnemonic – the ethnographic components of his *speech event* model (Hymes 1974: 52–64). This model and the way it embraced cultural diversity and social variation expanded the treatment offered by Levinson (1983) who drew the vast majority of his examples of usage from ordinary language philosophy and conversational analysis and from English language data. Hymes' ethnography of communication promised to expand the possibility of analyzing cultural contexts in which speakers would use their various languages and their appeal and utility, as both a type of analysis and as a method for gathering new data, and continues to be affirmed by its inclusion in introductory texts in linguistics, linguistic anthropology, communication studies, as well as other adjacent fields.

For the reader who may be unfamiliar with the S-P-E-A-K-I-N-G components, I will identify them briefly here and recommend a closer analysis of Hymes' more detailed treatments, as in his *Foundations in Sociolinguistics*, for example (Hymes 1974). In his mnemonic, S stands for *setting* – the time and place and the physical circumstances of the location in which the communication occurs. This can be a Kuna (Panama) congress hut, a Yakan (Phillipines) house, or a U.S. Law school classroom, and the cultural constraints these settings exercised on appropriate speech within them (Sherzer 1974; Frake 1980; Mertz 1998). P represents *participants* including speaker/addressor, hearer/receiver, and audience. Status relations between participants influence the manner of Wolof (Senegal) greetings and require the lower-status persons to greet first and inquire about the well-being of the higher-status persons and their families (Irvine 1974). The metalinguistics and metapragmatics of different cultural groups often recognize culture-specific configurations of participants. African-American *louding*, as described by Mitchell-Kernan (1972) is a speech act in which a speaker designs their remarks not only for their apparent hearer but for a targeted over-hearer who is in close proximity. Kuna shamans perform a curing ceremony in which the words they speak are not directed to the patient but rather to supernatural forces who are reached by addressing a bundle of ceremonial effigies placed below the patient's hammock (Sherzer 1974).

E stands for *ends* which Hymes further divides into "ends in view", or goals (of participants), and "ends as outcomes" – the communicative achievement (Hymes 1974: 57). Keith Basso's (1979) detailed study of Cibecue joking imitations of Euro-Americans provides a useful example as Apache jokers intentionally perform their code-switched impersonations for humor and to "soften" stiff interpersonal relations but the result produces a strong affirmation of Apache identity and its associated linguistic and embodied forms. A signifies *act sequence* which Hymes views as involving the introduction and flow of message content – a parallel in language use the ordering of elements in syntactic structure. Hymes explicitly calls attention to the interdependence of component speech acts and syntactic structures (Hymes 1974: 55). In Michael K. Foster's (1974) study of Iroquois Longhouse thanksgiving ceremonies, for example, he demonstrates a cultural order of thanking lower-ranking nature spirits in a hierarchical order that eventually leads up to the Creator, as an essential part of the ceremony. And while the orators performing this ceremony must be duly appointed over their required expressions of humility before it can begin, the performers of Apache joking impersonations of "the whiteman" give no hint that their surprise performance is about to happen (Basso 1979).

K represents *key* which includes "the tone, manner, or spirit in which an act is done" (Hymes 1974: 57). It is language use's counterpart to modality in grammar. Hymes notes its association with emotion and also its power to override apparent content through sarcasm and mockery. In the Apache imitative joking, for example, the jokes are both funny and risky because they involve an extended display of Euro-American norms (such as mutual gaze and health inquiries) that are offensive to Apaches (Basso 1979).

Next, I stands for *instrumentalities* which are "all the channels and forms of speech […] joined together as means or agencies of speaking" (Hymes 1974: 60) This includes all the choices of styles, registers, dialects, and languages in the speech community's linguistic repertoire as well as options for embodied communication and non-verbal accompaniment. In multilingual societies, this includes code choices according to communicative norms as well as code-choice designed to creatively alter "the definition of the situation" as in Jan Blom and John Gumperz's study of Bokmål and regional dialects in Norway (1972). As mentioned before, a code-switch to English in which Apache is normally expected can signal the abrupt beginning of an Apache joke, but silence is also culturally appropriate for Apaches in circumstances such as dealing with strangers or the recently bereaved – contrasting with European and Euro-American practices of "small-talk" and condolences (Basso 1970).

Turning to the final two components, N signifies norms, including both norms of interaction and interpretation (Hymes 1974: 60). The distinction usefully contrasts actual norms of conduct with ideal norms as in Elinor [Ochs] Keenan's study "Norm-makers, norm-breakers: Use of Speech by Men and Women in a Malagasy Community" (1974). In that study, the speech ideal of speaking in a beautiful and calm manner was not something many Malagasy women could achieve since the hard work of interpersonal confrontation and argument was often gendered as women's work, thus sparing the men from having to engage in these more despised forms and preserving their reputation as elegant speakers. In his discussion of norm-interpretation, Hymes mentions ethnomethodologist Harold Garfinkel's (1972) concept of *ad-hocing* as an example of how social actors attempt to creatively apply existing norms to ambiguous social situations (Hymes 1974: 61).

The final element, G represents *genre* – "categories such as poem, myth, tale, proverb, riddle, curse, prayer, oration, lecture, commercial, form letter, editorial, etc." (Hymes 1974: 61). While this list consists of categories familiar to those conversant with verbal folklore and English language media, it is also compatible with identifying the formal features associated with culture-specific genres such as Burundi proverbs (Albert 1972), Western Apache historical tales (*'agodzaahi*) (Basso 1996) or Tewa ceremonial speech, *te'e hiili* (Kroskrity 1998).

S-P-E-A-K-I-N-G provided a structure for discovering and representing the many ways socio-cultural considerations are intertwined with the contexted use that was critical for linguistic anthropology and clearly relevant for a socially engaged pragmatics. As part of the ethnography of communication, it provided a much-needed rebalancing of scholarly attention to languages in their sociocultural contexts, and enriched approaches to pragmatics that were sometimes too willing to assume the universality of ordinary language philosophy or English-language-based conversational analysis. Though Hymes' mnemonic is better seen as a sensitizing concept rather than a definitive one, it has had a lasting impact in demonstrating the importance of ethnography and in appreciating the intertwined nature of culture and language use. Alessandro Duranti, for example, in his "ethnopragmatic" study of Samoan, radically questions Western theories of meaning that are centered on the intentions of speakers, and demonstrates a Samoan system of communication more concerned with the assignment of responsibility than with "reading others' minds" (Duranti 1992: 24). Working at the interface of grammaticization, politeness theory, and Tewa ethnography of communication, Kroskrity (2011) provides an ethnopragmatic account of how language structure and cultural practices of language use have merged and materialized in the form of the Tewa (Kiowa-Tanoan) language's form of negation – a fusion of both language and culture that would not have been understandable without an anthropologically inflected pragmatics.

5. Hymes' own explorations of communicative competence

As mentioned above, Dell Hymes deserves considerable credit for shaping linguistic anthropology in the United States during the second half of the twentieth century and for providing conceptual resources for a more culturally informed pragmatics. His efforts were crucial in the transformation of linguistic anthropology from a "service" subfield that would provide necessary linguistic expertise to archeologists, biological, and cultural anthropologists, to a field of linguistic inquiry that was guided by anthropological theories and concerns. His mentor at Indiana University, C. F. Voegelin in 1949 had characterized linguistic anthropology's mid-century state of the art when he published his influential critique of a linguistics "without meaning" and an anthropological study of culture "without words". Though this critique deftly analyzed the deficiencies of Bloomfieldian linguistics in which meaning was ignored in favor of the formal rigor possible in phonological and morphological analysis and illuminated the lack of a linguistic emphasis in the British social anthropology-influenced American anthropology of the 1940s and early 1950s, it neither mobilized scholars nor demonstrated the potential of greater linguistic emphasis for anthropologists. But Hymes wrote voluminously to make the case for a socioculturally based linguistics and an anthropology with proper recognition of the many functions provided by language – as medium of data collection, as theoretical model, and as cultural practice – in various anthropological projects. In addition to his field-nucleating reader in linguistic anthropology, *Language in Culture and Society*, Hymes (1964) wrote extensively and influentially in three main but partially convergent areas – the ethnography of communication, ethnopoetics, and education and communication.

Hymes' pioneering efforts in creating a field of inquiry, which he named the Ethnography of Speaking (later generalized to the more inclusive focus on Communication), began with his recognition of how the study of language use had been neglected in both linguistics and anthropology. Linguistic grammars specified what was structurally possible but not what was actually said and by whom, to whom, and in what context. Anthropologists, on the other hand, have demonstrated the cultural relativity of technology, kinship, and religion but somehow neglected communication as a topic worthy of their attention. Anthropologists by mid-twentieth century had become especially familiar with the Sapir-Whorf hypothesis, also known as *linguistic relativity*, but Hymes used that familiarity to strategically demonstrate that the relativity of linguistic structure needed to be complemented by an appreciation of the cultural relativity of language usage (Hymes 1966). He argued persuasively for recognizing the importance of social, contextual and cultural criteria that members used in producing and evaluating culturally appropriate speech. As noted in the previous section, Hymes encouraged anthropologists and other language scientists to understand that cultural concerns mattered critically at the very time that Chomsky was constructing language as an asocial phenomenon. In 1964, Hymes and his colleague John Gumperz succeeded in co-editing a landmark collection of articles from the first major conference on the Ethnography of Communication as a special issue of the *American Anthropologist*. In a fortified and expanded version, a similar collection was developed by these co-editors in 1972 as *Directions in Sociolinguistics: The Ethnography of Communication*. These collections and the movement they represented did much to allow linguistic anthropology to shed its image and former role as a "service" subfield as Hymes and other scholars succeeded in an educational campaign to more fully recognize and confront the many roles of language and linguistic analysis in anthropological research. In their "service" role, linguistic anthropologists existed primarily to teach other anthropologists how to learn field languages and provide relevant linguistic expertise in research agendas set by archeologists and cultural anthropologists. In accord with "reflectionist" language ideologies (Silverstein 1979) that limited the role of language to providing labels for cultural things, language was typically viewed as an epiphenomenon.

Another key area in Hymes' research is a topic that has come to be known as *ethnopoetics* – the appreciation of narrative and other verbal art that uses both linguistic and anthropological analysis as a basis for understanding and interpretation. Dell Hymes' interest in this area, directed through his own original research was represented early on in research, dating to 1959 and the publication of his "Myth and Tale Titles of the Lower Chinook" in the *Journal of American Folklore* and continued throughout his life most visibly in the two major collections of his writing on the topic: *"In Vain I Tried to Tell You": Essays in Native American Ethnopoetics* (1981) and *"Now I Only Know So Far": Essays in Ethnopoetics* (2003). A major accomplishment in Hymes' work in this area was his recognition of what he called *measured verse* – linguistic patterning other than by rhyme and meter which often involved patterns of repetition of discourse features and forms of linguistic parallelism. Preferring to work on materials indigenous to his home area, Hymes often studied previously documented narratives from Chinookan and other Pacific Northwest communities. His detailed analysis and careful translation of narratives like "Seal and Her Younger Brother Lived There" revealed how attention to linguistic and cultural detail provided a basis for a more locally warranted reading of these texts – a reading which took into account the identities of the performers and their audiences. In that article, Hymes used several ethnopoetic details to reinterpret a myth previously collected by the psychological anthropologist Melville Jacobs. One of these details was the gender identity of the performer, Victoria Howard. This brief myth narrative involves the murder of Seal's brother and the repeated warnings of danger provided by Seal's young daughter of signs of danger. These are spoken warnings that Seal, conforming to gendered norms of politeness, chooses to ignore. In the climax of the story, the daughter discovers her murdered uncle and screams to her mother, "In vain I tried to tell you" – a commentary on how adhering to gender norms prevented the necessary intervention. Thus, Hymes' reinterpretation is one that restores the identity of the narrator as an important part of the myth performance and it confirms the value of using of a more ethnographic approach to understanding the local meanings of myth texts and performances rather than a decontextualized linguistic interpretation of texts.

A third area of sustained research, one that represents the intersection of Hymes' abiding interest in oral narrative with his service to the field of education, is one that may be termed *narrative inequality*. In work on this topic, which is sampled in his edited collection, *Ethnography, Linguistics, Narrative Inequality: Toward an Understanding of Voice* (Hymes 1996) he examines written and oral narratives of Native Americans and African Americans, and explores how many educational institutions enforce literacy – and social class-based ideals that reproduce class difference. Attempting to provide alternative goals, Hymes develops an ethnopoetic notion of voice as the individual's preferred languages and styles – his or her *voice* – for the narrative construction of self and society.

This emphasis on language and identity, genre, contexts of performance, and language and society clearly demonstrates the connection between his ethnography of communication and his ethnopoetics. He also develops a methodological emphasis on critical ethnography as a resource for social critique and pedagogical reform. This will also be taken up in the next section.

In addition to these main areas of sustained research, Hymes was an influential scholar who also made significant contributions, as a researcher, programmatic writer, and book and journal editor, including such topics as the history of linguistics and linguistic anthropology (for example, his 1974 *Studies in the History of Linguistics* and 1983 *Essays in the History of Linguistic Anthropology*), and studies of language contact and creolization (his 1971 edited collection *Pidginization and Creolization of Languages*). In other publications, he foreshadowed more contemporary interests in such works as his 1965 *The Use of Computers in Anthropology* and his 1972 edited collection *Reinventing Anthropology*. In the latter work he and other authors asked the radical question; If anthropology did not exist, would it have to be reinvented? The volume explores the uses of an activist anthropology in advocacy for the people it studies and as a basis for a socially engaged anthropology more generally. As in other aspects of Hymes' *oeuvre*, he displays here what has been described as his career-long linkage of "ethnography and democracy" (Blommaert 2009).

6. Continuing influence and recognition

Though many aspects of the research agenda promoted by Hymes became not only paradigmatic but also deeply inscribed in institutional practices of departments of anthropology and applied linguistics and schools of education, perhaps his most lasting influences are in the areas of ethnopoetics and the ethnography of educational contexts. I will mention two edited collections that explicitly advance his legacy in these domains. One of these emerged from a double session of the annual American Anthropological Association meetings, co-organized by Paul V. Kroskrity and Anthony Webster in Montreal in 2011, and devoted to honoring Hymes' many contributions to ethnopoetics. Twelve scholars, including the organizers, revisited, critiqued, and extended Hymes' research in further explorations of measured verse, voice, performance, and narrative inequality. That session was ultimately entextualized first as a special issue of the *Journal of Folklore Research* and later as the edited volume *The Legacy of Dell Hymes: Ethnopoetics, Narrative Inequality, and Voice* (Kroskrity and Webster 2015). Beyond applying ethnopoetic analysis to languages like Apache, Koryak, Mono, Yokuts, Kaska, Navajo, Yurok, and Hupa, the authors in these various chapters demonstrated both the importance of Hymes' pioneering work – especially in regard to narrative inequality and the voices of specific storytellers – as well as its continuing relevance. In the field of education, Teresa

McCarty's edited volume (2011) dedicated to Hymes, *Ethnography and Language Policy*, represents a similar testament to Hymes' ongoing relevance – especially in its attention to policy as sociocultural practice and to the importance of critical ethnography as a basis for pedagogical reform. In an important chapter dedicated to exploring new directions in language policy that would promote Indigenous language survival in a variety of Indigenous communities, the authors begin by returning to the Hymes-Chomsky ideological debate previously mentioned, and the Hymesian rejection of ideal speaker-listeners, homogenous speech communities, and "a liberal humanism which merely recognizes the abstract potentiality of all languages, to a humanism which can deal with [...] the inequalities that actually obtain, and help to transform them through knowledge of the ways in which language is actually organized as a human problem and resource" (Hymes 1980a: 55–56). In using ethnography both to confront social inequality and to provide a basis for social transformation, they rely heavily on Hymes' (1980b) emphasis on the special attributes of ethnography as a critically conscious and democratized way of knowing (McCarty et al. 2011: 31). This emphasis on allowing distinctive voices to exist, to survive, to emerge, as observed by Blommaert (2009), is a hallmark of Hymes that may make his work even more relevant going forward as democratic societies struggle with authoritarianism (Levitsky and Ziblatt 2018).

But it would be inappropriate to appreciate and otherwise celebrate Hymes' achievements as a scholar of sociolinguistics and language use without mentioning a significant gap between his high-minded achievements of social significance and the faults of his professional conduct. As Monica Heller and Bonnie McElhinney (2017: 215) have already noted: it was "alleged that he was responsible for sexually harassing a number of women, which had a major impact on the careers of more than one female scholar (this information comes from personal communication with a number of scholars)." While it is appropriate to note his professional achievements, the ethical standards of our time require accountability for personal misconduct affecting the professional lives of others and, indeed, the entire profession more generally.

References

Agha, Asif. 2003. "The social life of cultural value." *Language & Communication* 23: 231–73.
Agha, Asif. 2007. *Language and Social Relations*. Cambridge: Cambridge University Press.
Albert, Ethel M. 1972. "Cultural patterning of speech behavior in Burundi." In *Directions in Sociolinguistics*, ed. by John J. Gumperz and Dell H. Hymes, 72–105. New York: Holt, Rinehart, & Winston.
Alim, H. Samy, John R. Rickford, and Arnetha F. Ball, (eds). 2016. *Raciolinguistics: How Language Shapes Our Ideas about Race*. Oxford: Oxford University Press.
Bachman, Lyle and Adrian Palmer. 2010. *Language Assessment in Practice*. Oxford: Oxford University Press.

Basso, Keith H. 1970. "'To give up on words': Silence in Western Apache culture." *Southwestern Journal of Anthropology* 26 (3): 213–230.

Basso, Keith H. 1979. *Portraits of the Whiteman: Linguistic Play and Cultural Symbols Among the Western Apache*. Cambridge: Cambridge University Press.

Basso, Keith H. 1996. *Wisdom Sits in Places: Landscape and language among the Western Apache*. Albuquerque, NM: University of New Mexico Press.

Bauman, Richard and Joel Sherzer (eds). 1974. *Explorations in the Ethnography of Speaking*. Cambridge: Cambridge University Press.

Bernstein, Basil. 1964. "Elaborated and restricted codes: Their social origins and some consequences." In *The Ethnography of Communication*, ed. by John J. Gumperz and Dell H. Hymes, *American Anthropologist* 66 (6), Part 2, 55–69.

Blom, Jan P. & John J. Gumperz. 1972. "Social meaning in linguistic structures: Code-switching in Norway." In *Directions in Sociolinguistics*, ed. by John J. Gumperz and Dell H. Hymes, 407–434. New York: Holt, Rinehart, & Winston.

Blommaert, Jan. (ed). 1999. *Language Ideological Debates*. Berlin: DeGruyter.

Blommaert, Jan. 2009. "Ethnography and democracy: Hymes's political theory of language." *Text & Talk* 29: 257–276.

Bloomfield, Leonard. 1933. *Language*. Chicago: University of Chicago Press.

Briggs, Charles L. 1988. *Competence in Performance: The Creativity of Tradition in Mexicano Verbal Art*. Philadelphia: University of Pennsylvania Press.

Canale, Michael. 1983. "From communicative competence to communicative language pedagogy." In *Language and Communication*, ed. by J.C. Richard and R.W. Schmidt, 2–14. London: Longman.

Canale, Michael and Merrill Swain. 1980. "Theoretical bases of communicative approaches to second language teaching and testing." *Applied Linguistics* 1 (1): 1–47.

Caton, Steven C. 1987. "Contributions of Roman Jakobson." *Annual Review of Anthropology* 16: 233–260.

Cazden, Courtney. 2011. "Dell Hymes's construct of "communicative competence." *Anthropology and Education Quarterly* 42(4):364–369.

Celce-Murcia, Marianne, Zoltan Dornyei, and Sarah Thurrell. 1995. "Communicative competence: a Pedagogically motivated model with content specifications." *Issues in Applied Linguistics* 6 (2): 5–35.

Chomsky, Noam. 1965. *Aspects of the Theory of Syntax*. Cambridge MS: MIT Press.

Chomsky, Noam. 1966. *Cartesian Linguistics*. New York: Harper and Row.

Duranti, Alessandro. 1992. "Intentions, self, and responsibility: An essay in Samoan ethnopragmatics." In *Responsibility and Evidence in Oral Discourse*, ed. by Jane H. Hill and Judith T. Irvine, 24–47. Cambridge: Cambridge University Press.

Foster, Michael K. 1974. "When words become deeds: An analysis of three Iroquois longhouse speech events." In *Explorations in the Ethnography of Speaking*, ed. By Richard Bauman and Joel Sherzer, 354–367. Cambridge: Cambridge University Press.

Frake, Charles O. 1980. "How to enter a Yakan house." In *Language and Cultural Description: Essays by Charles O. Frake*, ed. By Anwar S. Dil, 214–232. Stanford: Stanford University Press.

Gal, Susan and Judith T. Irvine. 2019. *Signs of Difference: Language and Ideology in Social Life*. Cambridge: Cambridge University Press.

Garfinkel, Harold. 1972. "Remarks on ethnomethodology." In *Directions in Sociolinguistics*, ed. by John J. Gumperz and Dell H. Hymes, 309–324. New York: Holt, Rinehart & Winston.

Gumperz, John J. 1968. "The Speech Community." *International Encyclopedia of the Social Sciences* 9:381–386.

Gumperz, John J. and Dell Hymes. (eds). 1972. *Directions in Sociolinguistics: the Ethnography of Communication*. Holt, Rinhart, & Winston.

Gutierrez, Kris D. and Barbara Rogoff. 2003. "Cultural ways of learning: Individual ways or repertoires of practice." *Educational Researcher* 32 (5): 19–25.

Heller, Monica and Bonnie McElhinny. 2017. *Language, Capitalism, and Colonialism: Toward a Critical History*. Toronto: University of Toronto Press.

Huang, Yan. 2014. *Pragmatics* (second edition). Oxford: Oxford University Press.

Hymes, Dell. H. 1959. "Myth and tale titles of the Lower Chinook." In *The Journal of American Folklore*, 72 (284), 139–145.

Hymes, Dell. H. 1964. "Toward Ethnographies of Communication." In *American Anthropologist* 66 (6): 1–34.

Hymes, Dell H. 1966. "Two types of linguistic relativity (with examples from Amerindian ethnography). In *Sociolinguistics*, ed. by William Bright, 114–157. The Hague: Mouton.

Hymes, Dell H. 1967. "The anthropology of communication." In *Human Communication Theory*, ed. by Frank E. Dance, 1–39. New York: Holt, Rinehart & Winston.

Hymes, Dell H. 1971. "Competence and performance in linguistic theory." In *Language Acquisition, Models and Methods*, ed. by Renira Huxley and Elisabeth Ingram, 3–28. New York: Academic Press.

Hymes, Dell H. 1972. "On communicative competence." In *Sociolinguistics*, ed. by J. B. Pride and Janet Holmes, 269–293. New York: Penguin.

Hymes, Dell H. 1974. *Foundations in Sociolinguistics*. Philadelphia: University of Pennsylvania Press.

Hymes, Dell H. 1975. "Pre-war Prague school and post-war American anthropological linguistics." In *The Transformational-Generative Paradigm and Modern Linguistic Theory*, ed. by E. F. Koerner, 359–380. Amsterdam: John Benjamins.

Hymes, Dell H. 1980a. "Speech and language: On the origins and foundations of inequality among speakers. In *Language in education: Ethnolinguistic essays*, ed. by Dell H. Hymes, 19–61. Washington, D.C: Center for Applied Linguistics.

Hymes, Dell H. 1980b. "What is ethnography?" In *Language in education: Ethnolinguistic Essays*, ed. by Dell H. Hymes, 88–103. Washington, D.C.: Center for Applied Linguistics.

Hymes, Dell H. 1981. *"In Vain I Tried to Tell You": Essays in Native American Ethnopoetics*. Philadelphia: University of Pennsylvania Press.

Hymes, Dell H. 1992. "The concept of communicative competence revisited." In *Thirty Years of Linguistic Evolution*, ed. by Martin Pütz, 31–58. Amsterdam: John Benjamins.

Hymes, Dell H. 1996. *Ethnography, Linguistics, and Narrative Inequality: Toward an Understanding of Voice*. London: Taylor & Francis.

Hymes, Dell H. 2003. *Now I Only Know So Far: Essays in Ethnopoetics*. Lincoln, NE: University of Nebraska Press.

Hymes, Dell H. (ed). 1964. *Language in Culture and Society: A Reader in Linguistics and Anthropology*. New York: Harper and Row.

Irvine, Judith. 1974. "Strategies of status manipulation in the Wolof greeting. In *Explorations in the Ethnography of Speaking*, ed. by Richard Bauman and Joel Sherzer, 167–191. Cambridge: Cambridge University Press.

Jakobson, Roman. 1960. "Concluding Statement: Linguistics and Poetics." In *Style in Language*, ed. by Thomas A. Sebeok, 350–377. Cambridge, MS: M.I.T. Press.

Keenan, Elinor [Ochs]. 1974. "Norm-makers, norm-breakers: Uses of speech by men and women in a Malagasy community." In *Explorations in the Ethnography of Speaking*, ed. by Richard Bauman and Joel Sherzer, 125–143. Cambridge: Cambridge University Press.

Kroskrity, Paul V. 1998. Arizona Tewa kiva speech as a manifestation of a dominant language ideology. In *Language Ideology: Practice and Theory*, ed. by Bambi Schieffelin, Kathryn A. Woolard, and Paul V. Kroskrity, 103–122. New York: Oxford University Press.

Kroskrity, Paul V. 2011. "Getting negatives in Arizona Tewa: On the relevance of ethnopragmatics and language ideologies to understanding a case of grammaticalization. *Pragmatics* (IPrA) 20: 91–107.

Kroskrity, Paul V. (ed). 2000. *Regimes of Language: Ideologies, Polities, and Identities*. Santa Fe, NM: School of American Research.

Kroskrity, Paul V. and Anthony K. Webster (eds). 2015. *The Legacy of Dell Hymes: Ethnopoetics, Narrative Inequality, and Voice*. Bloomington, IN: Indiana University Press.

Leung, Constant. 2005. "Convivial communication: Recontexualizing communicative competence." *International Journal of Applied Linguistics* 15 (2): 119–144.

Levinson, Stephen C. 1983. *Pragmatics*. Cambridge: Cambridge University Press.

Levitsky, Steven and Daniel Ziblatt. 2018. *How Democracies Die*. New York: Crown.

McCarty, Teresa L. (ed). 2011. *Ethnography and Language Policy*. London: Routledge.

McCarty, Teresa L., Mary Eunice Romero-Little, Larisa Warhol, and Ofelia Zepeda. 2011. "Critical ethnography and Indigenous language survival." In *Ethnography and Language Policy*, ed. by Teresa L. McCarty, 30–51. London: Routledge.

Mertz, Elizabeth. 1998. "Linguistic Ideology and Praxis in a U.S. Law School Classroom." In *Language Ideology: Practice and Theory*, ed. by Bambi Schieffelin, Kathryn A. Woolard, and Paul V. Kroskrity, 149–162. Oxford: Oxford University Press.

Mitchell-Kernan, Claudia. 1972. "Signifying and marking: Two African-American speech acts." In *Directions in Sociolinguistics*, ed. by John J. Gumperz and Dell H. Hymes, 161–179. New York: Holt, Rinehart and Winston.

Moore, Robert E. 2008. Listening to Indians. *Reed Magazine, Winter*, 87(1): 12–17.

Morris, Charles W. 1938. "Foundations of the theory of signs. In *International Encyclopedia of Unified Science*, ed. by Otto Neurath, Rudolph Carnap, and Charles W. Morris, 7–138. Chicago: University of Chicago Press.

Murray, Stephan O. 1998. *American Sociolinguistics: Theorists and Theory Groups*. Amsterdam: John Benjamins.

Rosa, Jonathan. 2019. *Looking Like a Language, Sounding Like a Race: Raciolinguistic Ideologies and the Learning of Latinidad*. Oxford: Oxford University Press.

Sapir, Edward. 1949. *Selected Writings of Edward Sapir*. David G. Mandelbuam, ed. Berkeley, CA: University of California Press.

Schieffelin, Bambi, Kathryn A. Woolard, and Paul V. Kroskrity, (eds). 1998. *Language Ideology: Practice and Theory*. Oxford University Press

Sherzer, Joel. 1974. "Namakke, sunmakke, kormakke: Three types of Cuna speech event." In *Explorations in the Ethnography of Speaking*, ed. by Richard Bauman and Joel Sherzer, 263–282. Cambridge: Cambridge University Press.

Silverstein, Michael. 1979. "Language structure and linguistic ideology." In *The Elements: Parasesession on Linguistic Units and Levels*, ed. by, Paul R. Clyne, William F. Hanks and Carol L. Hofbauer, 193–247. Chicago: Chicago Linguistics Society.

Silverstein, Michael. 2003. "Indexical order and the dialectics of sociolinguistic life." *Language & Communication* 23(3–4): 193–229.

Silverstein, Michael. 2010. Dell Hathaway Hymes. *Language* 86: 933–939.

Slobin, Dan (ed). 1967. *A field manual for cross-cultural study of the acquisition of communicative competence*. Berkeley, CA: Psychology Department UC-Berkeley.

Verschueren, Jef. 1999. *Understanding Pragmatics*. London: Arnold.

Directives
(with a special emphasis on requests)

Nicolas Ruytenbeek
KU Leuven

1. Introduction

To date, a lot of attention has been devoted to the speech act of requesting, especially from the cross-cultural perspective pioneered by Blum-Kulka et al. (1989). In fact, requests have been the bread and butter of speech act theoretic pragmatics, with a clear focus on their various indirect realizations (see, e.g., Ruytenbeek 2017a for a review of experimental work and Ruytenbeek 2021 for a critical discussion). Unlike previous review articles devoted to (indirect) requests (e.g., Ruytenbeek 2017a; Walker 2013), I will leave aside the discussion of (in)directness, a phenomenon that is not specific to requests, nor to directives more generally, but applies to a wide range of speech act types (Ruytenbeek 2021). In the present article, I will focus on the philosophical and theoretical foundations underlying directive speech acts, including a discussion of the various proposals for distinguishing between the subtypes of directives.

Sometimes, in empirical research on directives, requests are equated with directives. This is, for example, the case in Freytag's (2020) study of business email directives. However, in the original tradition in philosophy of language (Searle 1969), requests are but one subtype of directives, alongside questions, suggestions, warnings, begging, commands, to only name a few. One of the aims of this chapter will therefore be to examine the properties of directives in general, and of requests in particular. Focusing on the directive speech act type, I will critically address the different definitions of the category of directive speech acts and of requests that have been proposed to this day.

Not only would a systematic review of the empirical literature on requests be difficult to achieve in a single chapter, but the results of such an endeavor would also be inconsistent for several reasons. To begin with, most of our knowledge about the form and structure of directives comes from discourse completion tasks (DCTs), a technique widely criticized for its artificial nature and which has led to different results compared to other data collection instruments such as naturally occurring discourse, role plays and multiple-choice questionnaires (Flöck 2016: 43–59). The methods that have been used to collect production data for requests and directives more generally are so diverse that any generalization of the findings of a particular study would be virtually impossible. Second, the fact that the form of requests is sensitive both to the modality of utterance (written, spoken or signed, including a multimodal dimension) and to social variables such as power, familiarity and gender makes it even more difficult to achieve a clear picture of how all these contextual ingredients shape the form of directives. Finally, there is a marked asymmetry in terms of the amount of data that have been collected for different languages; for instance, much more data on requests are available for English and Spanish than for minority languages or languages spoken by small populations.

This contribution is structured as follows. I first address the features that constitute the category of directives (Section 2) before zooming in on the features that allow us to distinguish between different subcategories of directives (Section 3). Then, in Section 4, I consider the face-threatening potential of directives and the politeness strategies that can be used to compensate for this risk. This issue leads me to the discussion of pre-requests (Section 5) and the variety of linguistic modifiers that can either minimize or intensify the imposition entailed by the performance of a directive (Section 6). In Section 7, I propose an explanation of how the force exerted by a directive typically results in an obligation for the addressee. Section 8 offers a summary of the main topics of this chapter; I also outline promising directions for future research on directives based on recent developments in multimodal pragmatics and neuropragmatics.

2. What is a directive?

In this section, I will first discuss the generic notion of a directive speech act based on the philosophical tradition from which it sprung, i.e., Searle's (1969) speech act theory, and compare the definitions of directives available in the literature. I will then review, in Section 3, the criteria that have been proposed to differentiate between the subtypes of directives (e.g., a request vs. a command).

2.1 Definitions in terms of necessary and sufficient conditions

An early attempt to define directive speech acts is Austin's (1962) discussion of the illocutionary category of *exercitives*, which encompasses utterances consisting in exercising a power, a right, or an influence, such as ordering someone to perform an action, or sentencing someone to death (Austin 1962: 150, 154–156). For Austin, an exercitive is "the giving of a decision in favour of or against a certain course of action, or advocacy of it" (1962: 154). In line with this definition, the category of exercitives is quite heterogeneous. While this category comprises requests, orders, commands, and beggings (these speech acts are nowadays usually referred to as *directives*), it also includes speech acts such as proclaiming and declaring a meeting closed/open, which constitute changes in institutional states of affairs, and thus require extralinguistic institutions for their performance to be successful.

In SAT, an *illocutionary act* (or, for short, a speech act) is the primary meaningful unit in the production and comprehension of natural language. It can be decomposed into an illocutionary force (F) applied to a propositional content (p), and has the form $F(p)$ (Searle 1969: 122–123; Searle and Vanderveken 1985: 1). The force of an utterance amounts to the utterance achieving an illocutionary act of a certain type, e.g., a directive. In Searle's version of speech act theory (SAT), the category of *directives* is more homogenous than Austin's exercitives. The speech acts of suggestions, requests, commands, and orders, which constitute the group of directives, consist in a speaker (S) telling (with varying degrees of strength) their addressee(s) to perform an action (Searle and Vanderveken 1985: 198–205; Vanderveken 1990: 189–198). The propositional content of a directive speech act is the state of affairs that the addressee (A) should bring about in order to comply with the directive. For example, the propositional content of the command performed with (1) is that A will close the door.

(1) Close the door.

In SAT, the understanding of *sentence meaning* (Grice 1989) determines which illocutionary act S intends to perform (Searle 1969: 48–49). According to Grice (1957), a speaker S who means p by uttering a sentence must have the following three intentions: the intention (i_1) to provoke an effect on A's mental states; the intention (i_2) that A recognizes i_1 (reflexive intention); the intention (i_3) that the satisfaction of the reflexive intention i_2 will not only be the cause but also the reason for the satisfaction of i_1. In line with Grice's (1957) definition, in SAT, illocutionary acts must be understood as originating from S's communicative intentions, which correspond to Grice's intentions i_1, i_2 and i_3, in order to be successful (Searle 1969: 42–50).

Identifying the intended illocutionary act is obvious when S is speaking 'literally', as in the imperative request in (1). In that case, S performs a literal directive illocutionary act because, in SAT, the imperative sentence type/mood directly encodes the directive illocutionary force. What A has to do is determine whether the illocutionary act S intended to perform by uttering (1) corresponds to the sentence meaning of (1). To do this, A resorts to their knowledge about what SAT takes to be the encoded meaning of imperatives and uses Gricean principles of conversational cooperation and background information. This knowledge enables A to infer S's communicative intentions.[1]

The illocutionary force of an utterance determines, in turn, a set of rules or conditions that must be met for the performance of a SA to be successful. These rules, which

---

1. According to Grice's (1975: 45–46) Cooperative Principle, speakers are expected to make "a conversational contribution such as is required, at the stage at which it occurs, by the accepted purpose or direction of the talk exchange in which [they are] engaged".

are called *felicity conditions* in SAT, are of the following types: the preparatory conditions (a), the propositional content condition (b), the sincerity condition (c), and the essential condition (d) (Searle 1969: 64–71; 1975: 71).

a. The preparatory conditions for a directive involve the assumption that (S believes that) A is capable of performing the action requested and that it is not obvious that A would perform that action otherwise.
b. The propositional content condition for a directive is the proposition that A will perform a future act.
c. For the sincerity condition to be met, S must entertain the desire that A carry out the action requested.
d. The essential condition means that S's issuing a directive illocutionary act *counts as* an attempt to get A to bring about the truth of the propositional content. The essential condition relates to the point of S's utterance: the "illocutionary point of a type of illocutionary act is that purpose which is essential to its being an act of that type" (Searle and Vanderveken 1985: 14). For a directive, the utterance has to count as an attempt to get A to carry out some action.

According to Searle and Vanderveken (1985: 21–23), if either the propositional content condition (b) or the essential condition (d) is not met, the directive will not be successful and the utterance will not be interpreted as a directive. By contrast, in cases where one of the preparatory (a) or sincerity conditions (c) does not obtain, the performance of the directive will not be successful, but the utterance will nevertheless be interpreted as such. In these cases, a *defective interpretation* will be triggered. An example of a defective directive corresponding to a violation of the sincerity condition is that of a general who commands their soldiers to climb a hill where they will meet a certain death. While they do not actually want them to go there (they do not want them to die), they nonetheless issue the command because it is part of their military duty to do so. In this case, their utterance will nonetheless be considered a directive. Another example is that of exam questions, which, for SAT, would qualify as defective too. Exam questions, in which S does not need to know the answer, but, rather, wants to know whether A knows it, are distinguished from 'real' questions in which S wants to know the answer to the question asked.

Another definition of directives in terms of necessary and sufficient conditions is proposed by Bach and Harnish (1979), for whom the performance of a directive entails S's intention to provide A with a reason to do some action. For Bach and Harnish (1979: 124), directives express "the speaker's intention that the [addressee] act because of S's desire or S's utterance itself"; the successful performance of a directive requires A's recognition of this intention. For example, S can command their child to shut up, just to keep up appearances in the presence of bystanders, and without intending their child to take their command as a reason to shut up. For Bach and Harnish, the directive would be successful because the utterance *expresses* S's intention that their child comply with the directive. By contrast, this example would be a non-successful directive in SAT because S's utterance would not *count as* an attempt to cause A's compliance, i.e., the essential condition would be violated.

For Alston (2000: 70–71), when S performs a SA, they are only taking responsibility for the fact that the conditions relevant to the SA are satisfied. An utterance thus constitutes a SA by virtue of a *normative* fact about S, i.e., that S has changed their normative position and is thus open to the possibility of being corrected or contradicted if some conditions for the performance of the SA are not satisfied. According to Alston's (2000: 97–103) normative definition of directives, what is required for the successful performance of a directive is not that A be obliged to do some action but, rather, that S take the responsibility for the obligation they are imposing on A. The successful performance of a directive also requires the satisfaction of appropriate background conditions (corresponding to SAT's preparatory conditions). What Alston means by *obligation* is that "whenever [A is] subject to blame for doing or not doing something, what lies behind this is some obligation on [A's] part [A] failed to carry out" (2000: 100). This obligation is a *prima facie* obligation in the sense that it is subject to being overridden by another, incompatible obligation (Alston 2000: 65). For instance, if I am told to arrive at the office at 8 AM, the obligation can be overridden if I need to bring my daughter to the hospital at the same time. For Alston (2000: 98), understanding an utterance as a directive thus amounts to recognizing that S purports to impose on A an obligation to do an action, but not that the purported obligation takes effect. Thus, in Alston's (2000) account, it is not S's intention that A do some action that is part of the schema for directives, but rather S's taking responsibility for the fulfilment of that intention. Whether the sincerity condition should obtain is therefore irrelevant to the (successful) performance of a directive.

Kissine's (2009, 2013: 104–116) proposal diverges from Bach and Harnish's (1979) because, instead of conceiving a directive as the *expression* of S's intention that their utterance be a reason to act, he claims that a directive *is* a reason for action. For Kissine (2009, 2013), to count as a directive with the content *p*, S's utterance must be, with respect to the conversational background, a sufficient and necessary reason for A to decide to bring about the truth of *p*. In such cases, the fact that S provides A with a reason to act will become part of their *common ground*, which is the set of propositions that S and A mutually assume can be taken for granted for the purpose of the conversational exchange at hand (cf. Stalnaker 2002).

2.2 Definitions in terms of graded membership

In the definitions we have discussed so far, scholars propose a set of necessary and sufficient conditions to be fulfilled (or assumed) for an utterance to *count as* a directive SA. From an alternative (specifically cognitive) perspective, however, the category of directives can be said to be graded in nature, and defined in terms of a number of features satisfied (or not) by the members of the category.

Cognitive linguistic definitions of speech act categories originate in Johnson's (1987) approach to meaning, developed against the framework of *embodied cognition* (see, e.g., Rohrer 2007). For Johnson (1987: 41–64), we experience physical forces that make their way into the conceptual structures, allowing us to understand meaning, to reason, and to communicate. The meaningful, *gestalt* structure that constitutes our notion of *force* can be decomposed into several features (Johnson 1987: 43–44). Force is experienced through interaction, and conceptualized as oriented in a certain direction. A force typically includes a single path of motion, has a source, is directed towards a target, with varying degrees of intensity, and is the means by which causal interaction is achieved between the source and the target. The first schema he proposed, *compulsion*, corresponds to the general notion of force (Figure 1).

Figure 1. Illustration of Johnson's (1987) compulsion schema

According to Johnson, it makes sense to consider that SAs are conceptually experienced in terms of force interactions. In fact, the speech act theoretic definition of an illocutionary act itself is based on the "conduit metaphor" identified by Reddy (1979) (see Johnson 1987: 58–60 for a discussion). Reddy argued that the semantic structures of a language are largely determined by how people conceptualize their roles of speaker and addressee. In English, a major such structure is the "figurative assertion that human language transfers human thoughts [...]" (Reddy 1979: 287): language is conceptualized as a channel (a *conduit*) through which thoughts and feelings are conveyed by words and sentences. According to Johnson (1987: 59), the conduit metaphor is an elaboration of the *compulsive force* image schema, which itself is a specification of the path schema: a force originates from a source, with a given magnitude, moving along a path in a certain direction. Accordingly, directives "exert a force to compel the [addressee] to realize some state of affairs" (Johnson 1987: 60). Issuing a directive SA thus amounts to a speaker exerting some degree of (mental) force towards the addressee's performance of an action.

2.3 Provisional conclusion

The cognitive linguistic approaches to directives are not that different from the traditional speech act theoretic studies. In Searle and Vanderveken (1985), for instance, all the subtypes of directives share a common core (illocutionary point), and differ according to several dimensions, such as degree of strength of the illocutionary point (or sincerity conditions). The schema of compulsive force would parallel the directive illocutionary point in SAT, and the more specific instances of this basic schema could alternatively be defined in terms of conditions on the performance of the corresponding particular directive subtypes. SAT and the cognitive linguistic approaches thus have a number of similarities as to the preconditions of directives and how particular directive subtypes are related to a common *directive core*. However, they diverge in several respects. For cognitive linguists, the successful performance of a directive does not entail that all the features of the directive category are checked; if the utterance exhibits at least some features (not necessarily the central ones), then this is sufficient for the utterance to convey the force of a directive. In such a case, the utterance will be considered by cognitive linguists as a non-prototypical directive, whereas, for SAT, it will not be considered a directive at all. The cognitive linguistic approaches are thus more flexible than SAT in that they make it easier to account for borderline cases of directives.

In Ruytenbeek (2017a), I proposed that the notion of a directive is a vague concept that does not come with a prototype (cf. Kamp and Partee 1995), and I defined the graded category of directives with respect to the quality of having some degree of force exertion. In effect, some exemplars of the category of directives involve a higher degree of force exertion than others. Exemplars of the category that involve a very weak degree of force exertion will count as peripheral members, while SAs that do not involve any degree of force exertion will count as non-exemplars of the category. This definition accounts for a variety of degrees of force exertion regardless of the expressions used to perform them. This definition is also compatible with force dynamic definitions of the categories corresponding to the subtypes of directives, as long as these categories include a feature of force exertion – which may or may not be satisfied by the members of these categories. Another advantage of this definition is that it also holds for non-verbal directives. For instance, it is possible to request that someone close the window by making gestures such as, to only name a few, a pointing finger, a hand movement, or turning the head towards the window and frowning. Like verbal directives, these gestures are conceptualized as forces exerted by an agent towards an addressee's performance of some expected action.

3. Subtypes of directives

Having addressed in some detail the features that constitute the macro-category of directive speech acts, let us move on to the discussion of the most influential studies bearing on the distinction of the different types of directives, including requests.

3.1 Definitions in terms of necessary and sufficient conditions

Alongside the illocutionary point, the preparatory conditions, propositional content condition, and sincerity conditions, two additional features make up the directive illocutionary force (Searle and Vanderveken 1985: 15–20). First, the *degree of strength* of the illocutionary force differentiates, for instance, requesting from insisting, the latter consisting in a stronger attempt to get A to perform an action. A difference in strength can have different sources. For instance, relative to requesting, pleading involves a stronger desire on the part of S that A perform the action. Second, some illocutionary acts require special preparatory conditions for their illocutionary point to be achieved. For example, for the performance of commands and orders to be successful, S must be in a position of authority relative to A and they must invoke that position when producing their utterance.

There is a consensus on the view that the class of directives comprises not only requesting, questioning, insisting, pleading, and commanding, but also suggesting, ordering, and begging (e.g., Bach and Harnish 1979; Pérez Hernández 2013; Pérez Hernández and Ruiz de Mendoza 2002; Searle 1969, 1975; Searle and Vanderveken 1985). However, it is less clear whether warning and advising too should be classified as directives. The main difference between advising and warning is that with advising the utterance counts as an undertaking to the effect that the action is beneficial to A, and with warning that the event is not in A's best interest (e.g., Searle 1969: 66–67). Even though they note that advising and warning can be either assertive or directive, Searle and Vanderveken (1985: 202–203) and Vanderveken (1990: 197) classify these two SAs as directives, arguing that the aim of issuing advice (or a warning) is in general to get A (not) to perform some vaguely defined action (see also Bach and Harnish 1979), as when saying *Watch out!* or *Be careful!*

Bach and Harnish (1979: 47–49) classify directives into *requestives, questions, requirements, prohibitives, advisories,* and *permissives*. With *requestives*, S intends their utterance to constitute a necessary reason for A to comply; for instance, requesting, begging, and inviting express both S's desire that A do something and S's intention that A perform that action at least in part because of S's desire. For Bach and Harnish, *questioning* is a special case of requesting, namely, requesting A to provide a piece of information by way of an answer. *Requirements* such as charging, demanding, ordering, and commanding differ specifically from requestives because they express S's intention that their utterance constitute a *sufficient* reason for A to act – the utterance being such a reason by virtue of S's authority over A. Another difference between requestives and requirements is that requirements do not involve S's desire that A perform the action. *Prohibitives*, such as forbidding or restricting, are requirements that A not do something. With *advisories*, S expresses the belief that A's doing something is in A's best interest, rather than S's desire that A perform that action; S also expresses the intention that A take S's belief as a reason to act. Warning is a particular type of advisory that implies the existence of a possible danger or inconvenience for A; this definition is close to Searle and Vanderveken's (1985), for whom these SAs are action-oriented and involve an informative component too. Finally, *permissives* such as agreeing, licensing, and excusing express A's entitlement to doing something, as well as S's intention that A take S's utterance as entitling them to perform the action.

Another possible criterion for differentiating between the variety of subtypes of directives is to consider the sort of obligation that S purports to impose on A when performing a directive. The difference between an order and a request, Alston (2000) explains, is that, with the former, the obligation is imposed on A by virtue of a valid institution and it is not up to A to decide whether or not they should perform the ordered action; the obligation is *categorical*. An example of a background condition for the existence of a categorical obligation is the power relationship between S and A. By contrast, with a request, A either is obliged to perform the action or must be prepared to give S an acceptable reason for not doing so; in this case the obligation is *disjunctive*.

3.2 Definitions in terms of graded membership

We have seen that, according to cognitive linguists such as Johnson (1987), speakers conceptualize (directive) SAs in terms of their strength. Accordingly, a stronger intensity in illocutionary force reflects a stronger force with which the sentence *container* is directed towards the addressee. This view is similar to Searle and Vanderveken's (1985) view of gradation in terms of strength of the illocutionary force. In line with this idea, the image schemata proposed by Johnson (1987) have been used by Pérez Hernández and Ruiz de Mendoza (2002) to distinguish between subtypes of directive SAs. The experiential structural basis of directives is essential for understanding why these SAs can be said to vary in strength. For instance, requests allow some space for refusal. In that respect, they are more tentative than commands, which are conceptualized as inexorable forces.

The force image schemata used by Pérez Hernández and Ruiz de Mendoza (2002) are a type of *idealized cognitive models* (ICMs). In cognitive linguistics, an ICM is a mental structure of conceptual representation (see Lakoff 1987: 284–285). ICMs have an ontology (the set of elements used in the model) and a structure (the properties of these elements and the relations between these elements) (Lakoff 1987: 285). Pérez Hernández and Ruiz de Mendoza classify the subtypes of directives in terms of prototypes according to which particular force image schemata are associated. These authors make use of Johnson's (1987: 45–48) force image schemata of compulsion, blockage, counterforce, removal of restraint, enablement, and iteration.

In this framework, orders and commands are conceptualized according to the *compulsive force* schema (Pérez Hernández and Ruiz de Mendoza 2002: 274–275) (see Section 2.2). The potential obstacles to the success of an order are that S lacks the power required to issue the order in question or that the order is perceived as unjustified. Rejecting the validity of the order amounts to "the building up of barriers to the force of the order" (Pérez Hernández and Ruiz de Mendoza 2002: 274).

Beggings are another subtype of directives (Pérez Hernández and Ruiz de Mendoza 2002: 278–279), not conceptualized as an inexorable or a tentative force, but in terms of the *iteration* schema. With prototypical beggings, the degree of S's desire that A perform the action is higher than with other directives, and this strong desire is manifested in the use of repetitions. For Pérez Hernández and Ruiz de Mendoza (2002), the iteration schema gets activated when a directive is performed more than once, which is the case, they propose, with prototypical beggings. The rationale behind the repetition of the directive is twofold: ensure that the obstacle of A's unwillingness to perform the action is removed, and show that S really wants the action to be performed while at the same time avoiding imposing on A.

According to Pérez Hernández and Ruiz de Mendoza, requests performed with utterances such as (2)–(3) exemplify the *removal of restraints* schema (2002: 275–276).

(2) Could you close the window?

(3) Would you mind closing the window?

The idea underlying this conceptualization is that, when S performs a request using a construction such as (2) or (3), typically instantiating *indirect requests* (IRs), they not only try to identify the existence of obstacles, but they also attempt to remove a possible obstacle to A's compliance with the request. In (2) the obstacle would be that it is not possible for A to close the window because of, e.g., a physical disability, and in (3) that A is not willing to close the window. These *indirect request* constructions are generally chosen when S does not want to impose on A. Therefore, the realization of A's future action is not intended to be ensured by S's exercising power. In an attempt to overcome possible obstacles, S resorts to linguistic mechanisms such as mitigation, cost minimization, and optionality (see Section 4).

Some of the variables proposed by Pérez Hernández and Ruiz de Mendoza (2002) are more essential to the analysis of requests than others. To begin with, unlike in SAT, S's desire that A perform the action is not necessary to define the subcategory of directives. Rather, they suggest that S's willingness that A perform the action should be conceived of as a gradable feature (2002: 264–265). For instance, the degree of S's willingness is higher for a begging than for a request, but in the case of advising, the degree of S's willingness is weaker. The three variables that, according to these authors, define a prototypical request are the cost–benefit assessment, the relatively high optionality of the action, and the presence of mitigating expressions.[2] To illustrate, (4) activates several components of the request ICM: a reference to the fact that the action is beneficial to S (*for me*), optionality of A's action (*if you don't mind*), and mitigation of A's costs (politeness marker *please*).

(4) Please, close the window for me, if you don't mind.

An evaluation of the cost–benefit of A's future action for both S and A is useful for distinguishing directive subtypes. In the case of requests and commands, the expected action involves a cost for A and a benefit for S. By contrast, for advising A to perform some action it is not required that the action be beneficial to S or that it be costly for A (but it is supposed to be beneficial to A).

The feature *degree of optionality* represents the extent to which A is free to perform the requested action (Pérez Hernández and Ruiz de Mendoza 2002: 265–268). Whereas a request conveys a high degree of optionality and the power relationship between S and A is immaterial, a command conveys low optionality and implies that S is more powerful than A. According to Pérez Hernández and Ruiz de Mendoza, optionality is (partially) signaled by the linguistic properties of the sentence uttered. For instance, the interrogative mood indicates higher optionality compared to the imperative and the declarative moods (Pérez Hernández and Ruiz de Mendoza 2002: 271), because the answer to the question asked (e.g., in (2) and (3)) gives A a way to avoid performing the requested action.

For Pérez Hernández and Ruiz de Mendoza (2002: 263–265, 274–275), another feature that distinguishes between the subtypes of directives is the power relationship required between S and A for a successful directive to take place. In the case of requests, there is no specific power relationship that holds between S and A, which distinguishes them from, e.g., commands.

3.3 Provisional conclusion

To sum up, cognitive linguists propose that directive SAs involve some degree of force exertion consisting in a psychological pressure from a speaker towards an addressee's performance of an action. While, in speech act theoretic approaches, the subtypes of directives are (like the macro category itself) defined in terms of necessary/sufficient conditions that have to be met for the directive to be felicitous, from the cognitive linguistic perspective working with ICMs, directives consist in scenarios defined relative to a prototype. These scenarios are made up of conceptual elements that can get activated

---

2. This view is debatable. For instance, as indicated by one reviewer, while the performative construction *I hereby request you to VP* does not include mitigating expressions, its form makes it very likely to be used as a request.

when an utterance is produced and understood. The nature of these components, and their centrality with respect to the scenario, result in a variety of subtypes of directives that can be related to different schemata.

4. Directives as face-threatening speech acts

We first saw that, according to most accounts of the category of directives, in a directive, a speaker/writer exerts some degree of psychological pressure or *force* towards an individual's performance of some action. Second, in cognitive linguistic approaches to directives, *optionality* is a key feature of requests. Here, I further explore these notions of force exertion and optionality and how they relate to politeness considerations.

Brown and Levinson (1987) define an individual's *negative face* as their desire that others do not impede their freedom of action. A directive SA constitutes a face-threatening act (FTA) insofar as A's negative face is threatened when S puts them under some degree of obligation/force exertion. When an individual is about to request someone to carry out a particular action, they have five ways to go (Brown and Levinson 1987: 69). First, they could refrain from performing the request altogether, e.g., if the threat to A's negative face is very high. Second, they could go off-record and use an ambiguous utterance that leaves the request interpretation of their utterance to A's discretion, as in (5).

(5) It's cold in here.

Third, the speaker could follow the on-record strategy, making it clear that their utterance has the meaning of a request, and including a redressive action, i.e., references to A's positive face and their want to be approved of (positive politeness), as in (6).

(6) Hey mate, would you be so kind and close the window?

The fourth strategy is to go on-record while including references to A's negative face (negative politeness) to redress the face-threatening potential of the request, as in (7).

(7) Would you mind closing the window?

The fifth strategy is to go on-record without redressive action (8), a strategy most likely to occur in situations of emergency or when face-threat considerations are not at issue.

(8) Close the window!

The choice of one of these strategies is based on an assessment of the weightiness of the request, which is determined by the power relationship between the conversational participants (P), the social distance between them (D), and the degree to which the request results in an imposition on A in the culture of the participants (*rank of imposition*, R).

The weight of a face-threatening act (W(FTA)) positively correlates with the values of each of these parameters: W(FTA) = P + D + R. To be more precise, the higher the social distance between S and A and the higher the rank of imposition, the higher the weight of the directive. Likewise, the higher the power of S relative to A, the higher the weight of the directive. Regarding the impact of the weight of the FTA on the ways to perform requests, the higher the weight of the request, the more rational it would be for the speaker to use an off-record strategy; the lower the weight of the request, the more they can afford to use an on-record strategy. Politeness is thus strategic behavior enacted by a speaker or writer to compensate for the threat that the directive speech act poses to the addressee's negative face.

Importantly, request utterances can be linguistically modified with *downgraders*, i.e., syntactic, lexical, or phrasal devices that soften the illocutionary force of the directive; by contrast, *upgraders* are linguistic elements that strengthen it (Blum-Kulka et al. 1989). While downgraders achieve politeness strategies, upgraders, also called "aggravating" devices, involve the use of impoliteness strategies, that is, strategies that may damage A's face instead of saving it (cf. Culpeper 1996). In some situations, such as in business exchanges (Freytag 2020), communicative efficiency is of primary importance to speakers/writers: they therefore resort to upgraders, which illustrate the transactional dimension of language use. These aggravating strategies, which run against A's negative face wants, are not incompatible with the relational dimension, and they can thus cooccur with mitigating strategies, as when saying *Can you send this email as soon as possible?*.

To illustrate the variety of downgraders and upgraders available, I provide a short explanation for each of them and examples that are authentic, corpus-extracted English utterances which originate from Freytag (2020) (FR), Flöck (2016: 106–113) (FL), or the *Corpus of Contemporary American English* (COCA, Davies 2008). For instance, with progressive aspect, S achieves a minimization of the temporal validity of the request, as in (9).

(9) I am hoping you will be able to do the same with the September ones. (FR)[3]

Another way to downgrade the force of the directive is the modal use of the past tense. For example, with the use of potentialis, S achieves a distancing effect, increasing A's chances to opt out, as in the case of (10).

(10) Could I change that meeting to 12.5? (FR)

---

3. This only seems to apply to stative verbs. By contrast, in English, using the progressive with dynamic verbs, as in *I'm telling you to VP*, would achieve the opposite effect, i.e., it would reinforce the strength of the directive. I thank the editors for this highly relevant remark.

Downgraders can also consist in dependent interrogative clauses such as the one in (11) and question tags, such as *can you?* in (12), that question A's ability or willingness to perform the action.

(11) I was gonna ask you if you could take care of Trace. (FL)

(12) Can't fit me in as well, can you? (FL)

With a negative interrogative such as (13), S expresses the expectation that A will not (be able/willing to) comply with the request.

(13) Can't you stand up and hold it? (FL)

Finally, in using a pseudo-cleft such as (14), S shifts the focus from A to another part of the sentence, i.e., *what I recommend*.

(14) What I recommend you do Tony is… (FL)

Another category of downgraders are lexical and phrasal downgraders. For instance, S can appeal to A's benevolent understanding (appealer), as in (15), try to establish social harmony with A (cajoler), as in (16), use the formulaic politeness marker *please* to bid for cooperation, as in (17), or seek to involve the addressee by bidding for their cooperation with a consultative device such as *don't you think*, as in (18).

(15) Don't touch anything yellow… Okay? (FL)

(16) But I do think that, you know, it might be worth getting in touch. (FL)

(17) Please can you respond to my emails? (FR)

(18) It's very hot in here, don't you think? (COCA)

Another type of downgrading device involves terms of endearment used to address A in a favorable way, as in (19).

(19) Get your work done dear. (FL)

Epistemic adverbs too can serve as downgraders: for example, in (20), the modifier *maybe* weakens the intensity of the directive illocutionary point, i.e., S's desire.

(20) Maybe we should head there? (FL)

In the case of the hedging strategy, S tries to avoid making the propositional content of the directive too specific, as in (21).

(21) You probably got to get a bit of help on that training or whatever. (FL)

By making a false start (*hesitation marker*), S makes the request sound more tentative.

(22) Oh, um, … just put it in here. Just put the paper in there. (FL)

Likewise, in the case of the understater *few* in (23), the modifier (e.g., an adjective) under-represents the state of affairs.

(23) Can you wash those few cups up please? (FL)

With a subjectivizer such as *I suppose*, S expresses their opinion about a state of affairs, as in (24).

(24) You could I suppose commission some prints of you yourself. (FL)

In contrast to internal modifiers that serve to downgrade the force of the directive speech act, some internal modifiers act as upgraders, i.e., they intensify the imposition entailed by the directive. For instance, while a higher vocal intensity can be used to emphasize the directive force in spoken utterances (25), it is usually mirrored by the use of capital letters or by adding multiple exclamation marks.

(25) [YELL Hey, stay out of it. Stay out of it, you're not involved in it. YELL] (FL)

Frequently used internal upgraders are intensifiers. For instance, in (26), the adverbial modifier intensifies the directive illocutionary point of the utterance, i.e., S's desire.

(26) I really want to get something agreed to get the [hotel] in his first edition. (FR)

Some intensifiers called *time intensifiers* increase the degree of urgency associated with the requested action, as in (27).

(27) Please let me know ASAP! (COCA)

Lexical uptoners consist in marked lexical choices that achieve a negative evaluation of the propositional content of the directive. For instance, in (28), unlike utterances containing more neutral action verbs (e.g., *Don't do that* or *Leave this*), the verb *to mess* denotes a negative attitude on the part of S with respect to A's behavior.

(28) Don't mess with this here. (FL)

In a similar vein, taboo words such as *shit* in (29) achieve a negative evaluation of the propositional content of the directive.

(29) Turn it off, I've had enough of that shit. (FL)

While this overview is not meant to be exhaustive, it illustrates the most frequent request modifiers found in empirical studies on languages such as English (e.g., Flöck 2016; Freytag 2020), French (e.g., Ruytenbeek 2017b, 2019), and Spanish (e.g., Freytag 2020). It is to be complemented by data documenting other less well studied languages of the world in different modalities and discourse genres.

5. Requests and pre-requests

In the conversational analytic (CA) tradition, requests are conceived of as a social practice, with attention paid not only to the form of the utterance, but primarily to the position of the request in the wider stretch of discourse and the responses from the other interactants (for a discussion, see Flöck 2016: 28–34). In addition, studies in the CA framework have shown that requests are best conceived of as *multi-turn* actions (Walker 2013). From the perspective of turns at talk, the performance of a request creates an expectation that a response will be produced by A. That is, in performing a request, S allocates the next turn to A, who can, in turn, produce the second part of the *adjacency pair* of requesting–(non-)complying. Interestingly, the second pair part of the adjacency pair can be used by S to verify that their illocutionary intent has been correctly recognized. While the preferred second pair part of a request is acceptance, the most dispreferred move following a request is a flat refusal, i.e., non-compliance with the directive (Figure 2).

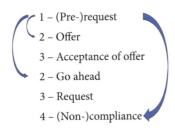

Figure 2. Adjacency pairs for requesting (adapted from Flöck 2016: 33)

A (pre-)request can also be followed by an offer to be accepted by the individual who performed the request in turn 1. While the request–compliance (1→4) adjacency pair comes first in the list of preferred sequences, the request–offer–acceptance (1→2→3) sequence is ranked second. The sequence that comes third is that in which the pre-request is not taken as a request and the addressee forces the interlocutor to clarify their directive intent, thus uncovering the full face-threatening potential of the directive (1→2 go ahead →3 request →4).

Within the framework of CA, constructions such as *Do you have X?* in (30) have been analyzed as "pre-requests", that is, requests for information that are performed prior to requests for action (Levinson 2012; Sacks 1992: 685; Schegloff 1980).

(30) Do you have any enchiladas? (Gibbs 1986: 183)

Indeed, questioning the availability of an item is a convenient preparation for S to request A to provide them with the item; if the item is available, (30) will easily be understood by A as a request to serve an enchilada. An affirmative answer to the pre-request will thus enable S to carry out a request in their next conversational turn. Note that, however, an affirmative answer to the *pre-request* is not always necessary and the pre-request can count as a request. For instance, the pre-request utterance could be immediately responded to with compliance, as is often the case in highly ritualized exchanges such as service encounters in small shops or in restaurants.

A plausible explanation concerning the form of questions used in the performance of indirect requests such as (30), which follows the conversational analytic approach, is proposed in Francik and Clark (1985). According to these authors' obstacle hypothesis, speakers have a tendency to phrase their requests so as to deal with the obstacles that would prevent their addressees from complying with their requests. For instance, if S wants to find out where John will go on holiday, they would utter (31) if they believed that the greatest obstacle for A to provide the requested information is that John did not tell A where he will go on holiday.

(31) Did John tell you where he will go on holiday?

Francik and Clark's explanation applies not only to indirect requests for information, but also to indirect requests for action in general. According to the obstacle hypothesis, *Can you* + verbal phrase (VP)? requests are used to remove very general obstacles to A's compliance, such as A's (physical) inability to carry out some action, which is why it is a common way to make a request.

6. Requests as speech events

In contrast to the traditional speech act theoretic view that a speech act, as the minimal unit of communication, is associated to a single utterance (Searle 1969), individual speech acts can also be approached in terms of *speech events* (Hymes 1972; see also Levinson's 1992 activity types) or *speech acts* (Murphy and Neu 2006), which consist in complexes of individual utterances that, taken together, achieve a common communicative goal. For example, a request performed via email can include, alongside the *request utterance*, greetings and closings.

Following the Cross-Cultural Speech Act Realization Pattern (CCSARP) (Blum-Kulka et al. 1989: 17), the "head act" of a speech event is the "part of the sequence which might serve to realize the [speech event] independently of other elements". A variety of constructions and discursive strategies can be used as directive head acts, including imperatives, deontic *You should/must* VP declaratives, and interrogatives, typically exemplified by the indirect request constructions *Could/Would you* VP? (for an overview, see Freytag 2020: 63; Ruytenbeek 2017b), some of them with a higher amount of *redressive action* compared to others. For instance, we saw that unmodified interrogative requests for action display a higher degree of optionality compared to imperatives and deontic declaratives. Interestingly, a request for action can be preceded by a pre-request, in which case the pre-request would not count as a request strictly speaking, but as a *supportive move* that modifies/prepares the head act of a request for action (for a discussion, see Flöck 2016: 100–101).

Unlike in the case of internal modification that is 'contained' in the directive head act itself, as with the down- and upgraders discussed in Section 4, external modification takes places outside the head act utterance. While some external modifiers pertain to the compensation of the threat to A's negative face (e.g., apologies and preparators), others reflect S's will to attend to A's positive face (e.g., appreciations and sweeteners). A large variety of downgrading devices can be used to externally modify the directive head act (cf. Flöck 2016 "FL"; Freytag 2020 "FR"). Starting with the strategies that minimize the threat to A's negative face, a first way to achieve this mitigation effect amounts to providing A with an alternative action to the one requested, as with the disjunctive clause in Example (32).

(32) Could you be so kind to tell me if I used the right email address or to forward my email to the relevant person? (FR)

Another strategy is to restrict the validity of the directive to a specific condition, as (33) illustrates.

(33) If you can save the bag, you can turn it inside out. (FL)

Other ways to minimize the threat of the directive to A's negative face is to apologize for the directive and/or ensuing imposition (34), or to try to reduce the imposition on A (*imposition minimizer*) (35).

(34) Sorry to be a pain but we have to send the program by tomorrow. (FR)

(35) I don't want to borrow your car since it's new, could I get a ride? (FL)

S can also downgrade their directive by providing A with information that facilitates compliance, as in (36), or specifying the content of the directive, as in (37).

(36) Would you get me a glass of ginger? There's a bottle of it, down in that bottle rack thing? (FL)

(37) Could you offer us something along these lines for these dates – it can be any hotel/apartment, not necessarily the hotels/apartments we have contracted. (FR)

Other downgraders have to do with the preconditions for the performance of the directive head act. For example, in the first sentence of (38), S prepares their request without expressing its content yet.

(38) Listen, may I ask you a favor? Is it possible to connect to another passenger? (COCA)

This *preparator* strategy is different from "getting a pre-commitment", illustrated in (39), in the sense that a preparator such as the *May I ask you a favor?* clause alone cannot stand for the head act of requesting. In (39), S checks on A's potential refusal while making the request at the same time.

(39) Please can I ask you to help me with the following? (FR)

In some cases, S provides a justification for the request before the head act (*pre-grounder*), as in (40), or after the head act (*post-grounder*), as shown in (41).

(40) Since he's not vomiting now, you can go ahead and feed him and stuff. (FL)

(41) Please can you email me your phone number so that I can give you a quick call? (FR)

Other downgrading strategies consist in boosting A's positive face. For instance, S can express their gratefulness regarding A's future compliance with the request, as in (42), or simply thank A.

(42) If you could relate these details to Susan we would be extremely grateful. (FR)

A "mitigation booster" consists in the use of an additional modifier to increase mitigation of the directive, as in (43).

(43) Could you either call me on [number] or I will try again later. Many thanks. (FR)

With a disarmer such as *I know it's tempting* in (44), S tries to discard A's potential objection regarding the request.

(44) Don't Steven. Please. I know it's tempting. (FL)

Other strategies for boosting A's positive face are to highlight the positive consequences of A's compliance (45), to positively evaluate either A as a person or A's (future) actions (46), to use small talk to put A into a positive mood (*sweetener*) (47), to offer a reward as a compensation for their compliance (48) and to use emoticons or emoji that express a positive attitude/emotion, e.g., ☺ (FR).

(45) This change would be perfect and definite. (FR)

(46) You know what you could do, that would be just really helpful? (FL)

(47) I hope you are well, [...] Please could you contact them? (FR)

(48) Can I use your car John old fellow? There's a hearty reward in it for you. (FL)

As we saw in the case of internal modification, external modifiers can also act as upgraders, that is, strategies that can, in the case of directives, aggravate the threat to A's negative or positive face. There is a variety of upgraders attested in spoken and written English corpora, which I illustrate with examples from Flöck (2016) ("FL") and Freytag

(2020) ("FR"). A possible way to intensify the directive would be to use an additional utterance ("addition"), such as *Don't argue* in (49); another upgrader is the use of a "determination marker" by means of which S expresses a higher degree of determination, which the second sentence of (50) illustrates.

(49) Now, you take that downstairs right now. And don't argue. (FL)

(50) Hey, don't start on me. And I said stay out of it, it's none of your concern. (FL)

Stating the consequence of A's non-compliance with the directive, as with the second utterance in (51), expressing one's disagreement with A (52), and negatively evaluating A's past or ongoing actions (53) will also increase the intensity of the directive.

(51) Don't holler like that. I'm gonna throw the masa on the floor. (FL)

(52) No no. Don't put it on now. (FL)

(53) You cannot dump them in here. It's not the way that it's done. (FL)

An upgrading strategy that we have encountered before – when discussing internal modification – is emphasis on urgency, which can also be expressed as a separate utterance, as in (54).

(54) Well make sure you don't even have a cup of coffee before you set foot on it. (FL)

Finally, another upgrader is the repetition of the directive in the same or in the next turn, as in (55).

(55) Come here, I wanna show you. Please come here. (FL)

While conceptually distinct from external modifiers, sequencing strategies also belong to directive speech events. However, rather than being specifically related to the nature of the speech act in question, they are an index of the conversational genre (Freytag 2020: 75–76). For example, the speech event of requesting via email often contains an opening formula to greet the recipient or a reference to a previous email exchange. The different sequencing strategies that have been identified in past empirical research on requests are greetings (e.g., *Hi dear* + first name), self-introduction (56), checking on preconditions, i.e., whether the preparatory conditions for the directive still hold (57), orientation moves in which S establishes orientation and shared knowledge with A (58), closing (e.g., *Kind regards*) and phatic closing (e.g., *Good afternoon*).

(56) Please let me introduce myself, my name is Charlotte and I am the new commercial Executive. (FR)

(57) If you still want your items to be sent with a code, send me a message. (Internet)

(58) Caroline is out of the office today so she has asked me to look at this matter in her absence. (FR)

Finally, it is important to mention that, as an individual speech act, a request head act can also be part of a different multi-component speech event or *speech act set* (e.g., Vásquez 2011). This is, for instance, the case with complaints (Decock and Depraetere 2018) and (typically negative) consumer reviews (Ruytenbeek et al. 2021), both of which can include requests for action. Following previous accounts of complaints (e.g., Olshtain and Weinbach 1993; Trosborg 1995), Decock and Depraetere (2018) propose that a complaint situation is made up of four constitutive components. One such component is the past or ongoing action/event that occurred and about which S is complaining (complainable). The second component is a negative evaluation about the complainable, and the third component is the entity, i.e., person, company, or institution, that is, according to S, responsible for the complainable. The fourth component of a complaint situation is S's wish for the complainable to be remedied, which can be expressed as a request for information, for a solution, or for compensation, as in *Can I get my money back?* as voiced by a dissatisfied customer (Depraetere et al. 2021).

7. The social effectiveness of directives

The theoretical approaches discussed in Section 2 agree that the performance of a directive typically creates an obligation on A. But how is it the case that a directive results in the creation of an obligation for A to act in a certain way? In Ruytenbeek (2017b), I propose that S's force exertion results in an obligation for A because, when confronted with force exertion, A feels entitled to comply with S's directive.

Social interactions such as requests for action and requests for help build on mutualistic collaboration and communicative cooperation (see, for instance, Tomasello 2008: 193–199). From S's perspective, it is crucial to discriminate addressees who will cooperate from those who will not, based on past experience and on current available evidence. And from A's own perspective, the performance of a directive SA gives rise to an inner conflict. On the one hand, A does not necessarily want to cooperate with S by providing the requested help, or even by giving a plausible justification for not complying. This corresponds to A's immediate desire to do only what they want to (cf. negative face). On the other hand, A's internalization of social values such as providing help and being cooperative goes against their immediate desire for short-term benefits.

The human tendency to orient towards social values because these offer long-term benefits could explain why directives typically create obligations. What is necessary for the obligation created by a directive to arise is that A's concern with the long-term benefits of their actions overrules their short-term egocentric benefits. The roles of S and A can be exchanged in the future, and the favor of complying be returned (Clayman and Heritage 2014: 64–65; Enfield 2014: 42–48). That is, the individual who is now A would be better off if, as S, they can count on their interlocutor's help (Frank 1988; Trivers 1971). Another sort of long-term benefit is reputation: in a society based on cooperation and reciprocity, it is important for the individual's *social survival* to be known as a cooperative person (Frank 1988: 71–95; see also Tomasello 2008: 206–208). Accordingly, it is reasonable for A to cooperate with S even in cases where it is highly unlikely that they will ever meet again, because there may be bystanders keeping track of who cooperates and who does not. If the person cooperates in such a situation, A will enhance their reputation as a cooperative individual. The upshot is that force exertion results in obligations because rational addressees favor long-term benefits over short-term benefits. As for the origins of compliance with requests for help, Tomasello (2008: 206) suggests that it "likely began in mutualistic collaboration, where compliance is always adaptive because it benefits the [helper], and then generalized to non-mutualistic situations owing to their positive effects on the reputation of the helper".

Turning to directives involving actions that are beneficial to A, such as advising and suggesting, it would also be rational for S to assume that A could help them in the future with some piece of advice when necessary. It is in A's long-term interest to follow S's suggestion or, if they do not follow it, to give a reason for their choice. A would not be pleased if, as an S, the suggestions they make for someone's well-being are dismissed without any justification, which accords with Alston's (2000) notion of disjunctive obligations. That is, in the case of directives in which a low or moderate degree of force is exerted on A, such as suggestions, advising but also requests, A is under a disjunctive obligation: they should either perform the suggested/requested action or provide a reason for not doing so.

Such an explanation based on the logic of reciprocity and long-term cooperation is in line with the view that directives can be defined as natural kinds. Following Millikan (1984), Ball (2014) assumes that a token of a device type functions normally if and only if it does what tokens of that type did in past cases in which they contributed to the evolutionary success of that type. The idea is that, over time, speakers continue to issue directives because they thereby come to produce obligations, and these obligations most often result in action. One can thus consider that a directive consists in S's exerting some degree of force towards A's performance of some action, and that S purports, by means of force exertion, to produce some degree of obligation for A to act; this is so because the normal function of directives is to produce obligations.

8. Conclusion, recent developments and future directions

In this contribution, I have addressed the defining features of the category of directive speech acts as well as of the directive subtypes, focusing on requests for action. To do this, I compared traditional speech act theoretic accounts involving necessary and sufficient conditions and cognitive linguistic accounts assuming prototype-based graded illocutionary categories. I concluded that, despite their divergences, in both frameworks the key feature of a directive is that the speaker/writer who issues it exerts some degree of psychological pressure towards the addressee's future performance of some action, which typically results in the creation of an obligation for A to carry out that action. Adopting an analysis of speech acts as *speech events*, I illustrated the variety of internal and external linguistic modifiers that can enable speakers/writers to either mitigate (downgraders) or reinforce (upgraders) the face-threatening potential of their directives. I would now like to look ahead and highlight recent developments and promising avenues in empirical studies on requests and directive speech acts more generally.

A first important advance in our knowledge about directives has been offered by studies in *multimodal pragmatics* (O'Halloran et al. 2014), a domain/approach that focuses on the different modalities involved in speech act production, such as the interaction between linguistic constructions and prosodic features. For instance, replicating Trott et al.'s (2023) findings for English indirect requests for action, Ruytenbeek et al. (2023) found that French negative state remarks such as *It's cold in here* with a more positive slope of fundamental frequency (i.e., the number of vocal cord vibrations per second) are more likely to be interpreted as requests, whereas French modal interrogatives such as *You can* VP? with a more positive fundamental frequency slope are more likely to be taken as questions. Second, they found that longer negative state remarks and shorter modal interrogatives are more likely to be interpreted as requests. Such studies provide valuable insights into the combined used of particular request forms as head act and a specific prosodic pattern achieving mitigation. In a similar vein, the relationship between the linguistic properties of requests and their prosodic characteristics has recently been addressed from the perspective of (im)politeness by Caballero et al. (2018). These authors found, in particular, that the acoustic properties of request utterances are influenced by the degree of imposition of the request: while low imposition imperative requests had a higher mean fundamental frequency and were uttered with a faster speech rate, low imposition *Can you* VP? indirect requests were uttered with a slower speech rate.

Another promising research avenue can be found in *neuropragmatics*, a subfield of (experimental) pragmatics that started flourishing about two decades ago (Bara and Tirassa 2000). While, to date, few studies have documented the brain activation patterns associated with the processing of directive speech acts, we can say that a pattern is already emerging (Tomasello 2023). For instance, requests for action (e.g., to pass an item) result in the activation of the cortical areas that attend to motor actions (Boux et al. 2021; Egorova et al. 2014; Van Ackeren et al. 2012). Regarding the difference between requests for information (questions) and requests for action, the former gave rise to a specific pattern of brain activation centered on the articulatory cortex (representing the movements of lips in spoken speech), as compared to requests for motor actions (e.g., to close a window) (Tomasello et al. 2022). It is, however, important to mention that these studies only considered single-utterance directives. As a result, additional work will be necessary to assess whether their findings also extend to directive speech events more generally.

To date, the production of requests has been documented in a variety of settings, ranging from daily family interactions (Zinken 2016) to the genre of business emails (Freytag 2020), using a plethora of methods of data collection, but with a high degree of imbalance in terms of the languages represented. In addition, the complex interactions between social and demographic variables and the data collection instruments remain under-researched when it comes to the form of directives. It is to be hoped that a more systematic investigation of both the social variables involved in the production of directives and the effects of the genre/modality on the form of directives will enable scholars to lay the foundations of a general theory of the production of directive speech acts, a view that has already been promoted regarding the comprehension of speech acts (Gibbs 2014).

References

Alston, William P. 2000. *Illocutionary Acts and Sentence Meaning*. Ithaca: Cornell University Press.

Austin, John L. 1962. *How to Do Things with Words*. Oxford: Clarendon Press.

Bach, Kent, and Robert M. Harnish. 1979. *Linguistic Communication and Speech Acts*. Cambridge: MIT Press.

Ball, Brian. 2014. "Speech acts: Natural or normative kinds? The case of assertion." *Mind and Language* 29: 336–350.

Bara, Bruno G., and Maurizio Tirassa. 2000. "Neuropragmatics: Brain and communication." *Brain and Language* 71: 10–14.

Blum-Kulka, Shoshana, Juliane House and Gabriele Kasper (eds). 1989. *Cross-Cultural Pragmatics: Requests and Apologies*. Norwood: Ablex.

Boux, Isabella, Rosario Tomasello, Luigi Grisoni and Friedemann Pulvermüller. 2021. "Brain signatures predict communicative function of speech production in interaction." *Cortex* 135: 127–145.

Brown, Penelope and Stephen Levinson. 1987. *Politeness: Some Universals in Language Usage*. Cambridge: Cambridge University Press.

Caballero, Jonathan, Nikos Vergis, Xiaoming Jiang and Marc D. Pell. 2018. "The sound of im/politeness." *Speech Communication* 102: 39–53.

Clayman, Steven E., and John Heritage. 2014. "Benefactors and beneficiaries: Benefactive status and stance in the management of offers and requests." In *Requesting in Social Interaction*, ed. by Paul Drew and Elizabeth Couper-Kuhlen, 55–86. Amsterdam: John Benjamins.

Culpeper, Jonathan. 1996. "Towards an anatomy of impoliteness." *Journal of Pragmatics* 25: 349–367.

Davies, Mark. (2008–). *The Corpus of Contemporary American English (COCA): 560 million words*, 1990–present. Available online at https://corpus.byu.edu/coca/

Decock, Sofie, and Ilse Depraetere. 2018. "(In)directness and complaints: A reassessment." *Journal of Pragmatics* 132: 33–46.

Depraetere, Ilse, Sofie Decock and Nicolas Ruytenbeek. 2021. "Linguistic (in)directness in Twitter complaints: A contrastive analysis of railway complaint interactions." *Journal of Pragmatics* 171: 215–233.

Egorova, Natalia, Friedemann Pulvermüller and Yury Shtyrov. 2014. "Neural dynamics of speech act comprehension: An MEG study of naming and requesting." *Brain Topography* 27: 375–392.

Enfield, Nick J. 2014. "Human agency and the infrastructure for requests." In *Requesting in Social Interaction*, ed. by Paul Drew and Elizabeth Couper-Kuhlen, 35–53. Amsterdam: John Benjamins.

Flöck, Ilka. 2016. *Requests in American and British English: A Contrastive Multi-Method Analysis*. Amsterdam: John Benjamins.

Francik, Ellen P., and Herbert H. Clark. 1985. "How to make requests that overcome obstacles to compliance." *Journal of Memory and Language* 24: 560–568.

Frank, Robert H. 1988. *Passions within Reason: The Strategic Role of the Emotions*. New York: Norton.

Freytag, Vera. 2020. *Exploring Politeness in Business Emails: A Mixed-Methods Analysis*. Bristol: Multilingual Matters.

Gibbs, Raymond W. 1986. "What makes some indirect speech acts conventional?" *Journal of Memory and Language* 25: 181–196.

Gibbs, Raymond W. 2014. "Is a general theory of utterance interpretation really possible? Insights from the study of figurative language." *Belgian Journal of Linguistics* 28: 19–44.

Grice, H. P. 1957. "Meaning." *Philosophical Review* 66: 377–388.

Grice, H. P. 1975. "Logic and Conversation." In *Syntax and Semantics, Vol. 3: Speech Acts*, ed. by Peter Cole and Jerry L. Morgan, 41–58. New York: Academic Press.

Grice, H. P. 1989. *Studies in the Way of Words*. Cambridge: Harvard University Press.

Hymes, Dell. 1972. "Models of the interaction of language and social life." In *Directions in Sociolinguistics: The Ethnography of Communication*, ed. by John J. Gumperz and Dell Hymes, 35–71. New York: Holt, Rinehart & Winston.

Johnson, Mark. 1987. *The Body in the Mind*. Chicago: University of Chicago Press.

Kamp, Hans, and Barbara Partee. 1995. "Prototype theory and compositionality." *Cognition* 57: 129–191.

Kissine, Mikhail. 2009. "Illocutionary forces and what is said." *Mind and Language* 24: 122–138.

Kissine, Mikhail. 2013. *From Utterances to Speech Acts*. Cambridge: Cambridge University Press.

Lakoff, George. 1987. *Women, Fire and Dangerous Things: What Categories Reveal about the Mind*. Chicago: University of Chicago Press.

Levinson, Stephen. 1992. "Activity types and language." In *Talk at Work: Interaction in Institutional Settings*, ed. by Paul Drew and John Heritage, 66–100. Cambridge: Cambridge University Press.

Levinson, Stephen. 2012. "Interrogative intimations: On a possible social economics of interrogatives." In *Questions: Formal, Functional, and Interactional Perspectives*, ed. by Jan P. de Ruiter, 11–32. Cambridge: Cambridge University Press.

Millikan, Ruth G. 1984. *Language, Thought and Other Biological Categories*. Cambridge: MIT Press.

Murphy, Beth, and Joyce Neu. 2006. "My grade's too low: The speech act set of complaining." In *Speech Acts Across Cultures: Challenges to Communication in a Second Language*, ed. by Susan M. Gass and Joyce Neu, 191–216. Berlin; New York: De Gruyter Mouton.

O'Halloran, Kay L., Sabine Tan and Marissa, K. L. E. 2014. "Multimodal pragmatics." In *Pragmatics of Discourse*, ed. by Klaus P. Schneider and Anne Barron, 239–268. Berlin: De Gruyter Mouton.

Olshtain, Elite, and Liora Weinbach. 1993. "Interlanguage features of the speech act of complaining." In *Interlanguage Pragmatics*, ed. by Gabriele Kasper and Shoshana Blum-Kulka, 108–122. New York: Oxford University Press.

Pérez Hernández, Lorena. 2013. "Illocutionary constructions: (Multiple source)-in-target metonymies, illocutionary ICMs, and specification links." *Language and Communication* 33: 128–149.

Pérez Hernández, Lorena, and Francisco José Ruiz de Mendoza. 2002. "Grounding, semantic motivation, and conceptual interaction in indirect directive speech acts." *Journal of Pragmatics* 35: 259–284.

Reddy, Michael. 1979. "The conduit metaphor: A case of frame conflict in our language about language." In *Metaphor and Thought*, ed. by Andrew Ortony, 164–201. Cambridge: Cambridge University Press.

Rohrer, Tim. 2007. "Embodiment and experientialism." In *Oxford Handbook of Cognitive Linguistics*, ed. by Dirk Geeraerts and Hubert Cuyckens, 25–47. New York: Oxford University Press.

Ruytenbeek, Nicolas. 2017a. "The comprehension of indirect requests: Previous work and future directions." In *Semantics and Pragmatics: Drawing a Line*, ed. by Ilse Depraetere and Raphael Salkie, 293–322. Cham: Springer.

Ruytenbeek, Nicolas. 2017b. The Mechanics of Indirectness: A Case Study of Directive Speech Acts. PhD dissertation, Université libre de Bruxelles.

Ruytenbeek, Nicolas. 2019. "Lexical and morpho-syntactic modification of student requests: An empirical contribution to the study of (im)politeness in French e-mail speech acts." *Lexique* 24: 29–47.

Ruytenbeek, Nicolas. 2021. *Indirect Speech Acts*. Cambridge: Cambridge University Press.

Ruytenbeek, Nicolas, Marie Verschraegen and Sofie Decock. 2021. "Exploring the impact of platforms' affordances on the expression of negativity in online hotel reviews." *Journal of Pragmatics* 186: 289–307.

Sacks, Harvey. 1992. *Lectures on Conversation*, vol. 1., ed. by Gail Jefferson. Oxford: Blackwell.

Schegloff, Emanuel A. 1980. "Preliminaries to preliminaries: 'Can I ask you a question?'" *Sociological Inquiry* 50: 104–152.

Searle, John R. 1969. *Speech Acts: An Essay in the Philosophy of Language*. Cambridge: Cambridge University Press.

Searle, John R. 1975. "Indirect speech acts." In *Syntax and Semantics, vol. 3: Speech Acts*, ed. by Peter Cole and Jerry L. Morgan, 59–82. New York: Academic Press.

Searle, John R., and Daniel Vanderveken. 1985. *Foundations of Illocutionary Logic*. Cambridge: Cambridge University Press.

Stalnaker, Robert. 2002. "Common ground." *Linguistics and Philosophy* 25: 701–721.

Tomasello, Michael. 2008. *Origins of Human Communication*. Cambridge: MIT Press.

Tomasello, Rosario. 2023. "Linguistic signs in action: The neuropragmatics of speech acts." *Brain and Language* 236: 105203.

Tomasello, Rosario, Luigi Grisoni, Isabella Boux, Daniela Sammler and Friedemann Pulvermüller. 2022. "Instantaneous neural processing of communicative functions conveyed by speech prosody." *Cerebral Cortex* 32: 4885–4901.

Trivers, Robert L. 1971. "The evolution of reciprocal altruism." *The Quarterly Review of Biology* 46: 35–57.

Trosborg, Anna. 1995. *Interlanguage Pragmatics: Requests, Complaints, and Apologies*. Berlin: Mouton de Gruyter.

Trott, Sean, Stefanie Reed, Dan Kaliblotzky, Victor Ferreira and Benjamin Bergen. 2023. "The role of prosody in disambiguating English indirect requests." *Language and Speech* 66: 118–142.

Van Ackeren, Markus J., Daniel Casasanto, Harold Bekkering, Peter Hagoort and Shirley-Ann Rueschemeyer. 2012. "Pragmatics in action: Indirect requests engage theory of mind areas and the cortical motor network." *Journal of Cognitive Neuroscience* 24: 2237–2247.

Vanderveken, Daniel. 1990. *Meaning and Speech Acts*, vol. 1. Cambridge: Cambridge University Press.

Vásquez, Camila. 2011. "Complaints online: The case of TripAdvisor." *Journal of Pragmatics* 43: 1707–1717.

Walker, Traci. 2013. "Requests." In *Handbook of Pragmatics: Pragmatics of Speech Actions*, ed. by Marina Sbisà and Ken Turner, 445–466. Berlin: De Gruyter.

Zinken, Jörg. 2016. *Requesting Responsibility: The Morality of Grammar in Polish and English Family Interaction*. New York: Oxford University Press.

Heteroglossia

Martina Björklund
Åbo Akademi University

1. Introduction

In the 1980s and 1990s, *dialogism*, *voice/double-voicing*, and *polyphony* were the foremost Bakhtinian notions among Western linguists, whereas *heteroglossia* turned up more rarely in linguistic studies. However, the beginning of the 21st century witnessed an increased interest in heteroglossia, especially among sociolinguists and other scholars interested in multilingualism. Heteroglossia is the English translation of Mikhail Bakhtin's (1895–1975) notion of *raznorechie*, which was introduced in the essay "Slovo v romane"/"Discourse in the Novel" written in 1934–1935 (English translation in Bakhtin 1981). In this essay Bakhtin discusses his view of linguistic diversity and stratification, and how they relate to the use of words/discourse in novels. Bakhtin was, however, not the first or the only one in the Soviet Union of the time to pay attention to the social stratification of language. As pointed out by Mika Lähteenmäki (2003, 2004, 2010) and discussed in detail by Craig Brandist and Lähteenmäki (2010), the idea of the social stratification of language was widely discussed in Soviet linguistics at the beginning of the 1930s, for instance, by Lev Iakubinskii and Viktor Zhirmunskii. Nonetheless, it is Bakhtin's thinking and his notion of *raznorechie* in its English translation of heteroglossia that has attracted the attention of contemporary linguists interested in living language as a social and ideological phenomenon. The translated term heteroglossia has actually attracted more attention and is more widely used by linguists than the Russian original, which to this day is most often used in literary analyses.

Because the term heteroglossia has enjoyed increasing appeal in both pragmatics and related fields devoted to multilingualism and multilingual discourse, this chapter will present a critical examination of the reception of Bakhtin's term. Linguists of various orientations have described their own understanding of the concept and proposed novel applications, some of which seem to distort Bakhtin's original idea. In section two of this chapter, therefore, I trace the origin and meanings of the term *raznorechie* and the coining of the term heteroglossia by the translators, and examine how *raznorechie* is related to other concepts of linguistic diversity distinguished by Bakhtin. This fairly detailed historical overview provides the background for the remainder of the chapter, which discusses how the concept of heteroglossia is utilized in different types of linguistic approach

https://doi.org/10.1075/hop.26.het1
© 2023 John Benjamins Publishing Company

and how its meaning has gradually been expanded to include other forms of diversity not originally contained in the concept (and for which Bakhtin had proposed other terms). In section three, I discuss how heteroglossia has been adopted in the study of discourse in a single language, while section four examines how it informs the study of multilingual practices. In this final section, I also define the position of heteroglossia in relation to competing new concepts that have recently been introduced in the study of multilingualism and argue for its continued relevance.

2. Bakhtinian concepts of linguistic diversity (and their English translations)

In the essay "Slovo v romane"/"Discourse in the Novel", Bakhtin discusses three types of linguistic diversity, and in his definition of the genre of novel he introduces three terms: *raznorechie, raznoiazychie,* and *raznogolositsa*. He writes:

> Roman – èto khudozhestvenno organizovannoe sotsial'noe *raznorechie*, inogda, *raznoiazychie*, i individual'naia *raznogolositsa*. (Bakhtin 1975: 76, my emphasis)

In Emerson and Holquist's translation, the definition goes as follows:

> The novel can be defined as a *diversity of* social *speech types* (sometimes even *diversity of languages*) and a *diversity of* individual *voices*, artistically organized.
> (Bakhtin 1981: 262, my emphasis.)

The three Russian compound nouns beginning with *razno-* are translated into three noun phrases with the head 'diversity', which corresponds to *razno-* in one of its meanings (cf. Shvedova 2008, s.v. *razno-* and *raznyi*). After a description of what the internal stratification of a national language includes (not reproduced here), the expression *sotsial'noe raznorechie* appears again. This time it is rendered into English as the "social diversity of speech types [raznorechie]" (Bakhtin 1981: 263), and thus the Russian word is added in brackets. For the third mention of *raznorechie*, the translators come up with the term *heteroglossia*, again adding the Russian word in brackets (Bakhtin 1981: 263). Using Greek stems meaning 'other, different' and 'tongue, speech, language', they created another Bakhtinian catchword – one that is in tune with the other famous Bakhtinian catchwords of foreign origin (dialogue, polyphony, carnival, chronotope, metalinguistics, and genre – in Russian *dialog, polifoniia, karnaval, khronotop, metalingvistika, zhanr*), which Bakhtin invested with his own terminological meanings. In contrast, the terminological use of the Russian nouns *raznorechie, raznoiazychie,* and *raznogolositsa* is similar to Bakhtin's special terminological utilization of ordinary Russian words, such as *slovo* ('word', 'discourse') and *golos* ('voice').

For *raznoiazychie* and *raznogolositsa* translators Emerson and Holquist did not coin new terms or consistently use the same words or expressions throughout the text. In addition to 'diversity of language(s)' and 'language diversity', *raznoiazychie* is translated as 'multi-languagedness', 'heteroglossia', 'polyphony', 'vari-languagedness', and 'polyglossia'. In addition to 'diversity of voices', the translation of *raznogolositsa* includes 'differing voices', 'variety of voices', and 'multiple voices'.

The words *raznorechie, raznoiazychie,* and *raznogolositsa* were all part of the Russian lexicon in the 1930s and are included in *Tolkovyi slovar' russkogo iazyka* ('Explanatory dictionary of the Russian language') edited by D.N. Ushakov (Vol. III, 1939). Their dictionary meanings are as follows. *Raznorechie* (Ushakov, ed. 1939, s.v. *raznorechie*) is given the stylistic label 'bookish' and is recorded with two meanings (in my translation): (1) "Contradiction in words, in meaning, disagreement"; (2) "Idiom, dialect, as a variant of some vernacular", a meaning marked as obsolete and belonging to the sphere of philology. *Raznoiazychie* (Ushakov, ed. 1939, s.v. *razniazychie*) is also labelled as 'bookish', and the following definition is given (my translation): "the presence/existence of different languages, of peoples/nations speaking different languages." *Raznogolositsa* is also recorded with two meanings (Ushakov, ed. 1939, s.v. *raznogolositsa*, my translation): (1) "discordant, dissonant singing" with the stylistic label "colloquial"; (2) "Multitude of opinions, lack of unity of opinions or decisions, disagreement."

Bakhtin invests these words with the special meanings he needed for his theoretical discussion of the workings of language/discourse in the novel. *Raznorechie* basically covers the stratification within one language (dialects, socio-ideological languages, etc.) and the orchestration and dialogization of the "languages of heteroglossia" in the novel, reflecting different worldviews:

> But the centripetal forces of the life of language, embodied in a "unitary language", operate in the midst of heteroglossia. At any given moment in its evolution, language is stratified not only into linguistic dialects in the strict sense of the word (according to formal linguistic markers, especially phonetic), but also – and for us this is the essential point – into languages that are socio-ideological: languages of social groups, "professional" and "generic" languages, languages of generations and so forth. (Bakhtin 1981: 271–272)

As we can see, *raznorechie* in the Bakhtinian sense encompasses "linguistic dialects in the strict sense of the word" and all other social and other variants of a language that are opposed to the standard language or, in Bakhtin's terms, "unitary language" which strives towards fixity "in the midst of heteroglossia." The Bakhtinian sense of *raznorechie* could thus be seen as an expansion of the second (obsolete) dictionary meaning, and possibly even as a kind of conflation of both meanings, since the different socio-ideological languages reflect different points of view that can be opposed to one another. They can thus be deployed, combined and contrasted by novelists to orchestrate their themes and express their intended views and values:

> all languages of heteroglossia, whatever the principle underlying them and making each unique, are specific points of view on the world, forms for conceptualizing the world in words, specific world views, each characterized by its own objects, meanings and values. [...] They may all be drawn in by the novelist for the orchestration of his themes and for the refracted (indirect) expression of his intentions and values. (Bakhtin 1981: 291–292)

In the quote above, dialects "in the strict sense" are included in *raznorechie*, but in some cases Bakhtin assigns them to *raznoiazychie* (see below).

Turning to the related concept of *raznoiazychie*, the multitude of different translations reflect Bakhtin's somewhat inconsistent utilization of the term, which ranges from "language-diversity (dialects)" (Bakhtin 1981: 299) to "extranational multi-languagedness" (Bakhtin 1981: 368). Thus, *raznoiazychie* applies both to dialects within a national language (also assigned to *raznorechie*) and to different "national" languages, a sense that is closer to the dictionary meaning of the word. In one instance, *raznoiazychie* is translated as 'polyglossia' (Bakhtin 1981: 285). Polyglossia brings us to the notion of *mnogoiazychie* – a fourth Bakhtinian term concerning linguistic diversity – but used only once in "Discourse in the Novel", when discussing the participation of linguistic consciousness "in the social multi- and vari-languagedness of evolving languages" (Bakhtin 1981: 326). Here *mnogo-iazychie* is translated as 'multi-languagedness', which is also one of the most frequent translations of *raznoiazychie*. However, in the essay "Iz predystorii romannogo slova"/"From the Prehistory of Novelistic Discourse", written in 1940 (English translation in Bakhtin 1981), where *raznoiazychie* does not appear at all, *mnogoiazychie* is the term used in reference to situations where several different "national" languages are in use. Bakhtin's use of the term *mnogoiazychie* coincides with the meaning of the corresponding adjective *mnogoiazychnyi* in Ushakov's dictionary (Ushakov, ed. 1938, s.v. *mnogoiazychnyi*): "with a multitude of national languages" (my translation). The translation of *mnogoiazychie* is 'polyglossia' throughout "From the Prehistory of Novelistic Discourse". Hence, whereas *raznoiazychie* and *mnogoiazychie* are both used about multilingual situations, only *raznoiazychie* may imply different dialects of a single national language.

The third word used by Bakhtin in the definition of the novel, viz. *raznogolositsa* refers to differing individual voices (cf. *individual'naia raznogolositsa*) which can be discerned thanks to the surrounding heteroglossia. This sense does not coincide with the dictionary meanings (see above). It is actually more in tune with one of the meanings of the adjective *raznogolosyj* 'with different voices', 'filling a space with a buzz of sounds, different voices' (Ushakov, ed. 1939, s.v. *raznogolosyj*). Naturally, differing voices might also convey different opinions and disagreement (cf. the second dictionary meaning of *raznogolositsa*).

To sum up, Bakhtin operates with three levels of linguistic diversity: the level of separate "national" languages, the level of different varieties of one "national" language, and the level of difference between individual speakers' voices/use of language. However, most of "Discourse in the novel" is concerned with the importance of *raznorechie* and its workings in the novel. *Raznorechie* (and the other two types of linguistic diversity) enter into the novel through narrators, characters' speeches and inserted genres (Bakhtin 1981: 263), but most interestingly for Bakhtin, through hybrid constructions, i.e. utterances that formally belong to one speaker but contain two mixed utterances (Bakhtin 1981: 304), which results in double-voiced internally dialogized discourse of a consciousness that speaks "indirectly, conditionally, in a refracted way" (Bakhtin 1981: 326).

As Bakhtin is not always explicit and consistent in the definitions and utilizations of his terms, it is sometimes necessary to infer from the surrounding text what exactly is meant in the current context, especially when it comes to the use of *raznorechie* and *raznoiazychie* in "Discourse in the novel". For a reader of the Western scholarly discourse on Bakhtin's view of language and English translations of his texts, the terminology is further complicated by Tzvetan Todorov's (1981) book on Bakhtin's dialogical principle and its English translation (1984). For *raznorechie* Todorov coins the neologism *hétérologie* (in the English translation 'heterology'), for *raznoiazychie* he uses *hétéroglossie* (translated as 'heteroglossia'), and *raznogolositsa* is called *hétérophonie* (translated as 'heterophony') (Todorov 1981: 89; Todorov 1984: 56).[1] Todorov thus coins neologisms for all three Bakhtinian terms, which he also takes to be Russian neologisms (Todorov 1981: 89; Todorov 1984: 56). The English translators and the French scholar thus coined the neologism *heteroglossia* in the translation of different Bakhtinian notions: *raznorechie* (English 'heteroglossia') and *raznoiazychie* (French 'hétéroglossie').

With the translation of Bakhtin's works into Western languages, notably English, not only literary scholars but also linguists found inspiration in Bakhtin's dialogical view of language. Holquist and Emerson's neologism heteroglossia found applications in various approaches and gradually grew in popularity, especially among sociolinguists. As demonstrated by Michael Edward Volek (2014), the treatment of heteroglossia in the scholarly literature diverges from the original in different ways. He concludes that "the various individual claims differ as much from each other as they do from Bakhtin" (Volek 2014: 188). In the following section, I will briefly touch upon a selection of different approaches in order to demonstrate different interpretations and applications of the attractive neologism heteroglossia and how it has come to subsume all three Bakhtinian concepts of linguistic diversity in the Western scholarly literature. I start out with approaches that apply the notion to discourse in individual languages and proceed to approaches that widen it to include bilingual and multilingual practices.

---

1. Todorov writes *raznogolosie*, a near synonym of *raznogolositsa* used by Bakhtin only once in "Slovo v romane" (p. 139, translated as "dissonances", cf. Bakhtin 1981: 325).

3. Heteroglossia in the study of discourse in a single language

Linguistic approaches that have found inspiration in the concept of heteroglossia may differ in their interpretation and use of the notion even when they are associated with one and the same scholarly tradition. I will exemplify this with two approaches that were constructed in accordance with M. A. K. Halliday's Systemic Functional Linguistics, where the notion of heteroglossia had already been "discovered" in the 1980s (Lemke 1995: 21). I start with Jay Lemke's social semiotic approach to discourse, where it is stated that heteroglossia "in Bakhtin's original sense" is "simply the diversity of social languages, socially defined discourse types in a community" (Lemke 1995: 32). Heteroglossic relations can be found between the texts and discourses of such communities. Lemke (1995: 21) links heteroglossia to the principle of *intertextuality*, since utterances must be read against the background of other utterances in the community.[2] Heteroglossic relations are characterized as social and political relations construed by someone from a particular (ideological) point of view (Lemke 1995: 33; for the relation between ideology and heteroglossia, see Määttä and Pietikäinen 2021). In Lemke's approach, heteroglossia remains on the level of diversity within a national language, observed in discourses where it creates ideological tensions. Lemke applies Bakhtin's ideas to non-fictional discourses and teases out what he sees as heteroglossic relations from texts written in standard English. This means that the tensions between standard "unitary" language and the "languages of heteroglossia" receive no attention.

The second approach identified as a branch of Systemic Functional Linguistics is Appraisal Theory (Martin and White 2005; see also White 2011). James Martin and Peter White study appraisal in (standard) English, and state that their approach is informed by Bakhtin's notions of dialogism and heteroglossia (2005: 92). What Martin and White set out to provide is a systematic account of how speakers/writers position themselves and "what sort of heteroglossic backdrop or other voices and alternative viewpoints they construct for their text and […] the way in which they engage with that backdrop" (2005: 93). They provide a reanalysis from a Bakhtinian, dialogistic perspective, of "wordings which have traditionally been treated under such headings as modality, polarity, evidentiality, intensification, attribution, concession, and consequentiality" (Martin and White 2005: 94). All locutions that function "to recognise that the text's communicative backdrop is a diverse one" are said to be heteroglossic (Martin and White 2005: 99). These locutions may also be grounded in individual subjectivities. Martin and White are thus interested in the linguistic mechanisms of introducing other viewpoints into a text or discourse (also called heteroglossic resources, Martin and White 2005: 102), but

---

2. Kristeva's (1968) concept of *intertextuality* (in French *inter-textualité*) stems from her understanding of Bakhtin's view of language in use and is connected to the concept of heteroglossia by several researchers, see Slembrouck (2011).

there is no mention of the social stratifications of language, "languages of heteroglossia" or standard "unitary" language.

As can be concluded, the two approaches discussed above stress different aspects of Bakhtin's dialogistic thinking on linguistic diversity. Lemke is interested in "socially defined discourse types in a community" (1995: 32) and studies heteroglossic relations between actual texts and discourses to reveal ideological and political tensions and points of view. Lemke's heteroglossia, like Bakhtin's, thus applies to the languages of different social groups. Martin and White, for their part, analyse ways of introducing alien points of view in a discourse or text, but demonstrate less interest in the social strata from which these points of view originate. However, the alien points of view might be those of individual voices or subjectivities, in which case the heteroglossia of appraisal theory incorporates *raznogolositsa* ('diversity of individual voices'). Thus, appraisal theory is concerned with the locutions of individual texts in one (standard) language and how they relate to other locutions of the same text or to voices from other texts. Incidentally, the appraisal approach seems to have much in common with (linguistic) *polyphony* in French linguistics (see, for example, Roulet 2011). Of the two approaches, appraisal theory is the one that departs the furthest from Bakhtin's concept.

One definition of heteroglossia that is concerned with the diversity of individual languages but that also includes *raznogolositsa* is that proposed by Vyacheslav Ivanov in the collection *Key Terms in Language and Culture* (Duranti 2001: 95): "the simultaneous use of different kinds of speech or other signs, the tension between them, and their conflicting relationship within one text." Ivanov also mentions that "Bakhtin had in mind both the stylistic and social differences within the language of any modern developed society" and individual differences among speakers (Ivanov 2001: 95). Further, he directs attention to Bakhtin's opposition between heteroglossia and monoglossia (the dominance of one language), and polyglossia (the co-existence of two languages). Thus, in Ivanov's reading of Bakhtin, heteroglossia is about the diversity and tensions within one language, but includes differences among individual speakers (*raznogolositsa*).

4. Heteroglossia as bilingual and multilingual practices

The most conspicuous application of the concept of heteroglossia during the first decades of the 21st century involves a widening of the concept to include not only the linguistic diversity of individual languages and individual voices but also elements from different named ("national") languages. Nina Møller Andersen (2010: 17) is of the opinion that the translated term heteroglossia covers all three notions of linguistic diversity discussed by Bakhtin, and Birgitta Busch (2014: 24) declares that she uses "the term heteroglossia in a large sense, embracing the multifaceted and multi-layered plurality which in Bakhtin's view is inherent to living language." In her opinion this is customary in "today's reception" (ibid.) and corresponds to Emerson and Holquist's translation where only the term heteroglossia is used and not three different ones as in Todorov's book. Turner and Lin (2020: 426) find a motivation for the inclusion of polyglossia in heteroglossia in Bakhtin's own discussion in the essay "From the Prehistory of Novelistic Discourse". Bakhtin (1981: 67–68) writes that the question of polyglossia (*mnogoiazychie*) is inseparable from the question of heteroglossia (*raznorechie*) and that intra-language heteroglossia was prepared for by active polyglossia during the Middle Ages and intense interanimation of languages during the Renaissance. According to Turner and Lin (2020: 426), today's active polyglossia is "an important tool for the creativity and speech diversity" of individual speakers and can thus be seen as part of heteroglossia. Viewing heteroglossia in this perspective makes sense and shows that multilingual heteroglossia is not too far from Bakhtin's own thinking.

However, mention of heteroglossia in connection with the use of elements from different (named) languages can already be found in linguistic anthropological works from the 1980s and 1990s (for example, Hill and Hill 1986; Duranti 1992). An early proponent of the view that code-switching is a particular manifestation of heteroglossia is Joan Pujolar (2001: 174). Benjamin Bailey's (2007, 2012) widely used definition of heteroglossia can be seen as the definite leap of the concept into theories and studies of bi- and multilingualism. Bailey rephrases Ivanov's (2001; see above) definition, breaking it up into two parts: First, "the simultaneous use of different kinds of forms or signs", and second, "the tensions and conflicts among those signs, based on the sociohistorical associations they carry with them" (2007: 257; 2012: 499). Bailey includes forms from different languages among the forms that are simultaneously used in heteroglossia, although he is aware of the fact that Bakhtin had intra-language variation in mind. After deciding to include both monolingual and multilingual forms, Bailey suggests that the concept of heteroglossia "allows a level of theorizing about the social nature of language that is not possible within the confines of a focus on code-switching" (2007: 258; for code-switching, see Auer and Eastman 2010). For many researchers who study and theorize practices of juggling between languages and the fusion of features from different languages in multilingual communities (ranging from playing children to multilingual classrooms, youth culture, new media communication and web 2.0 discourse), the concept of heteroglossia has thus become more attractive than code-switching. These researchers see bilingual and multilingual knowledge as consisting not of separate linguistic systems or codes (L1, L2, etc.) but as one single repertoire of linguistic features associated with different named languages and language varieties with the possibility of choosing among them and combining them. They avoid the notion of code-switching due to its history of association with stigmatized behaviour and with an ideology of languages as codes that should be kept separate and pure (García and Li 2014: 12, 58).

Most of these authors refer to Bailey's (2007, 2012) articles and commend the concept of heteroglossia for being flexible enough to be applicable to multilingual, multicultural, and multimodal settings, and for not presupposing strict boundaries between languages, language varieties, and codes. A further advantage is that heteroglossia takes into account different (ideological) points of view, in addition to social and historical processes. It is acknowledged that such a "fuzzy" concept is difficult to operationalize in a clear-cut way, but the potential disadvantage of such an open and flexible concept can also be seen in a positive light, as it offers the possibility of spotting relations between various kinds of signs and structural properties at different levels of discourse. There is also a felt need to pin down the understanding of heteroglossia while still incorporating the diversity of its meaning (Blackledge and Creese 2014: 4). Adrian Blackledge and Angela Creese (2014: 4–11) propose fitting the various facets of heteroglossia, also discussed by Bakhtin himself, under three headings: indexicality, tension-filled interaction, and multivoicedness. Indexicality relates to the fact that language in use "indexes" a certain point of view or social position; tension-filled interaction accounts for the constant pull between forces of standardization (*centripetal* forces) and heteroglossic disunification (*centrifugal* forces); and multivoicedness, finally, is a consequence of the dialogic nature of language, and focuses upon the relation of the word not only to other words of the past, but also anticipates future words of the other.

While some of these authors in their analyses explicitly rely on the concept of heteroglossia (for example, Androutsopoulos 2011; Busch 2014; Kyratzis et al 2010; Leppänen et al. 2009; Leppänen 2012; Peuronen 2011; Pietikäinen and Dufva 2014; Sultana 2014; Tagg 2016), others may prefer other notions, but they usually still discuss how their own terms relate to heteroglossia. Such terms are: *crossing* (Rampton 1995, 2005), *polylingual languaging* (Jørgensen 2008), *translanguaging* (Canagarajah 2011; Creese and Blackledge 2011; Garcia 2009, Li 2011, 2018; García and Li 2014), *metrolingualism* (Otsuji and Pennycook 2010; Jaworsky 2014), *flexible bilingualism* (Creese and Blackledge 2011) *code meshing* (Canagarajah 2011), *code play* (Jaworska 2014), and *transglossia* (Sultana et al. 2015). These terms do not overlap completely but each covers a different aspect of flexible and fluid multilingual practice, pedagogy, and ideology. Often, they apply to immigration and postcolonial contexts (for a discussion, see Jaspers and Madsen 2019).

Throughout this discussion, the term heteroglossia occurs in various relationships with these alternative notions. Creese and Blackledge (2011) see their concept of flexible bilingualism as identical to Bailey's (2007) heteroglossia (stemming from Bakhtin). Jaworski (2014) views metrolingualism as a manifestation of heteroglossia. García and Li (2014: 14–15) see heteroglossia as the umbrella concept under which the other terms fall, while Sultana, Dovchin, and Pennycook (2015) wish to place the heteroglossic language practices of young adults into what they call a transglossic framework. Thus, heteroglossia may be directly applied to actual multilingual practices, it may be viewed as an umbrella term for various more specific practices, or, finally, it may be fitted into a larger framework of transglossia. According to Jaspers (2018), the related notion of translanguaging has gradually become more widely used than the rival terms in socio- and applied linguistics, but it has also come to be deployed in too many senses, viz. an innate instinct, fluid language use, a bilingual pedagogy (the original sense), a theory of language, and a process of personal and social transformation. Jaspers (2018) also notes that code-switching is used more often than the new terms (for code-switching and translanguaging, see Bhatt and Bolonyai 2019).

As a theoretical framework for the study of functional and communicative language use in which various linguistic forms and features combine and intermingle, heteroglossia has certain advantages over the other proposed terms. First, heteroglossia in itself is not associated with specific contexts, places, cultures or ideologies like most of the newer competing notions, which are associated with, for instance, immigrational and urban contexts; an anticolonial stance, liberation and transformation (see Jaspers and Madsen 2019). It is the different "languages" and practices of heteroglossia that may have ideological and other meanings and connotations. Second, heteroglossia is not used for as many different purposes as, for instance, translanguaging (see above). And third, the concept of heteroglossia acknowledges (named) standard (unitary) languages and the constant tension between processes of standardization (centripetal forces) and all sorts of fluid linguistic practices (centrifugal forces). An increasing number of publications recognise the need to study both types of force and to acknowledge the usefulness of boundaries and naming languages (see, for example, the chapters in Jaspers and Madsen (eds.) 2019; McLelland 2021; Slembrouck 2022; Prinsloo 2023). An example of research using the theoretical perspective of heteroglossia to study the tensions between the use of standard and vernacular Finnish as well as linguistically heterogeneous urban slang, is Leppänen and Westinen (2022).

I will end this section with a discussion of a short exchange of texting between two schoolmates, to illustrate how the lens of heteroglossia can be used to analyze pragmatic functions of fluid language use and how it is related to interactional and interpersonal processes. Examples (1) and (2) were texted by two Finland-Swedish/Finnish bilingual schoolmates (A and B), closest friends attending a Swedish-speaking high school in Southwestern Finland.[3] As foreign languages they studied English, Russian, and Spanish, and in their communication, both in speech and texting, they loved playing with forms and features from their whole linguistic repertoire. Example (1) contains three quick short messages by A to check whether B, who is late, will come to her place as agreed in earlier texting (in "colloquial" Finland-Swedish) the same day.

---

[3]. A corpus of texting between A and her schoolmates was given to me by A in 2015, with informed consent by her and all schoolmates that the material could be used in anonymized form for research purposes. For a fuller discussion, see Björklund (in press).

(1) A: Helo   21:13
       It me   21:13
       You comes?   21:13

The three short messages in (1) are examples of A's and B's use of deliberately broken English in their own heteroglossic joking jargon. According to A (personal communication), the greeting *Helo / It me* is meant to reflect a Russian accent. The "innovative" spelling <Helo> instead of <Hello> is heteroglossic in the sense that it is supposed to reflect a Russian accent of pronunciation, whereas the message *It me* is a heteroglossic fusion of the English phrase *It's me* and Russian syntax without a copula in the present tense. This very private greeting is used only between A and B. The grammatically incorrect question *You comes?* plays with the deliberately broken English used in the so-called doge memes (popular Internet memes that typically feature pictures of a dog and its internal dialogue in broken English). In pragmatic terms, A mitigates her reminder that B is late by using their private heteroglossic jargon. B's answer also comes in quick, short messages, the first two resuming the same heteroglossic jargon:

(2) B: Helo   21:13
       Much chaps   21:13
       Chaos   21:13
       No shower   21:13

In interpersonal terms, the greeting with Russian accent and the doge meme-inspired explanation of the delay *Much chaps* confirms A's and B's affectionate friendship. The explanation continues in two short, standard English phrases, which creates heteroglossic tension between standard English forms (learned at school) and English used in a specific humorous internet context. In their private communication in Examples (1) and (2), they chose, combined and played with forms and features from two languages that were foreign to both of them. When it comes to the possibility of applying the rival concepts in the analysis, translanguaging in the sense of fluid language use would apparently qualify, but I would hesitate to regard at least the fusion of English and Russian features as code-switching. Hence, because of the many disparate meanings of translanguaging, out of which only one might be relevant here, and since code-switching is about the *juxtaposition* of speech from two different systems (cf. Auer and Eastman 2010), the heteroglossic perspective is preferable over these alternatives.

5. Conclusion

In this chapter I have traced Bakhtin's terms denoting three levels of linguistic diversity back to four existing Russian words: *raznorechie, raznogolositsa*, and *raznoiazychie/*

mnogoiazychie. The neologism heteroglossia, coined by Holquist and Emerson in translation of *raznorechie*, turned out to be a success and has attracted the attention not only of literary scholars but also of linguists of different orientations. There are even scholars writing in Russian who use the transliteration *geteroglossiia* instead of the Russian original. Since the term heteroglossia was coined, its meaning has expanded to encompass all three levels of linguistic stratification covered by the four Bakhtinian terms, but it also continues to be used in the original intra-lingual sense (see, for example, Simpson 2018). Both in the intra-lingual and the multilingual sense heteroglossia offers a theoretical framework for the study of pragmatic functions, whether in its own right or as the umbrella term for various practices.

The story of heteroglossia, in fact, illustrates an important Bakhtinian idea, viz. that a word gets its actual meaning(s) only in living utterances – "no living word relates to its object in a *singular* way" (Bakhtin 1981: 276, original emphasis). As Volek (2014: 256) points out, "in speaking about speech, Bakhtin is both a language theorist and a participant in a real speech situation." In his "living" utterance, at least the Russian words *raznorechie* and *raznogolositsa* used by him acquire actual meanings that go beyond their mere linguistic significations. Similarly, linguists who take part in the scholarly discussion on various types of text and discourse have endowed heteroglossia with meanings that are absent from both the Russian original text and its English translation in order to put forward their own views.

References

Androutsopoulos, Jannis. 2011. "From variation to heteroglossia in the study of computer-mediated discourse." In *Digital Discourse. Language in the New Media*, ed. by Crispin Thurlow and Kristine Mroczek, 277–298. Oxford: Oxford University Press.

Auer, Peter, and Carol M. Eastman. 2010. "Code-switching." In *Handbook of Pragmatics* 14, ed. by Jan-Ola Östman and Jef Verschueren, 1–34. Amsterdam/Philadelphia: John Benjamins Publishing Company.

Bailey, Benjamin. 2007. "Heteroglossia and boundaries." In *Bilingualism: A Social Approach*, ed. by Monica Heller, 257–274. Basingstoke and New York: Palgrave Macmillan.

Bailey, Benjamin. 2012. "Heteroglossia." In *The Routledge Handbook of Multilingualism*, ed. by Marilyn Martin-Jones, Adrian Blackledge, and Angela Creese, 499–507. London and New York: Routledge.

Bakhtin, Mikhail. 1975. *Voprosy literatury i èstetiki. Issledovaniia raznykh let*. Moscow: Khudozhestvennaia literatura.

Bakhtin, Mikhail. 1981. *The Dialogic Imagination*, ed. by Michael Holquist, transl. by Caryl Emerson and Michael Holquist. Austin and London: University of Texas Press.

Bhatt, Rakesh., M. and Agnes Bolonyai. 2019. "Code-switching and translanguaging." In *Handbook of Pragmatics* 22, ed. by Jan-Ola Östman and Jef Verschueren, 61–78. Amsterdam/Philadelphia: John Benjamins Publishing Company.

Björklund, Martina. In press. "*Amazing* – the use of English in texting between a Finland-Swedish high school girl and friends." In *Structures in Discourse: Studies in Interaction, Adaptability, and Pragmatic Functions in Honour of Tuija Virtanen*, ed. by Martin Gill, Aino Malmivirta and Brita Wårvik. John Benjamins Publishing Company..

Blackledge, Adrian, and Angela Creese. 2014. "Heteroglossia as practice and pedagogy." In *Heteroglossia as Practice and Pedagogy, Educational Linguistics* 20, ed. by Adrian Blackledge and Angela Creese, 1–20. Dordrecht: Springer.

Brandist, Craig and Mika Lähteenmäki. 2010. "Early Soviet linguistics and Mikhail Bakhtin's essays on the novel of the 1930s." In *Politics and the Theory of Language in the USSR 1917–1938*, ed. by Craig Brandist and Katya Chown, 69–88. London: Anthem Press.

Busch, B. 2014. "Building on heteroglossia and heterogeneity: The experience of a multilingual classroom." In *Heteroglossia as Practice and Pedagogy, Educational Linguistics* 20, ed. by Adrian Blackledge and Angela Creese, 21–40. Dordrecht: Springer.

Canagarajah, A. Suresh. 2011. "Codemeshing in academic writing: identifying teachable strategies of translanguaging." *The Modern Language Journal* 95 (3), 401–417.

Creese, Angela and Adrian Blackledge. 2011. "Separate and flexible bilingualism in complementary schools: Multiple language practices in interrelationship." *Journal of Pragmatics* 43 (5): 1196–1208.

Duranti, Alessandro. 1992. "Heteroglossia in Samoan oratory." *Pacific Studies* 15 (4): 155–175.

Duranti, Alessandro (ed). 2001. *Key Terms in Language & Culture*. Oxford: Wiley-Blackwell.

García, Ofelia. 2009. "Education, multilingualism and translanguaging in the 21st century." In *Multilingual Education for Social Justice: Globalising the local*, ed. by Ajit K. Mohanty, Minati Panda, Robert Phillipson and Tove Skutnabb-Kangas, 126–158. New Delhi: Orient BlackSwan.

García, Ofelia and Wei Li. 2014. *Translanguaging. Language, Bilingualism and Education*. London: Palgrave Macmillan.

Hill, Jane H. and Kenneth C. Hill. 1986. *Speaking Mexicano: The Dynamics of Syncretic Language in Central Mexico*. Tucson: University of Arizona Press.

Ivanov, Vyacheslav. 2001. "Heteroglossia." In *Key Terms in Language and Culture*, ed. by Alessandro Duranti, 95–97. Oxford: Blackwell.

Jaspers, Jürgen. 2018. "The transformative limits of translanguaging." *Language & Communication* 58: 1–10.

Jaspers, Jürgen and Lian Malai Madsen. 2019. "Fixity and fluidity in Sociolinguistics. Theory and Practice." In *Critical Perspectives on Linguistic Fixity and Fluidity. Languagised Lives*, ed. by Jürgen Jaspers and Lian Malai Madsen, 1–26. New York and London: Routledge.

Jaspers, Jürgen and Lian Malai Madsen (eds). 2019. *Critical Perspectives on Linguistic Fixity and Fluidity. Languagised Lives*. New York and London: Routledge.

Jaworska, Sylvia. 2014. "Playful language alteration in an online discussion forum: The example of digital code plays." *Journal of Pragmatics* 71: 56–68.

Jaworski, Adam. 2014. "Metrolingual art: Multilingualism and heteroglossia." *International Journal of Bilingualism* 18: 134–158.

Jørgensen, J. Normann. 2008. "Polylingual languaging around and among children and adolescents." *International Journal of Multilingualism* 5 (3): 161–176.

Kristeva, Julia. 1968. "Problèmes de la structuration du texte." In *Tel Quel, Théorie d'ensemble*, 298–317. Paris: Éditions du Seuil.

Kyratzis, Amy, Jennifer F. Reynolds and Anna-Carita Evaldsson. 2010. "Introduction: Heteroglossia and language ideologies in children's peer play interactions." *Pragmatics* 20 (4): 457–466.

Lähteenmäki, Mika. 2003. "On the interpretation of Baxtin's linguistic ideas: The problem of the texts from the 1950–60s." *Russian Linguistics* 27: 23–39.

Lähteenmäki, Mika. 2004. "On the origins of Bakhtinian sociolinguistics. In *Papers from the 30th Finnish Conference of Linguistics, Joensuu, May 15–16, 2003*, ed. by Marja Nenonen, 101–106. Joensuu: University of Joensuu.

Lähteenmäki, Mika. 2010. "Heteroglossia and voice: Conceptualising linguistic diversity from a Bakhtinian perspective." In *Language Ideologies in Transition: Multilingualism in Russia and Finland*, ed. by Mika Lähteenmäki and Marjatta Vanhala-Aniszewski, 15–29. Frankfurt am Main: Peter Lang.

Lemke, Jay L. 1995. *Textual Politics: Discourse and Social Dynamics*. London and Bristol, PA: Taylor & Francis.

Leppänen, Sirpa. 2012. "Linguistic and generic hybridity in web writing: The case of fan fiction." In *Language Mixing and Code-switching in Writing: Approaches to Mixed-language Written Discourse*, ed. by Mark Sebba, Shahrzad Mahootian and Carla Jonsson, 233–254. London: Routledge

Leppänen, Sirpa, Anne Pitkänen-Huhta, Arja Piirainen-Marsh, Tarja Nikula, and Saija Peuronen. 2009. "Young people's translocal new media uses: A multiperspective analysis of language choice and heteroglossia." *Journal of Computer-Mediated Communication* 14: 1080–1107.

Leppänen, Sirpa and Elina Westinen. 2022. "Sociolinguistic upsets and people of color on social media performances." *International Journal of the Sociology of Language* 2022 (275): 129–151.

Li, Wei. 2011. "Moment analysis and translanguaging space: Discursive construction of identities by multilingual Chinese youth in Britain." *Journal of Pragmatics* 43: 1222–1235.

Li, Wei. 2018. "Translanguaging as a practical theory of language." *Applied Linguistics* 39 (1): 9–30.

Martin, James R. and Peter R. R. White 2005. *The Language of Evaluation: Appraisal in English*. New York: Palgrave Macmillan.

Määttä, Simo and Sari Pietikäinen. 2021. "Ideology." In *Handbook of Pragmatics Online* 18, ed. by Jan-Ola Östman and Jef Verschueren, 1–24. Amsterdam/Philadelphia: John Benjamins Publishing Company.

McLelland, Nicola. 2021. "Language standards, standardisation and standard ideologies in multilingual contexts." *Journal of Multilingual and Multicultural Development* 42 (2): 109–124.

Møller Andersen, Nina. 2010. "Talesprog og sproglig polyfoni. Bachtins sproglige begrebsapparat i anvendelse." *TidSchrift voor Skandinavistik* 3 (2): 3–23.

Otsuji, Emi and Alastair Pennycook. 2010. "Metrolingualism: fixity, fluidity and language in flux." *International Journal of Multilingualism* 7 (3): 240–254.

Peuronen, Saija. 2011. "'Ride hard, live forever': Translocal identities in an online community of extreme sports Christians." In *Digital Discourse. Language in the New Media*, ed. by Crispin Thurlow and Kristine Mroczek, 154–176. Oxford: Oxford University Press.

Pietikäinen, Sari and Hannele Dufva. 2014. "Heteroglossia in action: Sámi children, textbooks and rap." In *Heteroglossia as Practice and Pedagogy, Educational Linguistics* 20, ed. by Adrian Blackledge and Angela Creese, 59–74. Dordrecht: Springer.

Prinsloo, Mastin. 2023. "Fixity and fluidity in language and language education." *Journal of Multilingual and Multicultural Development* Published online 08 Feb 2023.

Pujolar, Joan. 2001. *Gender, Heteroglossia and Power: A Sociolinguistic Study of Youth Culture.* Language, Power and Social Process 4. Berlin and New York: Mouton de Gruyter.

Rampton, Ben. 1995. "Language crossing and the problematisation of ethnicity." *Pragmatics* 5 (4): 485–513.

Rampton, Ben. 2005. *Crossing: Language & Ethnicity among Adolescents* (Second Edition). Manchester, UK and Northampton MA: St. Jerome Publishing.

Roulet, E. 2011. "Polyphony." In *Discursive Pragmatics. Handbook of Pragmatics Highlights* 8, ed. by Jan Zienkowsky, Jan-Ola Östman, and Jef Verschueren, 208–222. Amsterdam/Philadelphia: John Benjamins Publishing Company.

Shvedova, N. Iu. (ed). 2008. *Tolkovyj slovar' russkogo iazyka. S vkliucheniem svedenii o proizkhozhdenii slov.* Moscow: RAN.

Simpson, Ashley. 2018. *The Dialogism of Ideologies About Equality, Democracy and Human Rights within Finnish Education. Many Voices and Many Faces.* Helsinki Studies in Education, 26. Helsinki: University of Helsinki https://helda.helsinki.fi/bitstream/handle/10138/231872/Thedialo.pdf?sequence=1&isAllowed=y

Slembrouck, Stef. 2011. "Intertextuality." In *Handbook of Pragmatics Online* 8 (2011), ed. by Jef Verschueren, Jan-Ola Östman, Jan Bloammert and Chris Bulcaen. Amsterdam/Philadelphia: John Benjamins Publishing Company.

Slembrouck, Stef. 2022. "The various guises of translanguaging and its theoretical airstrip." *Journal of Multilingual and Multicultural Development* Published online 05 Dec 2022.

Sultana, Shaila. 2014. "Heteroglossia and identities of young adults in Bangladesh." *Linguistics and Education* 26: 40–56.

Sultana, Shaila, Sender Dovchin and Alastair Pennycook. 2015. "Transglossic language practices of young adults in Bangladesh and Mongolia." *International Journal of Multilingualism* 12 (1): 93–108.

Tagg, Caroline. 2016. "Heteroglossia in text-messaging: Performing identity and negotiating relationships in a digital space." *Journal of Sociolinguistics* 20 (1): 59–85.

Todorov, Tzvetan. 1981. *Mikhaïl Bakhtine. Le principe dialogique. Suivi de. Écrits du cercle de Bakhtine.* Paris: Éditions du Seuil.

Todorov, Tzvetan. 1984. *Mikhail Bakhtin. The Dialogical Principle.* Transl. by Wlad Godzich. Theory and History of Literature 13. Manchester: Manchester University Press.

Turner, Marianne, and Angel M.Y. Lin. 2020. "Translanguaging and named languages: Productive tension and desire." *International Journal of Biligual Education and Bilingualism*, 23 (4): 423–433.

Ushakov, D. N. (ed). 1938. *Tolkovyj slovar' russkogo iazyka.* Vol. 2. Gosudarstvennoe izdatel'stvo inostrannykh i natsional'nykh slovarei.

Ushakov, D. N. (ed). 1939. *Tolkovyj slovar' russkogo iazyka.* Vol. 3. Gosudarstvennoe izdatel'stvo inostrannykh i natsional'nykh slovarei.

Volek, Michael Edward. 2014. *Speaking of Bakhtin: A study of the sociolinguistic discourse on Bakhtin and language.* Vancouver: University of British Columbia. http://hdl.handle.net/2429/48413

White, Peter R. R. 2011. "Appraisal." In *Handbook of Pragmatics Online* 8 (2011), ed. by Jef Verschueren, Jan-Ola Östman, Jan Blommaert and Chris Bulcaen. Amsterdam/Philadelphia: John Benjamins Publishing Company.

Michael Alexander Kirkwood (M.A.K.) Halliday

Jonathan James Webster
City University of Hong Kong

1. Introduction

Alexander Kirkwood Halliday, whose pioneering approach to the study of language is known as Systemic Functional Linguistics (SFL), was born on Easter Monday, 13 April 1925 in Leeds, Yorkshire, England. He passed away on 15 April 2018 in Sydney, Australia, at the age of 93. Halliday recognized complementarity where some see only dichotomy, such as between system and text, grammar and lexis, speech and writing, the congruent and the metaphorical (Halliday 2008). Distinctive to Halliday's systemic-functional model is the functional organization of language, register variation according to use (Matthiessen 2015), and prioritizing the paradigmatic over the syntagmatic. Halliday envisioned linguistics as a human science encompassing the various dimensions of language in social life, integrating the *socio* and the *pragma* (see for example Lecompte-Van Poucke's 2021 'pragma-functional' approach 'combining systemic functional linguistics with argumentation theory, critical discourse studies and postcolonial insights'). Also discussed are the various influences that contributed to Halliday's unique emphasis on developing an *appliable* linguistics (see Mahboob and Knight 2010).

2. Metafunctional hypothesis

The influence of the Prague School is evident in the functional orientation of Halliday's approach to the study of language, particularly in Halliday's assignment of microfunctions to describe a child's protolanguage, reflecting a more commonsense perspective "where function equals use" (Halliday 1995/2003: 397–404, 429–430; Martin 2013: 79; Interviewer: Paul J. Thibault, 1985). However, when children transition from protolanguage into language, typically around the second year of life, the microfunctions are generalized into an opposition between demanding (i.e. the pragmatic) and describing (i.e. the mathetic), possibly realized through intonation and/or voice quality (Halliday 1994/2003: 401). In the final step in the child's development of human language, this opposition between the pragmatic and the mathetic is reconstrued into "a new metafunctional organization of language" (Halliday 1994/2003: 402). The pragmatic develops into grammar for enacting interpersonal relationships; the mathetic into grammar for construing experience. In addition, the child develops "grammar in its role of building up commonsense logic, construed as 'and', 'or', 'is', 'so', 'then', 'says', 'thinks', and so on" (Halliday 1994/2003: 403). The child also develops the grammar for creating text, "as a parallel 'virtual' universe that is made of meaning, and that has its own structure as metaphor for the structures it is imposing on the material world" (Halliday 1994/2003: 403).

Halliday's use of the term *metafunction* represents "a higher order abstraction than the notion of 'function' as in Bühler (1990), or as used in speech act theory with terms such as promise or command (Searle 1969)" (Hasan 2009: 265–266). Comparing his approach to Bühler's, Halliday noted the following similarities and differences:

> My own ideational corresponds very closely to Bühler's representational, except that I want to introduce the further distinction within it between experiential and logical, which corresponds to a fundamental distinction within language itself. My own interpersonal corresponds more or less to the sum of Bühler's conative and expressive, because in the linguistic system these two are not distinguished. Then I need to add a third function, namely the textual function, which you will not find in Malinowski or Bühler or anywhere else, because it is intrinsic to language: it is the function that language has of creating text, of relating itself to the context – to the situation and the preceding text.
> (Parret 1974: 94–96, cited in Wylie 2019: 76)

The ideational function "is the content function of language, language as about something" (Halliday 1975/2007: 183–184). Ideational meaning expresses our observations about "the phenomena of the environment: the things – creatures, objects, actions, events, qualities, states and relations – of the world and of our own consciousness, including the phenomenon of language itself; and also the 'metaphenomena', the things that are already encoded as facts and as reports" (Halliday 1975/2007: 184). Included under the heading of ideational meaning, Halliday distinguishes between experiential and logical sub-components. While the experiential concerns the speaker-as-observer's construal of experience, the logical "embodies those systems which set up logical-semantic relationships between one clausal unit and another" (Halliday 2003: 17). Logical meaning "extend[s] the experiential power of the grammar by theorizing the connection between one quantum of experience and another (note that their 'logic' is grammatical logic, not formal logic, though it is the source from which formal logic is derived" (Halliday 2003: 17). The logical is more iterative than configurational, complementing the power of experiential meaning by "form[ing] sequences of (most typically) clauses into a dynamic progression" (Halliday 2003: 18). The interpersonal function "is the participatory function of language, language as doing something" (Halliday 1975/

2007: 184). Interpersonal meaning expresses the role relationships between participants both as defined by the context of the situation and "by language itself, relationships of questioner-respondent, informer-doubter and the like" (Halliday 1975/2007: 184). The textual function "expresses the relation of the language to its environment, including both the verbal environment – what has been said or written before – and the non-verbal, situational environment" (Halliday 1975/2007: 184).

The metafunctions are not claimed to be innate, but instead seen "as one aspect of the evolution of the human species" (Halliday 2003: 18). In order to survive, we need a way to construe experience – "making sense of what we perceive as 'reality', both the world outside us and the world of our own inner consciousness"; enact interpersonal relationships – "setting up both immediate and long-term interaction with other persons, and in this way establishing each one's identity and self-awareness"; and create discourse – "formulating a distinct 'semiotic reality' in which [ideational] and [interpersonal] are combined into a single flow of meaning, as spoken or written text" (Halliday 1975/2007: 183–184; 1995/2005: 216). The metafunctions explain how "the world of semiosis unfolds alongside the material world, interpenetratingly" (Halliday 1997/2003: 249). The metafunctions relate "the semiotic construction of the culture as instantiated in particular situations" (Martin 2013: 82; Interviewer: Paul J. Thibault, 1985) with how "[they] are typically represented by different kinds of grammatical organization" (Martin 2013: 82; Interviewer: Paul J. Thibault, 1985). "The overall meaning potential of a language," states Halliday, "is organized by the grammar on functional lines" (Halliday 2003: 18). Halliday describes "the functional organization of meaning in language" as being "built in to the core of the linguistic system, as the most general organizing principle of the lexicogrammatical stratum" (Halliday 1975/2007: 184). Halliday maintains that "different patterns of realization taken by the linguistic system relate to these metafunctional distinctions" (Martin 2013: 82; Interviewer: Paul J. Thibault, 1985).

Each metafunctional component produces its own distinct dimension of structure. Butler argues that the novelty of Halliday's metafunctional hypothesis comes from the fact that the metafunctions "are not simply extrinsic imposed from outside, as uses to which language can be put, but are integrated into the basic organisation of language, in that they correspond to relatively discrete blocks of options in meaning within the linguistic system" (Butler 1988: 86). Choices made within these blocks of options are distinctively realized in the grammar. Experiential meaning is structurally realized by the configuration of process, participant(s) and circumstance(s), or what Halliday calls *transitivity structure*. Logical meaning is realized by linking words like conjunctions. Interpersonal meaning is realized by mood (giving or receiving information or goods & services) and modality (possibility, probability, obligation, etc.). Other phenomena related to the interpersonal metafunction include "the vocative, deixis, attitudinal lexical items, uses of conjunctive items invoking the speaker's communicative role (Halliday and Hasan 1976: 240), as well as prosodic, intonational features" (Davidse & Simon-

Vandenbergen 2008: 3). Martin's Appraisal Theory (Martin 2000; Martin & White 2005) "extended [Halliday's] notion of interpersonal 'prosody' to the lexical realization of 'APPRAISAL' meanings scattered over whole texts" (Davidse & Simon-Vandenbergen 2008: 5). Martin's "extensive lexico-semantic subcategorization of appraisal meanings" (Davidse & Simon-Vandenbergen 2008: 5) is intended to answer "very concrete questions arising from the analysis of text: how do we deal with subjectivity in text and to what extent can evaluative lexis be treated in a more systematic way than was hitherto the case?" (Davidse & Simon-Vandenbergen 2008: 12). Textual meaning is realized by theme (what occurs clause-initial) and information structures (given and new) (Halliday and Webster 2014). A text is Complementing the clausal orientation of systemic-functional grammar, Rhetorical Structure Theory, as developed by William C. Mann and Sandra Thompson (1988), and Christian Matthiessen (2015), investigates the relations that occur between functionally-significant text spans at clause level and above. Webster et. al. (2013) present "a framework for visualizing functional semantic information realized across functionally significant spans of text ranging from a text's constituent clauses up to the text as a whole" (2013: 302).

A metaphorical step – Halliday refers to it as "the Knight's move" – takes place in the construction of text-as-discourse, enabling the story "which Homo sapiens evolved, and that gave it an evolutionary advantage" (Meares 2016: 165). This story "had the structure of myth, depending upon the coordination of two forms of language and modes of thought, which have different development pathways and neurological bases. One concerns syntactical development (i.e.'verbal'), the other symbolic ('mythical')" (Meares 2016: 165). "Every theory", writes Halliday (2005/2013: 210), "is a metaphor for what it is theorizing". The semogenic strategies in verbal science and verbal art are related (Halliday 2005/2013: 207), both employ symbols to articulate second-order semiosis. Hasan calls it *symbolic articulation* (Butt and Webster 2019); Halliday prefers Mukařovský's term *de-automatization* since what is happening, whether in verbal art or verbal science, is "the partial freeing of the lower-level systems from the control of the semantics so that they become domains of choice in their own right" (Halliday 1987/2002: 86). In verbal art, symbolic articulation is achieved by the writer in mobilizing the habitual pattern of grammatical choice into a new automatic, a new pattern specific to the text (Butt forthcoming). The poet thus creates an automatization against which to de-automatize, creating a background against which to foreground. The poet's aim is to create a theory, i.e. "a hypothesis about some aspect of the life of social man" (Hasan 1985: 97; Carol Webster 2021). On the other hand, the language of science has seen a steady drift in the direction of nominalizing grammar, foregrounding 'things' over qualities, processes and relations (Webster 2009: 116–138). These shifts away from the congruent – grammatical metaphor/de-automatization – re-occur with such an intensity that the shifts eventually become a drift in the direction of a new automatic in verbal science (Butt, forthcoming). This *nominalizing grammar* has given scientists enormous power over their environment, so much so that they can make the world standstill, or even "create new, virtual realities" (Webster 2004: viii). Paradoxically, the more abstract the theorizing, the more concrete the world has become.

3. Context of situation

Halliday traces the influence behind his approach to dealing with context back to Malinowski, who first used the expression *context of situation* (Halliday 1991/2007: 271), and Malinowski's younger colleague and Halliday's mentor, J. R. Firth, who "saw the possibility of integrating this notion, of the "situation" as a kind of context, into a general theory of language" (Halliday 1991/2007: 272). Halliday credits Malinowski (1923), "an anthropologist, who became a linguist in the service of his ethnographic pursuits" (Halliday 1991/2007: 272), with distinguishing between *context of culture* – as-potential and *context of situation* – as-actual (Halliday 1971/2007: 44). This distinction is at the heart of the complementarity between "two founding traditions of the study of language in context", the British, with Malinowski and Firth, and the American, with Sapir and Whorf, as being complementary. Whereas the British tradition "stress[es] the situation as the context for language as text; and they see language as a form of action, as the enactment of social relationships and social processes", the American tradition "stress[es] the culture as the context for language as system; and they see language as a form of reflection, as the construal of experience into a theory or model of reality" (Halliday 1991/2007: 273).

Firth focused on the *context of situation* – as-actual, "since he preferred to study generalized patterns of actual behaviour, rather than attempting to characterize the potential as such" (Halliday 1971/2007: 45) – "[Firth's] interest was in the way people used language, spoken or written, as it might be, and the situations, the environments in which they used it" (Martin 2013: 144; Interviewer: Caroline Coffin, 1998). From "accurate observations", Firth sought to relate the actual to "a set of options specific to a given environment" (Halliday 1971/2007: 46). This set of options, i.e., a system, corresponds to "a behaviour potential" (ibid.).

Halliday re-interpreted the Malinowski-Firth concept of *context of situation* in terms of the three concepts of field, tenor and mode. Field of discourse "refers to what the participants in the context of situation are actually engaged in doing" (Halliday 1974/2007: 111). What one is doing, including what one is saying, is reflected in the speaker's choices of "different words and different grammatical patterns" (Halliday 1974/2007: 110). Tenor has to do with "role relationships in the situation in question: who the participants in the communication group are, and in what relationship they stand to each other" (Halliday 1974/2007: 112). The tenor of discourse, according to Hasan (2009: 213), "concerns the enacting of human relationships in language: who is interacting with whom? The focus is not on specific individuals but on features that establish their positioning in society (Bernstein 1990), e.g., mother-child, teacher-pupil, colleagues, neighbours, and so on." Mode deals with questions like "what function is language being used for, what is its specific role in the goings-on to which it is contributing? To persuade? To soothe? to sell? to control? to explain? or just to oil the works, as in what Malinowski called 'phatic communion'" (Halliday 1974/2007: 112). Choice of which mode, or *channel* of communication, "influences the speaker's selection of mood (what kind of statements he makes, such as forceful, hesitant, gnomic, qualified or reassertive; whether he asks questions and so on) and of modality (the judgement of probabilities); and also, in the distinction between speech and writing, it affects the whole pattern of grammatical and lexical organization, the *density* of the lexical content" (Halliday 1974/2007: 113). Increased lexical density results from "packing more content words into each phrase or clause or sentence" (Halliday 1974/2007: 113).

The three situational variables – field, tenor, mode – are instantiated by "features from amongst the vast number of systemic possibilities" (Hasan 2009: 264). The configuration of these "systemically related contextual features (Hasan 1999: 274–314)" are "'encapsulated' in the wording of the text" (Hasan 2009: 264). Halliday describes these three situational dimensions as "the backdrop, the features of the context of situation which determine the kind of language used" (1974/2007: 112). Together they determine the *register*: "the configurations of semantic options that typically feature in this environment, and hence also about the grammar and vocabulary, which are the realizations of the semantic options" (Halliday 1975/2003a: 292). Halliday credits T. B. W Reid (1956), professor of Romance Philology at Oxford, for the term *register* (Martin 2013: 150; Interviewer: Caroline Coffin, 1998). O'Donnell (2019) notes that Reid attributed the concept (not the name) to Firth's idea of *levels of diction*.

Depending on our interpretation of the semiotics of the situation, we can "make certain predictions about the linguistics properties of the text" (Halliday 1975/2003a: 292). This ability to pair the appropriate register with a given situation, or even "to 'place' a 'displaced text' in its original context of situation" (Hasan 2009: 264), "appears to arise because the categories of field, tenor and mode, which we are using to describe the semiotics of the situation, are in their turn associated in a systematic way with the functional components of the semantic system" (Halliday 1975/2003a: 292). Corresponding to field is the ideational component, tenor with the interpersonal, and mode with the textual (Halliday 1975/2003a: 293). Hasan describes metafunctions of language as underlying "the entire realizationally related assemblage of features" from the context of situation, "and the specialized features of semantics and of lexicogrammar: the functionality of language resonates through context to the higher strata of the linguistic system" (2009: 265).

Halliday describes a *register* "as essentially the clustering of semantic probabilities" (Martin 2013: 88; Interviewer: Paul J. Thibault, 1985). Drawing on the global set of probabilities in language, speakers re-align the probabilities in relation to the context of situation configured in terms of field, tenor and mode (Martin 2013: 80; Interviewer: Paul J. Thibault, 1985). Responding to critics who argue that "any text is in some register or other, some genre or other, so it doesn't make sense to talk about the global properties of language", Halliday gives the analogy of global climate whose probabilities may be "look[ed] at more delicately when we get to the climate of Brazil or Britain or whatever" (Martin 2013: 170; Interviewers: Geoff Thompson and Heloisa Collins,1998).

4. Paradigmatic basis

What distinguishes Halliday's approach from other functional grammars is its systemic or paradigmatic basis (Martin 2013: 79; Interviewer: Paul J. Thibault, 1985). Priority is given to the system over structure: "the fundamental aspects of language are not the structures themselves, but the choices which underlie those structures, and which are translated into them in the process of realization" (Butler 1988: 87). Explaining the inspiration behind "represent[ing] the whole thing as potential – as a set of options", Halliday stated that "this was certainly influenced by my own gut feeling of what I call 'language as a resource' – in other words, language was a mode of life, if you like, which could be represented best as a huge network of options. So that kind of came together with the notion that it had to be the system rather than the structure that was given priority" (Martin 2013: 109; Interviewers: Ruqaiya Hasan, Gunther Kress and J.R. Martin, 1986).

A text is the actualization of meaning potential "formed out of a continuous process of choice among innumerable interrelated sets of semantic options" (Halliday 1975/2003a: 285). These sets of semantic options represent the meaning potential in language. An act of meaning is a linguistic instance of meaning produced from out of this infinite meaning potential for construing the world and then sharing that experience with others. The choices made from among available options corresponding to the metafunctions are realized in the clause as "the main gateway between the semantics and the grammar" (Martin 2013: 81; Interviewer: Paul J. Thibault, 1985). Rather than see the clause syntagmatically as "a "lexicon" of words stuck together by grammatical cement" (Halliday 1996/2002: 404), the clause as most basic lexico-grammatical unit in a paradigmatic model represents the single output from passes through a network of options relating to different kinds of meaning (Martin 2013: 81; interviewer: Paul J. Thibault, 1985). In other words, semantic instead of structural considerations "determine the construal of the lexicogrammatical space" (Halliday 1996/2002: 403). The lexicogrammar unites lexis and grammar along a cline of delicacy ranging from the 'most grammatical' to 'most lexical', the lexis being most delicate grammar (Halliday 1996/2002: 404).

Halliday employs a system network formalism to represent how choices are subsequently realized in the grammar and lexis. The system network formalism applies throughout the process of meaning-making, at each level/stratum – context, semantics, lexico-grammar, phonology – and in each component – experiential, logical, interpersonal, textual; and is of "the form "if *a*, then either *b* or *c*"" (Halliday 1977/2002: 223).

Adding probabilities to the options available in the system network turns what would otherwise be a static form of representation into one that is dynamic. Every path made through the system network changes the probabilities. Halliday distinguishes between global probabilities of the language as a whole, and the probabilities local to some specific context of situation, such as the register of "weather forecasting (and no doubt other kinds of forecasting as well), where future becomes more probable than past; or one in which negative and passive suddenly come to the fore, like that of bureaucratic regulations (Halliday 1991a&b)" (Halliday 1996/2002: 401).

Butler illustrates how the choice of passive voice "may depend on the field (e.g. passives are said to be frequent in certain kinds of technical language), tenor (passives are probably used more in formal situations with a large social distance between participants than in informal language between intimates), and mode (passives are probably more frequent in written than in spoken language)" (Butler 1988: 99). Butler argues the attractiveness of "a model in which choice is the fundamental organizing principle" to those interested in "explaining the relationships between different ways of expressing things, and between these different ways and the factors conditioning the choices" (Butler 1988: 97). Butler further sees this dual emphasis on semantics and paradigmatic relations as "hav[ing] made systemic grammars extremely successful as the basis for various practical applications in stylistics, educational linguistics and artificial intelligence" (Butler 1988: 97; 1985a: 193–213; 1985b). The reason given by Halliday for "privileging the paradigmatic axis of representation" over the syntagmatic, included such practical concerns as "computational (machine translation), educational (first and second language teaching; language across the curriculum); sociological (language and cultural transmission, in Bernstein's theoretical framework, see Bernstein 1971); functional-variational (development of register theory) and textual (stylistics and analysis of spoken discourse)" (Halliday 1996/2002: 403).

5. Influences in Halliday's life[1]

During WWII, after having learned Chinese through the national services' foreign language training course, Halliday was called back to London from his assignment with the Chinese Intelligence Unit in Calcutta. For the next two years, Halliday taught Chinese to British recruits, prompting his first sortie into linguistics in search of answers to his pedagogical questions. After the war, Halliday returned to China to continue his studies. After passing the University of London examination on Modern Chinese language

---

1. biographical information from Webster 2005 and O'Donnell 2019

and literature in 1948, Halliday stayed on in China for another two years, working with Wang Li, Dean of the Faculty of Arts at Lingnan University in Canton, who Halliday describes as having "not only taught me grammar and phonology, and the history of Chinese linguistics, but also trained me in dialectology and field work" (Martin 2013: 184; Interviewer: Anne Burns, 2006). Wang Li was carrying out a dialect survey of the varieties of Cantonese spoken in the Pearl River Delta region. "I am deeply indebted to Wang Li", writes Halliday, "for having really made me work at the phonetics and phonology and also sociolinguistics – the whole notion of language in social and cultural context" (Martin 2013: 101; Interviewers: Ruqaiya Hasan, Gunther Kress and J. R. Martin, 1986).

After returning to England at the height of McCarthyism, Halliday's communist sympathies resulted in him being witch-hunted out of the SOAS. Subsequently admitted into Cambridge, Halliday began working on a linguistic analysis of the earliest known text in the Mandarin dialect, *The Secret History of the Mongols*. Following the death of Gustov Haloun, who was Halliday's supervisor at Cambridge, Halliday was allowed to transfer to J. R. Firth's supervision, even though still a student at Cambridge. Halliday describes Firth as "his other great teacher" (after Wang Li). However, when it came to applying Firth's system/structure theory to talking about the language of the *Secret History*, although Firth assumed what worked for phonology should work for grammar, still it seemed to Halliday that "there was a sort of hole in the middle. [Firth] did a lot of work at the phonology-phonetics end, and he did a lot of work at the context of situation end, but he didn't work with grammar" (Martin 2013: 161; Interviewers: Geoff Thompson and Heloisa Collins, 1998). Influenced by his "gut feeling of what I [Halliday] call "language as a resource"" (Martin 2013: 109; Interviewers: Ruqaiya Hasan, Gunther Kress and J. R. Martin, 1986), Halliday turned his attention to developing his notion of system as "a huge network of options" (Martin 2013: 109; Interviewers: Ruqaiya Hasan, Gunther Kress and J. R. Martin, 1986).

Around this time, Halliday joined the Communist Party Linguistics Group whose core members were Jeffrey Ellis, Jean Ure, Dennis Berg, Trevor Hill and Peter Wexler (Halliday 2015: 95). Explaining what the notion of 'Marxist linguistics' meant to him, Halliday wrote:

> It did not mean discarding or combating all previous wisdom about language; that would obviously be absurd. It did mean examining previous scholarship objectively, and trying to recognize and correct distortions that might arise from 'bourgeois' habits of thought; … we felt that a Marxist linguistics should give value to languages, and varieties of language, that were usually regarded as of little value, and often ignored altogether: minority languages, unwritten languages, languages of hybrid origin (creoles), non-standard, or non-literary, varieties, spoken languages (especially casual speech), trade languages, underworld languages and so on. Language planning meant working out policies and priorities, particularly educational policy, to determine how limited funding and energy should be distributed among competing agencies and institutions. (2015: 95)

Over the years, however, Halliday began to move away from "what you might call a classical Marxist view, which was very much technology driven and therefore seeing language as a kind of second-order phenomenon, where essentially it was reflecting rather than construing" (Martin 2013; 163; Interviewers: Geoff Thompson and Heloisa Collins, 1998). While still maintaining his approach is Marxist, or perhaps better characterized as neo-Marxist (although he expressed his dislike for the "neo-" label), he takes a different position: "instead of seeing language as essentially technology-driven, I [Halliday] would want to see it as a product of the dialectic between material processes and semiotic processes, so the semiotic become constructive – constitutive, if you like" (Martin 2013: 163; Interviewers: Geoff Thompson and Heloisa Collins, 1998).

In the 1960's, Halliday became "much influenced by the work of Basil Bernstein (1971, 1973)", who Halliday describes as "one of the great minds of that time" (Martin 2013: 184; Interviewer: Anne Burns, 2006). What interested Halliday about Bernstein's work "[was] that he seemed to me to be unique among social theorists in not merely paying lip service to language, as everyone does – saying yes, of course, language is important – but actually building it into his interpretative framework and seeing it as an essential part of the process of cultural transmissions" (Martin 2013: 90; Interviewer: Paul J. Thibault, 1985).

In 1963, Halliday became director of the Communication Research Centre at University College, London. The Nuffield Foundation funded the Schools Council Project in Linguistics and English teaching (1964–1970). This experience working with his colleagues and teachers impressed on him the need "to get a much more secure grounding both in an overall theory, an overall model of language, and also specifically in grammar and semantics" (Martin 2013: 162; Interviewers: Geoff Thompson and Heloisa Collins, 1998). Working with teachers on the project, whenever education psychology came up in the discourse, Halliday "found it profoundly unsatisfying" (Martin 2013: 226; Interviewers: J.R. Martin and Paul Thibault, 2011). Alternatively, Halliday suggested focusing instead on "the inter-organism perspective on language" (Martin 2013: 226; Interviewers: J.R. Martin and Paul Thibault, 2011). The inter-organism orientation, unlike one that is intra-organism, rejects the competence-performance dichotomy between what the speaker knows and what he does. After all, Halliday argues, it is not as though our mother is "some sort of a grammar book with a dictionary attached" (Halliday 1974/2007: 71). Rather, it is "in the sense of knowing how to use it; we know how to communicate with other people, how to choose forms of language that are appropriate to the type of situation we find ourselves in, and so on. All this can be expressed as 'know how to': we know how to behave linguistically" (Halliday 1974/2007: 71–2). Halliday "consciously tried to feed back into [his] thinking about language what came from, say, the experience of working with teachers […] I [Halliday] have always tried consciously to build teachers 'resources into my own thinking about language" (Martin 2013: 118; Interviewers: Ruqaiya Hasan, Gunther Kress and J.R. Martin, 1986).

Another important influencer who shaped Halliday's thinking about how we learn how to mean was his infant son. Taking advantage of an interlude in his professional life in the early 1970s (thanks to the Canadian government's refusal to admit Halliday into the country to take up a position at the University of British Columbia) Halliday conducted an intensive study as a participant-observer of his own son's developing linguistic ability from 9 months to 2½ years of age. The methodology was simple – using a notebook and pencil to transcribe everything that his son said (see Halliday 1975/2003b: 28–59). The insights from this intensive study contributed to the development of Halliday's metafunctional hypothesis.

However, the most significant influence on Halliday's thinking has to have come from Ruqaiya Hasan, who came to Edinburgh in 1960 and became one of Halliday's Ph.D. students. They collaborated on the Nuffield Schools Council Project in Linguistics and English teaching, during which time, Hasan began specializing on cohesion. In 1976, together with Halliday, she co-wrote the book *Cohesion in English*. Commenting about Hasan's contribution, Halliday stated that "she [Hasan] contributed substantially to the "core" levels of grammar and semantics and to sociolinguistics as well […] She has always had this sort of perspective where she has been able to work on the inside of language but to look at it from round about; and I [Halliday] have certainly learnt a great deal from her" (Martin 2013: 154; Interviewer: Manuel A. Hernÿndez, 1998).

6. Appliable linguistics

Halliday prefers the expression *appliable linguistics* over *applied* or *applicable* (even over the insistence of spell-checkers). On the one hand, he was concerned that to many *applied linguistics* narrowly applies to education (Martin 2013: 239; Interviewer: J. R. Martin and Paul Thibault, 2011). On the other hand, *applicable* "refers specifically to some task or at least some particular sphere of action" (Martin 2013: 188; Interviewer: Anne Burns, 2006). Instead, Halliday wanted a term that would give a more general sense of being "capable of and designed for being applied" (Martin 2013: 188; Interviewer: Anne Burns, 2006). Here, his knowledge of Chinese paid off. This distinction between *applicable* and *appliable* is captured in the Chinese language by the expressions *yingyong* 应用, meaning 'actually applied to something', and *shiyong* 适用, which means 'suitable for or capable of being applied' (Martin 2013: 239; Interviewer: J. R. Martin and Paul Thibault, 2011). As evident from Halliday's own pioneering work in applying insights from linguistics to translation, language development, linguistic computing, stylistics, and education (see Halliday 2013), a systemic-functional approach is particularly well suited to being applied wherever needed. While Halliday's own work in English (see Halliday 2005) and Chinese (see Halliday 2006) contributed significantly to the development of systemic-functional theory, the last two decades have seen systemic-functional descriptions of other languages and significant advances in functional language typology, in general, and systemic typology, in particular' (Mwinlaaru and Xuan 2016).

Halliday advocates for "a kind of linguistics which is able to be used in the ways that I [Halliday] would see as humanistic, progressive, forward looking – such as defending the individual against the excesses of this kind of society" (Martin 2013: 90; Interviewer: Paul J. Thibault, 1985), excesses such as one encounters in "mass consumer discourse, or bureaucratic (Hardaker 1982) or political or militaristic discourse" (Martin 2013: 93; Interviewer: Paul J. Thibault,1985). What we need, argues Halliday, is a theory of grammar "to account for, and hence enable us to control, the languages that are now construing this information-based society" (Martin 2013: 93; Interviewer: Paul J. Thibault, 1985). Halliday coined the term *grammatics* to refer to theorizing about the grammatical resources we use to make meaning, in contradistinction to the term *grammar* which refers to the stratum of language through which meaning comes to be realized. If our grammar is a theory of experience, then grammatics is "a grammar of grammars, a theory of theories of experience, or a metatheory in one sense of this term" (Halliday 1992/2002: 365).

References

Bernstein, Basil. 1971. *Class, Codes and Control: Theoretical Studies towards a Sociology of Language*. London: Routledge & Kegan Paul.

Bernstein, Basil. (Ed). 1973. *Class, Codes and Control 2*. London: Routledge & Kegan Paul.

Bernstein, Basil. 1990. *The Structuring of Pedagogic Discourse*. London: Routledge.

Bühler, Karl. 1990. *Theory of Language: The Representational Function of Language* (trans D. F. Goodwin). Amsterdam: Benjamins.

Burns, Anne. 2006. "Applied Linguistics: thematic pursuits or disciplinary moorings? – a conversation between Michael Halliday and Anne Burns." *Journal of Applied Linguistics* 3 (1): 113–28.

Butler, Christopher S. 1985a. *Systemic linguistics: Theory and applications*. London: Batsford.

Butler, Christopher S. 1985b. "The applicability or systemic theories". *Australian Journal of Applied Linguislics* 8 (1): 1–30.

Butler, Christopher S. 1988. "Pragmatics and Systemic Linguistics". *Journal of Pragmatics* 12, pp. 83–102.

Butt, David. Forthcoming. "Disciplinary English: the 'knight's move' in Halliday's theories of verbal science and verbal art."

Butt, David and Jonathan Webster. 2019. "From the workbench: the 'knight's move' in Halliday's long conversation between verbal art and verbal science" in *The Bloomsbury companion to M. A. K. Halliday*, ed. by Jonathan Webster, 467–488. London: Bloomsbury.

Davidse, Kristin & Anne-Marie Simon-Vandenbergen. 2008. "Introduction: The realization of interpersonal meaning." *Word*, 59:1–2, 3–23.

Halliday, M.A.K. 1971/2007. "Language in a Social Perspective." in J. Webster (Ed.) *Language and Society, Volume 10 Collected Works of M.A.K. Halliday*, ed. by Jonathan Webster, 43–64. London: Bloomsbury. First published in 1971, *Educational Review*, 23 (3), 165–188.

Halliday, M.A.K. 1974/2007. "Language and Social Man." in *Language and Society, Volume 10 Collected Works of M.A.K. Halliday*, ed. by Jonathan Webster, 65–130. London: Bloomsbury. First published in 1974, in *Schools Council Programme in Linguistics and English Teaching: Papers, Series II, Vol. 3*, London: Longman. Pearson Education Limited.

Halliday, M.A.K. 1975/2003a. "The Social Context of Language Development." in *The Language of Early Childhood, Volume 4, Collected Works of M.A.K. Halliday*, ed. by Jonathan Webster, 281–307. London: Bloomsbury. First published in 1975, in *Learning How to Mean: Explorations in the Development of Language*. London: Edward Arnold, 120–45.

Halliday, M.A.K. 1975/2003b. "Learning how to mean." in *The Language of Early Childhood, Volume 4, Collected Works of M.A.K. Halliday*, ed. by Jonathan Webster, 28–59. London: Bloomsbury. First published in 1995, in *Foundations of Language Development. A Multidisciplinary Perspective*, ed. by Eric Lenneberg and Elizabeth Lenneberg. London: Academic Press, 239–65.

Halliday, M.A.K. 1975/2007. "Language as Social Semiotics: Towards a General Sociolinguistic Theory." in *Language and Society, Volume 10 Collected Works of M.A.K. Halliday*, ed. by Jonathan Webster, 169–202. London: Bloomsbury. First published in 1975, in *The First LACUS Forum*, ed. by Adam Makkai and Valerie Becker Makkai 17–46. Hornbeam Press: California.

Halliday, M.A.K. 1977/2002. "Text as semantic choice in social contexts." in *Linguistic Studies of Text and Discourse, Volume 2 Collected Works of M.A.K. Halliday*, ed. by Jonathan Webster, 23–84. London: Bloomsbury First published in 1977, in *Grammars and Descriptions*, ed. by Teun A. van Dijk and Janos S. Petofi, Walter de Gruyter, 176–225. Mouton de Gruyter.

Halliday, M.A.K. 1987/2002. "Poetry as Scientific Discourse: The Nuclear Sections of Tennyson's "In Memoriam."" In *Linguistic Studies of Text and Discourse, volume 2 Collected Works of M.A.K. Halliday*, 149–67. First published in 1988, "The nuclear sections of Tennyson's "In Memoriam"", in *Functions of Style*, ed. by David Birch and Michael O'Toole, 31–44. University of California: Pinter.

Halliday, M.A.K. 1991/2007. "The Notion of "Context" in Language Education." in *Language and Education, Volume 9 Collected Works*, ed. By Jonathan Webster, 269–290. London: Bloomsbury. First published in 1991, in *Language Education: Interaction and Development, Proceedings of the International Conference, Vietnam April 1991*, ed. by Thao Lê and Mike McCausland, published by University of Tasmania (Launceston).

Halliday, M.A.K. 1991a. "Towards probabilistic interpretations", in *Functional and Systemic Linguistics: Approaches and Uses*, ed. by Eija Ventola, 39–62. Berlin: Mouton de Gruyter.

Halliday, M.A.K. 1991b. "Corpus studies and probabilistic grammar.", in *English Corpus Linguistics: Studies in Honour of Jan Svartvik*, ed. by Karin Aijmer and Bengt Altenberg London: Longman.

Halliday, M.A.K. 1992/2002. "How do you mean?" in *On Grammar, Volume 1 Collected Works of M.A.K. Halliday*, ed. by Jonathan Webster, 352–368. London: Bloomsbury. First published in 1992, in *Advances in Systemic Linguistics: Recent Theory and Practice*, ed by Martin Davies and Louise Ravelli, 20–35. London: Pinter.

Halliday, M.A.K. 1995/2003. "On language in relation to the evolution of human consciousness" in *On Language and Linguistics, Volume 3 Collected Works of M.A.K. Halliday*, ed. by Jonathan Webster, 390–432. London: Bloomsbury. First published in 1995, in *Of Thoughts and Words (Proceedings of Nobel Symposium 92: The Relation between Language and Mind)*, ed. by Sture Allen, published by Imperial College Press, Reprinted by permission of World Scientific Publishing Co.

Halliday, M. A. K. 1995/2005. "Fuzzy Grammatics: A Systemic Functional Approach to Fuzziness in Natural Language" in *Computational and Quantitative Studies, Volume 6. Collected Works of M.A.K. Halliday*, ed. by Jonathan Webster, 213–238. London: Bloomsbury. First published in 1995, Reprinted, with permission, from *Proceedings of 1995 IEEE International Conference on Fuzzy Systems. The International Joint Conference of the Fourth IEEE International Conference on Fuzzy Systems and The Second International Fuzzy Engineering Symposium*. Piscataway NJ.

Halliday, M. A. K. 1996/2002. "On grammar and grammatics." in *On Grammar, Volume 1 Collected Works of M.A.K. Halliday*, ed. by Jonathan Webster, 384–418. London: Bloomsbury. First published in 1996, in *Functional Descriptions: Theory inPractice*, edited by Ruqaiya Hasan, Carmel Cloran and David G. Butt, 1–38. Amsterdam: John Benjamins Publishing Company.

Halliday, M. A. K. 1997/2003. "Linguistics as Metaphor." in *On Language and Linguistics, Volume 3, Collected Works of M.A.K. Halliday*, ed. by Jonathan Webster, 1–49. Bloomsbury. First published in 1997, in *Reconnecting Language: Morphology and Syntax in Functional Perspectives*, ed. by A.-M. Simon-Vandenbergen, K. Davidse and, D. Noel, 3–28. John Benjamins Publishing Company.

Halliday, M. A. K. 2003. "Introduction: On the "Architecture" of Human Language" in *On Language and Linguistics, Volume 3 Collected Works of M.A.K. Halliday*, ed. By Jonathan Webster, 1–49. London: Bloomsbury.

Halliday, M. A. K. 2005. *Studies in English Language. Volume 7. Collected Works of M.A.K. Halliday*. London: Bloomsbury.

Halliday, M. A. K. 2005/2013. "On matter and meaning: the two realms of human experience" in J. Webster (Ed.) *Halliday in the 21st Century, Volume 11 Collected Works*, ed. by Jonathan Webster, 191-214. London: Bloomsbury. First published in 2005, in *Linguistics and the Human Sciences*, ed. by Jonathan J. Webster, Equinox, 59–82.

Halliday, M. A. K. 2006. *Studies in Chinese Language. Volume 8. Collected Works of M.A.K. Halliday*. London: Bloomsbury.

Halliday, M. A. K. 2008. *Complementarities in Language*. The Halliday Centre series in Appliable Linguistics. Beijing: Commercial Press.

Halliday, M. A. K. 2013. *Halliday in the 21st Century*. Volume 11. *Collected Works of M.A.K. Halliday*. London: Bloomsbury.

Halliday, M. A. K. 2015. "The Influence of Marxism" in *Bloomsbury Companion to M.A.K. Halliday*, ed. By Jonathan Webster, 94–100. London: Bloomsbury.

Halliday, M. A. K., and Jonathan J. Webster. 2014. *Text Linguistics: The How and Why of Meaning*. Sheffield: Equinox Books.

Halliday, M. A. K., and Ruqiaya Hassan. 1976. *Cohesion in English*. London: Routledge.

Hardaker, D. 1982. Language in a Regulative Context. Honours Thesis, Department of Linguistics, University of Sydney.

Hasan, Ruqaiya. 1999. "Speaking with reference to context." in *Text and Context in Functional Linguistics*, ed. By Mohsen Ghadessy, 219–328. Amsterdam: Benjamins.

Hasan, Ruqaiya. 2009. "A view of pragmatics in a social semiotic perspective." *Linguistics and the Human Sciences*, 5: (3), 251–279.

Kress, Gunther, Ruqaiya Hasan and James R. Martin. 1986. "Interview – M. A. K. Halliday." *Social Semiotics* 2 (1): 176–195 and 2 (2): 58–69.

Lecompte-Van Poucke, Margo. 2021. The value of a pragmafunctional approach to intercultural conflict discourses. *Language, Context and Text*, 3(1): 130–173.

Mahboob, Ahmar, Naomi K. Knight (Eds). 2010. *Appliable Linguistics*. London: Bloomsbury Publishing.

Malinowski, Bronislaw. 1923. "The Problem of Meaning in Primitive Languages." *Supplement 1 to C. K. Ogden and I. A. Richards The Meaning of Meaning*, London: Kegan Paul (International Library of Psychology, Philosophy and Scientific Method).

Mann, William C., Sandra A. Thompson. 1988. "Rhetorical structure theory: Toward a functional theory of text organization." *Text- interdisciplinary Journal for the Story of Discourse* 8(3), 243–281. Berlin/New York: Walter de Gruyter.

Martin, James R. 2000. "Beyond exchange: APPRAISAL systems in English." in *Evaluation in Text, authorial stance and the construction of discourse*, ed. by Susan Hunston and Geoff Thompson, 142–175. Oxford: Oxford University Press.

Martin, James R. 2013. *Interviews with M. A. K. Halliday: Language Turned Back on Himself*. London: Bloomsbury Publishing.

Martin, James R. and Paul Thibault. 2011. "Interview with M.A.K. Halliday." In *Interviews with M. A. K. Halliday: Language Turned Back on Himself*, ed. by James R. Martin. London: Bloomsbury Publishing.

Martin, James R., and Peter R. R. White. 2005. *The Language of Evaluation: Appraisal in English*. Palgrave Macmillan.

Matthiessen, Christian M. I. M. 2015. "Register in the Round: registerial cartography", *Functional Linguistics*. 2: 9.

Meares, Russell. 2016. *The Poet's Voice in the Making of Mind*. London: Routledge.

Mwinlaaru, Isaac N., and Winfred Wenhui Xuan. 2016. "A survey of studies in systemic functional language description and typology". *Functional Linguistics*. 3:8.

O'Donnell, Mick. 2019. *Michael Alexander Kirkwood Halliday A Personal Biography*. Information on Systemic Functional Linguistics http://www.isfla.org/Systemics/History/HallidayLifePart1-2-vOct08.pdf

Parret, Herman. 1974. "Discussing Language", *Janua linguarum* 93, 94–96 The Hague: Mouton.

Reid, Thomas B. W. 1956. "Linguistics, structuralism, philology". *Archivum Linguisticum* 8, 28–37.

Searle, John R. 1969. *Speech Acts: An Essay on the Philosophy of Language*. London: Cambridge University Press.

Thibault, Paul J. 1985. "An Interview with Michael Halliday." In *Language Topics: Essays in Honour of Michael Halliday. Vols. 1 and 2*, ed. by Ross Steele and Terry Threadgold (eds), 601–27. >Amsterdam: John Benjamins Publishing Company.

Thompson, Geoff and Heloisa Collins. 1998. "An interview with M. A. K. Halliday, Cardiff, July 1998." *D.E.L.T.A* 17 (1): 131–53.

Webster, Carol L. 2021. The Functions of a Second Order of Symbolic Articulation: Linguistic Stylistics and Dialogue in "The Sunset Limited" of Cormac McCarthy. PhD Dissertation, Macquarie University.

Webster, Jonathan J. 2004. "Preface" *The Language of Science*, Volume 5 Collected Works. London: Bloomsbury, vii–ix.

Webster, Jonathan J. 2019. "Michael Alexander Kirkwood (M.A.K.) Halliday – A brief biography" in *Bloomsbury Companion to M.A.K. Halliday*, 2nd edition, ed. by Jonathan Webster. London: Bloomsbury.

Webster, Jonathan J. Joe Chan, Victor Yan, and Kim Wong. 2013. "Visualizing the Architecture and Texture of a Text: A case study of selected speeches of US President Barack Obama" in *Eastward Flows the Great River Festschrift in Honor of Professor William S-Y. Wang on his 80th Birthday*, ed. by Gang Peng and Feng Shi, 309–332. City University of Hong Kong Press.

Wylie, Peter K. 2019. A Pragmatic Reconstruction of M.A.K. Halliday's Systemic Functional Grammar. Ph.D. Dissertation. Macquarie University

Wakimae

Yoko Yonezawa
The University of Sydney

1. Introduction

This chapter discusses the notion of *wakimae*, known in pragmatics by its English translation 'discernment', and reconsiders both its relevance and challenges in analysing different aspects of communication.

The notion of *wakimae* was first introduced by Hill, Ide, Ikuta, Kawasaki and Ogino (1986) in their comparative sociolinguistic investigation of American English and Japanese and subsequently developed by Ide (1982, 1989, 1990, 1992, 2005, 2006, 2012,). Hill et al. (1986: 347–348) explain *wakimae*/discernment as follows:

> No single English word translates *wakimae* adequately, but 'discernment' reflects its basic sense. In ordinary colloquial usage, *wakimae* refers to the almost automatic observation of socially agreed-upon rules and applies to both verbal and non-verbal behavior. A capsule definition would be 'conforming to the expected norm'.

In subsequent research on *wakimae*/discernment, Ide (1992: 299) further articulates the explanation:

> *Wakimae* is sets of social norms of appropriate behavior people have to observe in order to be considered polite in the society they live. One is polite only if he or she behaves in congruence with the expected norms in a certain situation, in a certain culture and society. Just like a set of rules you follow when you play a game, you follow *wakimae* in your game of life. Thus, speaking within the confines of *wakimae* is not an act of expressing the speaker's intention, but rather of complying with socially expected norms. The speaker's attention is paid not to what he or she intends to express, but rather to what is expected of him or her by social norms.

These explanations express two salient aspects of the notion of *wakimae*/discernment. First, they argue that the speaker's conformity to discernment is almost automatic behaviour in following the social norm in a given society. Second, this almost automatic linguistic practice is not the speaker's conscious intention, or rationality-based 'strategy', as Brown and Levinson's (1987) universal theory of politeness claims, but is done simply in conformity to what is regarded as appropriate behaviour in society.

https://doi.org/10.1075/hop.26.wak1
© 2023 John Benjamins Publishing Company

The contribution made by the studies of discernment is that they have identified another way of viewing politeness, namely, "adherence to the rules, whether a culture frames them in terms of face and FTA-avoidance or as something else", in other words, "adherence to conventional standards, i.e., the expectation that the rules will be followed" (Lakoff and Ide 2005: 4).[1] As will be discussed in Section 2, this aspect is often observed in the use of conventionalized expressions and phrases in certain situations, and formal forms, such as honorifics and address terms, in a given speech community.

Hill et al. (1986) discuss another aspect of politeness, one which allows the speaker to make a considerably more active choice in accordance with the speaker's intention, as being complementary to discernment, and they call this aspect 'volition'. This conceptualization was generated from a survey asking American English speakers and Japanese speakers how to make a polite request to borrow a pen in a wide range of social relationships. The results showed that the Japanese subjects' responses were more tightly clustered when choosing appropriate expressions. Their chosen answers predominantly aligned with the social norms of appropriate expressions based on the relative social status, power balance, and distance between the speaker and the addressee, as well as the distinction between 'in-group' and 'out-group'. On the other hand, American English speakers' responses showed more variation, and the distribution of their responses was very broad. The study interprets these results as showing that speakers' discernment plays a greater role in decision-making among Japanese speakers, whereas Americans may put greater emphasis on volition.

Hill et al. (1986) and Ide (1989) state that discernment and volition should be viewed as complementary, and these two aspects exhibited only relative prominence within the two sociocultural groups they surveyed. Ide (1989: 232) states:

> Discernment and volition are points on a continuum and in most actual language usage one finds that most utterances are neither purely one nor the other, but to some extent a mixture of the two.

However, as Kádár and Mills (2013) note, subsequent discussions about politeness have viewed the concepts of discernment and volition more as if they were proposed as dichotomic notions and discrete categories (Kasper 1990; Janney and Arndt 1993; Cook 2011; Dunn 2011), which may be seen as a polarization of cultures in that East Asian cultures are characterized as 'discernment cultures', whereas Western cultures are deemed to be 'volitional' cultures (Kádár and Mills 2013).

However, Ide (2006: 75–76) in fact states that it is not accurate to think that linguistic practices in Japanese are entirely governed by discernment and those in English are entirely governed by volition. The two are complementary in the sense that Japanese

---

1. FTA means 'Face Threatening Act'. See Brown and Levinson (1987) for the discussion of politeness to mitigate FTAs.

speakers also use 'strategies', while certain linguistic practices of English speakers, such as greetings, fixed phrases, and address terms, are highly relevant to the notion of discernment (Ide 2006). Kádár and Mills (2013) point out that the problem of the polarization of 'discernment culture' and 'volition culture', which exhibits stereotypes and does not capture the complexities of cross-cultural examinations of politeness, is not the concept of discernment itself, but the fact that a discernment vs. volition dichotomy has been uncritically used by numerous scholars in discussing politeness. In line with Kádár and Mills (2013), this chapter discusses the notion of discernment in its own right and explores the concept as providing a useful analytical perspective on language use in interaction involving (im)politeness.

This chapter is organized as follows. Section 2 starts by discussing conventional and ritualistic phrases, because discernment is fundamentally regarded as performance of the "observation of social norms" (Ide 1992: 299), and phenomena of conventions and rituals are connected directly to the discernment aspect of politeness in the sense that members of a speech community almost automatically follow them. The section also discusses some examples of certain linguistic practices, such as the use of honorifics and person reference terms, which include a relatively clear display of discernment. Section 3 discusses discernment at the macro level by viewing discernment – one's observation of social norms and adherence to them – as close to what is broadly regarded as default practice among members of a speech community who share common ground. The section looks at some examples from languages beyond Japanese to explore cross-cultural relevance. Section 4 examines discernment at the micro level, that is, how the notion of discernment situates in discursive interaction, the dynamic of discourse. Section 5 returns to the term *wakimae* in Japanese. While Hill et al. (1986) and Ide (1982, 1989, 1990, 1992, 2005, 2006, 2012) have used *wakimae*/discernment as technical terms, the Japanese word *wakimae* has its own connotation based on a Japanese emic notion. The section examines the emic notion of *wakimae* shared by the Japanese speech community. In so doing, it sheds light on the challenges of translating culturally loaded concepts into English. Section 6 concludes the chapter by expressing the importance of closely examining cultural conceptualization when analysing language and communication.

2. Discernment as the social norm

2.1 Conventions and rituals

Linguistic behaviours that are achieved by observing social norms and conforming to what is expected in a given speech community can be seen as part of conventional and ritualistic behaviour. As Kádár and Mills (2013: 143) point out, discernment is strongly related to conventions and rituals. Kádár and Mills (2013: 143) argue:

> [I]f we accept Ide's claim that discernment is a matter of degree and it exists in every culture and language, including non-honorific-rich ones, it is logical to argue that discernment should be interpreted as observance of whatever counts as normatively conventional, and potentially ritualistic, within a society. Thus, we should see discernment as the theoretical translation of a folk-theoretical concept, which describes the socially dominant norms of relationally constructive conventional and ritualistic behaviour.

Ide (2006:116) discusses conventions as part of discernment-governed social practices. For example, in Japan, when visiting someone's house and entering, one must use the fixed phrase *ojamashimasu* 'excuse me' (lit. I am humbly interrupting) rather than other alternative expressions. Backhouse (1993:182) uses the term "social formulas", which aligns with this aspect of linguistic practice, and states that Japanese has a large number of fixed formulae in social interaction, the use of which is "linguistic etiquette and protocol". A general expression of thanks, *arigatoo gozaimasu* 'thank you', is replaced by fixed expressions in certain situations: *itadakimasu* 'thank you for the meal' (lit. (I) humbly receive (the meal)) before a meal and *gochisoosamadeshita* 'thank you for the meal' (lit. (it) was a treat) after a meal are both said purely as etiquette by those who eat the meal. When leaving work ahead of other colleagues, *osakini shitsureishimasu* 'excuse me for leaving ahead of you' is expected (Backhouse 1993:184). The speaker uses these expressions in the appropriate situations, simply as expected protocol.

Terkourafi (2015:11) argues that at the heart of (im)politeness lies "conventionalization as a three-way relationship between expressions, contexts and speakers". Terkourafi explains this by drawing on different studies which show counter-evidence to the claim that politeness and indirectness are linearly correlated. This is counter to Leech (1983:108), who suggests that if the propositional content is the same, it is possible "to increase the degree of politeness by using a more and more indirect kind of illocution". Leech (1983:108) continues: "Indirect illocutions tend to be more polite (a) because they increase the degree of optionality, and (b) because the more indirect an illocution is, the more diminished and tentative its force tends to be". However, Blum-Kulka (1987) argues that, contrary to the idea that politeness and indirectness linearly correlate, more indirectness does not necessarily mean being more polite. Supporting Blum-Kulka, Terkourafi (2015) points to other studies which align with this argument. For example, Holtgraves and Joong-Nam (1990) compare American English speakers and Korean speakers in making requests. Their questionnaire results show that, in some respects, Korean speakers prefer conventionally indirect requests to those that convey greater indirectness, suggesting that more indirectness does not necessarily convey a higher degree of politeness. Terkourafi and Kádár (2017:181) argue that "[w]hen the speaker wants to implicate politeness she is on safer grounds doing so using an expression already established for this purpose rather than an illocutionarily ambiguous one".

Terkourafi (2015:13) visually makes the point in Figure 1 that what is regarded as polite correlates to conventionality more closely than to indirectness.

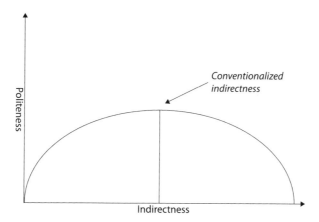

Figure 1. Politeness as a matter of conventionalization (Terkourafi 2015: 13)

Terkourafi (2015: 13) explains this as follows:

> [P]oliteness increases in proportion to the amount of indirectness but only up to a point, after which politeness begins to decrease although indirectness continues to increase. That point is achieved by conventionalized indirectness, which consists in using "phrases and sentences that have contextually unambiguous meanings (by virtue of conventionalization) which are different from their literal meanings" (Brown and Levinson 1987: 132).

Terkourafi's argument has commonality with what Hill et al. (1986) identified as the foundation of their proposal of discernment. Recall that they compared, between American English and Japanese, the request for a pen, made to various addressees. They reported that while many American English speakers gave one response for each person/situation category, a significant minority listed a variety of possible expressions (up to 22). However, all Japanese respondents gave only one expression as appropriate in each person/situation category. Hill et al. (1986) present Figures 2 and 3 and explain that American English speakers' responses are spread out, meaning there are more varieties allowed in a given situation, but Japanese speakers' responses are tightly clustered around certain expressions in a given relationship/context, meaning that there is greater consensus about the appropriate expression, i.e., a conventionalized set phrase which people tend to use in a given situation.

From this, it is possible to consider discernment in relation to socially conventionalized communicative patterns. These are "based on *consensus* among a group of language users rather than found in nature independently of such a group" (Terkourafi and Kádár 2017: 173) (emphasis by the authors). In this sense, thinking about discernment is thinking about two facets of communication at the same time: the consensus among members of a particular speech community on the one hand and the diversity between groups on the other hand, which means that the parameters of discernment are different from culture to culture. This point will be further discussed in Section 3.

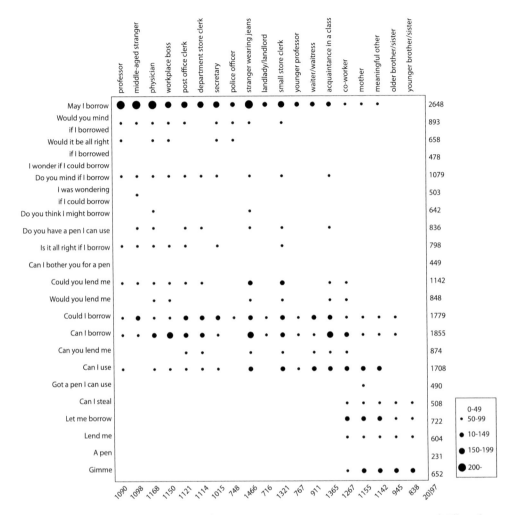

Figure 2. Correlation of request forms and people/situation categories – Americans (Hill et al. 1986: 358)

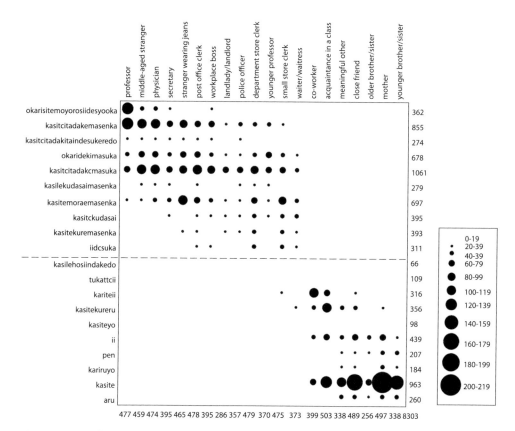

Figure 3. Correlation of request forms and people/situation categories – Japanese (Hill et al. 1986: 357)

2.2 Honorifics

While discernment has often been discussed in relation to Japanese honorific forms, the notion is not simply related to formal forms. That said, as the use of honorific forms indeed displays some fairly clear discernment-governed aspects (which does not mean it is 'entirely' governed by discernment), this section starts by drawing on examples of honorific language in Japanese provided by Ide (2006).

Two sentences in Example (1) (Ide 2006: 72) show the use and non-use of honorific forms.

(1) a. *Kyoo=wa ame da.*
today=TOP rain COP.NPST
'(It's) raining today.'

b. *Kyoo=wa   ame des-u.*
      today=TOP rain COP.POL-NPST
      '(It's) raining today.'

Examples (1a) and (1b) are identical except for the plain form of copula *da* at the end of the sentence in (1a) and its polite form *desu* in (1b). The propositional meaning of these sentences is the same: '(It's) raining today'. However, when speaking Japanese, the speaker must make a decision about which form to use depending on the context of the interaction. Matsumoto (1988) also argues that the choice is obligatory. Normatively, the speaker would use (1a) when talking to a friend or family, that is, those who are close to the speaker in an informal setting. When talking to someone who is higher in social status than the speaker or who is not socially close to the speaker, (1b) would be chosen. Ide (2006) states that even for such spontaneous, non-FTA utterances as talking about the weather, speakers of Japanese distinguish the style of the sentence almost automatically based on the context of the interaction.

Importantly, as Ide and Ueno (2011) point out, formal honorific forms are chosen not only in relation to the addressee but also in relation to the referent, who may not be the addressee in the immediate conversational situation.

(2) a. *Sensei=wa   hon=o   o-yom-i-ni.nat-ta.*
       Professor=TOP books=ACC HON-read-INF-RESP-PST
       'The professor read books.'
    b. ?*Sensei=wa   hon=o   yon-da.*
       professor=TOP books=ACC read-PST
       ?'The professor read books.'

In (2a), a subject honorific form is used in referring to the action of the subject referent, in this case, a professor. Ide and Ueno (2011) state that the social rules of Japanese society require the speaker to show deference to the professor and subject-predicate pragmatic agreement is determined not by grammatical agreement (as in person and number agreement) but by what they refer to as the 'social rule(s)' of the society where the language is spoken. In Japanese society, (2a) is regarded as pragmatically appropriate; thus, Ide and Ueno (2011) call it a 'socio-pragmatic agreement', differentiating it from the verbal strategies for mitigation of FTA in relation to the addressee.

2.3 Person reference

That the speaker must choose one form over another based on observation of the social norm can be seen in systems of person reference in some speech communities. In many cultures, terms of address and reference towards a person in everyday conversation are formulated by certain linguistic etiquette. European T/V systems are understood as being different from the English *you*, which can be used without considering the social characteristics of the interlocutor (e.g., Brown and Gilman 1960). In many languages in Asia, a wealth of linguistic resources for person reference is common, such as elaborate systems of pronominal choices as well as open-class alternative terms (Enfield and Comrie 2015: 8). Terms of address and reference in these languages include names, titles, occupational terms, kin terms, and other nouns. Their use is primarily determined by the social characteristics of the interlocutors, such as their age, gender, social status, kin relations, and the social distance between them, as well as the level of formality in the conversational setting.

In Japanese, to address/refer to older kin members, the speaker uses kinship terms. Names without respectful titles and second-person pronouns are not used from junior to senior. For example, when talking to one's father, kinship terms *otoosan, otoochan, papa* etc., all of which mean 'father', are normatively used, as seen in (3a) (Suzuki 1973: 151).

(3) a. *Kono hon otoosan=no?*
 this book father=GEN
 'Is this book father's (yours)?'
 b. **Kono hon anata=no?*
 this book 2SG=GEN
 '*Is this book yours?'

Kinship terms are used as both vocatives and interlocutor reference when talking to a superior addressee; thus, (3b) would not be normatively used. On the other hand, older members do not use kinship terms to address or refer to younger members, but use names and pronouns.

This kinship model may apply almost unchanged to social situations outside the family (Suzuki 1973). The speaker would address or refer to a hearer of higher social status in a range of different ways appropriate to a given context, such as the use of occupational terms, position titles, surnames with respectful title suffixes and so forth. Again, names only or second-person pronouns cannot normatively be used. For example, the use of *sensei* is expected when addressing/referring to teachers, professors, medical doctors, politicians, and so forth as follows (Suzuki 1973: 155).

(4) a. *Sensei=no oku-sama okagen ikaga des-u ka*
 teacher=GEN wife-HON condition how COP.POL-NPST Q
 'How is teacher's (your) wife?'
 b. **Anata=no oku-sama okagen ikaga des-u ka.*
 2SG=GEN wife-HON condition how COP.POL-NPST Q
 *'How is your wife?'

Ide (2006) argues that in Japanese society, the use of *sensei* does not necessarily occur out of an individual's decision to show respect towards the addressee. Rather, speakers use the term *sensei* because they are supposed to do so; in other words, society expects them to do so. These address practices can be said to be normatively governed by discernment.

3. *Wakimae*/Discernment at the macro-level: Common ground

Given the above brief discussion of examples which involve discernment aspects of linguistic behaviour, it is reasonable to think of discernment as a general norm or default linguistic protocol in a given speech community, the formulation of which is virtually automatic.

It should be noted, however, that when discussing the notions of 'social norms', 'default' practices, and 'common ground', a fundamental difficulty arises in that the discussion may well appear to entail what one may call 'cultural stereotyping'. Enfield (2004) discusses the notion of 'cultures' as opposed to 'culture'. Enfield agrees that it is highly problematic to characterize 'a culture' and/or generalize about its people, their practices, values, and/or beliefs by identifying an overarching category such as 'Japanese culture', 'Australian culture', or 'Russian culture', especially if the claim is that 'the culture' is empirically definable. However, he makes the point that it is possible to think about cultural generalizations as "what is collectively assumed to be 'normal' – or, more precisely, what is assumed to be assumed to be normal" (Enfield 2004: 17).

For example, according to Enfield (2004: 17), the statement "egalitarianism is part of Anglo Australian culture" can be interpreted in different ways as follows:

a. Egalitarianism exists in Anglo Australian society.
b. Anglo Australians hold egalitarian values (regardless of the truth of (a)).
c. A certain community of people may be defined by their knowledge that there may be assumed, among (Anglo) Australians, a popular belief that egalitarian values are widely held by (Anglo) Australians (regardless of the truth of (a–b)).

Among these descriptions, (c) is close to what Enfield means by "what is assumed to be assumed to be normal". He goes on to make the following statement which is helpful to our discussion of sociocultural norms:

> It is the stereotype ideas themselves, mythical or not, that are important in accounting for cultural logic, and emotional disagreements over whether it is valid to generalize about human groups or 'cultures' usually arise out of confusion as to whether the generalization intended is extensional (hardly tenable) or intensional (more like it; cf. Green 1995: 13) – i.e., whether the stereotype claims to describe the facts or whether it claims to describe some context-based default premises for cultural logic, which must be known about, but not necessarily committed to (cf. Putnam 1975: 249ff). (Enfield 2004: 17)

This statement is relevant to the remainder of this chapter in the sense that discernment is based on what is generally 'known about' norms in communication in a given language or speech community. It can be considered as an aspect of the broader notions of 'common ground' and 'linguistic ideology', which includes notions of "what is assumed to be assumed to be normal", and shared common experiences as well as shared expectations.

Regarding the notion of common ground, Tomasello (2008), in his discussion of the origin of human communication, uses the metaphorical example of a pointing gesture and explains how it is understood in relation to common ground: When you are walking to the library with your friend, and if out of the blue the friend suddenly points to a bike in front of the library, you would have no idea as to the meaning of the pointing. However, if you had broken up with your partner recently and the bike was your ex's, the exact same pointing gesture may mean 'your ex-partner is in the library (so we should not go in)'. If it is your bicycle which was stolen recently and your friend knows about it, then the pointing gesture would mean something completely different.

Tomasello (2008) argues that what is crucial in this example is that the physical aspects of the immediate context remain identical, i.e., your friend is pointing at bicycles in front of the library. The difference is not the actual content of the communication but only its background, i.e., the shared background knowledge. To share this background, not only must your friend know the bicycle is your ex-partner's and that you broke up with them recently, or that your bicycle was stolen recently, and the one pointed to is yours, but also that you both know that both of you know these facts. These facts "must be mutually known common ground" between the two of you. This is the foundation of communication and the use of language is fundamentally based on common ground.

There are three important points in relation to the discussion of common ground as the foundation of human communication and its relationship to the notion of discernment. First, the practice of discernment – "sets of social norms of appropriate behaviour people have to observe in order to be considered polite in the society they live" (Ide 1992: 299) – is only possible among people who have common ground. Second, the precise nature of shared common ground certainly varies group by group. Therefore, what is regarded as discernment may be different in different societies. Also, as Hill et al. (1986) suggest, the idea of discernment may be prominent in some societies but not in other societies. Third, the concept of common ground encompasses both pragmatic aspects and the grammar of language. The following statement by Evans (2010: 70) captures these points.

> It is increasingly clear that our ability to construct and participate in a shared mental world, to coordinate our attention and our goals, and to keep track of who knows, feels and wants what, lies at the heart of being human. It is this intense sociality that powered our quantum leap out of the company of all other animal species by enabling us to build that constantly evolving shared world we call culture. This achievement rests on an ability to keep constant tabs on the social and psychological consequences of what happens around us. But, although this skill is universal at a generic level, different grammars bring very different aspects of social cognition to the fore.

The term "social cognition" in the above statement is highly relevant to the notion of discernment, the *observation of socially-agreed-upon rules* (Hill et al. 1986). Be it grammar or pragmatics, understanding "our ability to participate in a shared mental world" and the "constantly evolving shared world we call culture" is key to understanding language and communication. Evans (2010: 70) paraphrases Roman Jakobsen's well-known point that, "[l]anguages differ not so much in what you *can* say as in what you *must* say" (emphasis by Evans), which is insightful for the discussion about not only the grammar of language but also its pragmatic aspects, including politeness in communication, which requires members of the group "to attend constantly to facets of the worlds that other languages let you ignore" (ibid).[2] In this sense, what we have seen in Section 2 are some aspects of communication to which Japanese speakers must constantly pay attention.

Further, as Evans (ibid) says, the shared mental world we call culture, whether it is culture in broader society or culture in a particular group within a community, constantly evolves. Thus, it is important to recognize both macro-level broader social changes and discursive interactions at the micro-level, because what is regarded as discernment can change along with societal change, and it interacts with individuals' understandings of local communications.

Regarding macro-level change, Jarkey (2021: 60) for example, points out that broader political and societal changes in Japan's history have been associated with "the growing importance of ingroup/outgroup social relationships as well as with a dramatic increase in interaction with non-intimates in the public sphere", which has led to a change of honorific usage, and consequently led to further grammaticalization, from subjective to intersubjective meanings, as explained below.

> These changes in Japanese society were accompanied by changes in the Japanese language, including an increasing attention to both ingroup/outgroup distinctions and to 'horizontal' social relations in the use of the Japanese honorific system. Processes of grammaticalization involving the development of some types of referent honorifics (subjective) into addressee honorifics (intersubjective), have accompanied these changes (Traugott and Dasher 2002: 226–278). The system has broadened its functions significantly, from simply acknowledging social hierarchy to indexing social and psychological 'distance', with a strong focus on deference to the addressee. (Jarkey 2021: 60)

Jarkey's statement is important for our discussion of discernment in the sense that what is regarded as discernment, or the specific set of norms involved, inevitably situates at a point in history, and it can change; the processes of grammaticalization in Japanese honorifics reflect a change in social values and their development at a macro-level. In this sense, discernment also interacts with history.

Regarding cultural diversity and the variations in discernment between cultural groups, the almost automatic and obligatory choices of linguistic items based on the

---

[2]. "Languages differ essentially in what they must convey and not in what they may convey" (Jakobson 1992 [1959]: 149).

observation of social norms are not unique to languages like Japanese and Korean, which are rich in formal honorific forms. As a number of anthropological studies show, in many societies, speakers are "highly attuned" to their social position in any interaction, and members of the society have "culturally mandated patterns of deference/avoidance" (Foley 1997: 309).

Some societies have so-called 'Mother-in-law' languages, which consist of special vocabularies that replace all or part of the everyday terms in speech in the presence of kin members who fall into certain avoidance relationships with each other. Mother-in-law languages have been reported from different parts of the world (Haviland 1979), and are relatively well-described in Australian languages. For example, in Dyirbal, spoken in north-east Queensland, one must avoid direct contact with a real or classificatory mother-in-law, father-in-law, son-in-law, or daughter-in-law (Dixon 2021).[3]

> Two people in such a relation should not sit close; they must not look at each other, nor speak directly with each other. When talking to anyone in the presence of an avoidance relative, a special speech type had to be employed, called – in all dialects – Jalnguy /'jalŋuy/.
> (Dixon 2021: 144)

In Jalnguy, vocabulary in everyday language, such as *buran* 'see, look at, notice, read', has to be replaced by *ñuriman*. Other verbs in everyday language, such as *waban* 'look up at', *barrmin* 'look back at', *gindan* 'look at after dark with the aid of a light', *rugan* 'watch someone who is going', and *jaymban* 'find', lose distinction when speaking Jalnguy, and all these verbs are expressed in one nuclear word *ñuriman*, with further specifications added to it as needed (Dixon 2021: 151). Speakers of Dyirbal must obligatorily use Jalnguy when standing in the presence of an avoidance relative. It is possible to think that the notion of discernment is relevant to the discussion of this type of linguistic practice.

In terms of person reference, while the norms in Japanese have been discussed in Section 2.3, complex social protocols in the use of kinship terms are known in a variety of languages. Chinese is well known for its elaborate kinship terms, which distinguish the maternal or paternal side of relatives in combination with an age difference (e.g., Fêng 1967; Usmanova and Ismatullayeva 2020; Liu 2021). For example, to address one's aunt, the speaker must use different terms for mother's younger sister, mother's older sister, father's younger sister, and father's older sister. Enfield (2022: 107) describes the Kri language spoken in Lao, which also has maternal and paternal distinctions in kinship terminology, and states as follows:

---

3. Dixon (2021: 144) notes that "[t]he Jalnguy speech style ceased to be actively spoken around 1930. However, a number of older people (born about 1900 or earlier) still had good knowledge of it, which they were eager to share with me".

> [Y]ou cannot get by in life as a member of Kri-speaking society if you don't monitor the specific kinship distinctions that are encoded in the language. The distinction between *jaa* (your father's older sister) and *qoo* (your father's younger sister) has consequences for what you expect from the person and what she expects from you. [...] [F]or Kri speakers, the different categories of aunt imply different behaviors.

These practices are acquired in socialization, and speakers learn the expected way of addressing/referring to kin members. When children make errors in relation to the language used towards senior kin, parents may reprimand them, saying, for example, "You can't speak to her like that. She's not your *jaa!*" (Enfield 2022: 107).

Evans (2010: 160) shares an episode that illustrates an aspect of children's socialization regarding the acquisition of the complex system of kinship terms in the Kunwinjku people of the Northern Territory, Australia.

> In one Kunwinjku children's game, someone calls out the kin group name of another, who must respond instantly by calling out the name of the kin group that is in their *kakkak* (matrilineal grandparent) relation. I suffered a series of humiliating defeats at the hands of children playing this game one night at Yikarrakkal outstation in the heart of Arnhem Land. Although I understood both the term *kakkak* and the kin group system in theory, I needed to think through the calculations, whereas they could give immediate answers, drawing on the same overlearned and rapid-fire fluency that oils their language use.

The socially expected way to address/refer to a person may be utterly natural from a cultural insider's perspective and invisible to members of the same speech community because it is virtually automatic. The types of linguistics practices discussed in this section can be thought of as the discernment aspect of communication.

4. *Wakimae*/Discernment at the micro-level: Dynamics of interaction

The above notwithstanding, communication is complex and unavoidably discursive. Interaction is an accumulation of the ongoing negotiation of relationships, attempts to achieve certain interactional goals, and expressions of participants' identities, amongst other things. As Haugh (2013: 56) notes, "evaluative social actions and pragmatic meanings are interactionally achieved by participants".

Given this, the notion of discernment as an analytical tool has tended to be associated with a static view of language and society and has been critiqued by scholars, especially from the perspective of social constructionists. For example, regarding the use of honorific forms in Japanese, as the referent-predicate agreement is pragmatically governed, it is possible to deviate from the generally assumed social norms of honorific usage. Cook (2006) argues that social relationships and identities are fluid, and they are negotiated during the moment-by-moment dynamics of interaction. A range of studies have found discursive and more fluid aspects of the use of honorifics (Cook 1996, 1998, 2006, 2008, 2011; Barke 2010; Okamoto 2011; Obana and Haugh 2021) as well as address terms (Maynard 2001a, 2001b; Yonezawa 2019, 2021). While we have seen in Sections 2.2 and 2.3 that the use of honorifics and person reference terms quite clearly displays discernment-governed aspects, it is also noted that this does not mean it is 'entirely' governed by discernment.

What is important to note is that communication cannot be entirely free from the influence of assumed cultural norms and expectations, be they truth or ideology. In other words, interpretations of certain expressions and phrases and the ongoing negotiation of the conversation participants' interactional goals in discursive and dynamic communication are inevitably entangled in assumed cultural norms and common ground. As Heritage (1984: 117) explains, linguistic practices are not a disorganized pursuit of an individual's random interests, but "normative accountability is the 'grid' by reference to which whatever is done will become visible and assessable"; it is against the background of norms and common ground that behaviours are made meaningful.

Returning to the use of Japanese honorifics, while it is discursive, this does not mean there are no pragmatic norms and discernment is irrelevant (Hasegawa 2012). Native speakers would agree that it is odd that, for instance, a student enters a professor's room and starts talking with non-honorific forms in normal circumstances, or the speaker conducts their entire presentation with plain forms in a formal business meeting. It is due to the background of socio-pragmatically governed expectations, that is, what is regarded as the discernment aspect of politeness, that makes it possible for the speaker, at times, to strategically or creatively depart from the norm to achieve particular interactional goals and create marked meanings in the style they choose.

It is fruitful to integrate the notion of discernment into the discursive approach by looking closely at how discernment-governed norms intersect with the speaker's negotiation of relationships and their attempt to achieve their interactional goals, and how their actions are evaluated during the dynamics of interaction in relation to both macro and micro levels of expected norms.

Hasegawa (2012) shows an example of a piece of *manzai* 'comedy duo', where one performer's failure to observe the social norm of polite language appears ridiculous, which demands acknowledgement of the notion of discernment. Observe the following extract from Hasegawa (2012: 252–253). The title of the comedy is *Tameguchi@robii* 'tameguchi at a hotel reception desk' (*tameguchi* means a casual/equal mode of talking, but the word itself is slang). At the hotel reception, the guest is asking if there is a room available. As a social norm, the receptionist is expected to use a high level of honorifics towards the customer, but he uses the plain form exclusively. This sounds rude and oddly unusual, thus inviting the audience's laughter.

(G: guest; R: receptionist; A: audience)
1 G: *Ano: suimasen, watashi yoyaku shitain desu kedo heya tte aitemasu ka ne.*
  'Excuse me. I'd like to make a reservation. Do you have a room available?'
2 R: *Kyoo?* (plain)
  'Today?'
3 G: *Hai.*
  'Yes.'
4 R: *Kyoo wa moo umatteru kara naa...* (plain)
  'It's all booked for today...'
5 G: *A so ka nnto kyuuna shutchoo de dokomo aitenakute komatterun desu yo.*
  'Is that so? I'm on a business trip on short notice and can't find a hotel.'
6 R: *Nanpaku yotee?* (plain)
  'How many nights?'
7 A: (laughter)
8 G: *Ano ippaku nan desu kedo.*
  'Well, just one.'
9 R: *Nannin?* (plain)
  'How many are (you)?'
10 G: *Ano hitori desu.*
  'Eh, one.'
11 R: *Ja shinguru ga ii yo ne.* (plain)
  'Well then you want a single room, don't you?'
12 A: (laughter)
13 G: *Soo-ssu ne.*
  'That's right.' [snip]
14 R: *A tsuin no heya nara aiteru kedo doo suru?* (plain)
  'Oh, there's a twin room available. How about that?'
  A: (laughter)
15 G: *Aa, tsuin ka tsuin doo shi...*
  'Oh, a twin room. Well, what shall I...'
16 *E ippaku ikuragurai desu ka.*
  'How much is the charge for one night?'
17 R: *Ippaku ichi-man ni-sen en.* (plain)
  '¥12,000 per night.'
18 G: *Ichi-man ni-se... kekkoo suru naa.*
  '¥12,000 ... Well, it's a little too expensive.'
19 R: *Demo soko shika aitenai yo.* (plain)
  'But that's the only room available.'
20 A: (laughter)

The receptionist constantly uses plain form as seen in lines 2, 4, 6, 9, 11, 14, 17, and 19, where, as a hotel receptionist speaking to a customer, he is expected to use polite style.[4] Initially, the guest puts up with the receptionist's blatant rudeness, but after this extract, he eventually becomes angry and asks why the receptionist speaks to him in plain form, *tameguchi*. The receptionist has no clue why the guest is angry and tries to calm him down in plain form, which makes the guest even angrier, and the comedy becomes funnier. Hasegawa (2012) makes the point that this comedic situation could not be funny if there were no socially agreed norms of speech style. She states that discernment prevails in situations like this in Japanese society, and that is precisely the reason that makes the receptionist's use of plain form, *tameguchi*, ridiculous and achieves the comedic goal.

Haugh (2018: 620) states that in politeness research, our interests lie not only "in abstracted and aggregated understandings of relevant concepts, but also in situated understandings of the various evaluative concepts that are invoked by users and observers" on which their evaluations rely to judge a particular (linguistic) behaviour as (im)polite. The above comedy is funny because (a) the receptionist has no discernment in his use of language and (b) he does not understand why the guest gets angry. In other words, his evaluation of what is happening in the ongoing interaction also is out of place. The audience's laughter shows that the receptionist has no sense of discernment throughout the ongoing interaction.

Norms exist not only in broader society but also operate in different domains of our lives. Barke (2010) draws on the notion of Community of Practice (CofP) (Eckert and McConnell-Ginet 1992; Holmes and Meyerhoff 1999) and pragmatic markedness (Jakobson 1971 [1957]; Levinson 2000) as useful tools for examining the shift between honorifics and plain form, analysing data from a TV drama series. Barke (2010: 457) argues that:

> [W]hen choosing between use and non-use of honorific forms, speakers take into account both macro-level knowledge of culturally-based interactional norms associated with a particular context, plus at a micro level, their own need to fulfil personal interactional goals.

Beyond broader societal norms, CofPs also exist in numerous areas of our social lives, such as workplaces, particular groups, local communities, families, or only between a couple or best friends, and so on. The speaker may follow the norm but may also deviate from the norm to achieve certain communicative goals. When certain linguistic behaviour is normative, it is unmarked; thus, it is unnoticed, but when the speaker departs from the norm, their behaviour is marked and creates expressive effects.

---

4. Hasegawa (2012) notes that the audience does not laugh to the utterance in line 4 because this utterance is regarded as soliloquy, which 'does not include interactional devices, or addressee-oriented elements' (262).

Research outside of honorifics also depicts aspects of marked uses of linguistic items. For example, in studies of terms of address and reference in Japanese, it is known that the most generic second-person pronoun *anata* 'you' is usually avoided. This is because, in Japanese, there is a range of socially expected terms from which to choose to acknowledge the speaker's social relationship with the addressee, as discussed in Section 2.3. The use of *anata* lacks this relationship acknowledgement; thus, it is problematic to use (Yonezawa 2021). However, the speaker, at times, does indeed deliberately use *anata* to generate particular expressive effects, such as strong impoliteness or extreme sincerity (ibid). Other second-person reference terms are also used in a manipulative manner, generating strong pragmatic effects. For example, a demonstrative, *sotchi* 'you (lit. that side)', is found to be used by a daughter in a TV drama to refer to her father cynically, to convey her anger towards him and create distance (Yonezawa 2019: 202).

These examples show the speaker deviating from the norms and strategically using linguistic resources such as honorifics and person reference terms to achieve particular interactional goals. Marked linguistic practices become visible precisely because there are unmarked ways of saying things. It is against the background of default, normative, conventionalized language use that non-normative language is made visible and generates special meanings.

Okamoto (2011) argues that the speaker's decision about what stance to take and what choice to make in a given context is influenced by their language ideology and specific contextual contingencies. About the use of honorific and plain forms, Okamoto (2011: 3686–3687) states that:

> interpretation of honorific and plain forms may vary depending on the context as well as on the interpreter, […] their situated meanings are potentially diverse, multiple, and ambiguous. That is, these linguistic forms may be construed as implicating diverse and multiple features of the context (e.g. status difference, degree of intimacy, speech act, setting) as social and pragmatic meanings. […] [M]eanings such as politeness/deference and formality are not inherently associated with honorifics, but rather represent their stereotypical interpretations in contexts in which they are believed to be typically used (e.g. status difference, lack of intimacy), and hence that these meanings may vary across context and across time.

At the micro-level, how a concept like discernment relates to individuals' discursive interactions still leaves much to be investigated. A constructive discussion involving discernment can be generated through the examination of how it operates in discursive interactions.

5. *Wakimae* as an emic metalanguage

Thus far, I have discussed *wakimae*/discernment as a general notion and a technical term used as an analytical tool, following Hill et al. (1986) and Ide (e.g., 1992, 2006, 2012), and treated it rather broadly: observation of and adherence to expected social norms or default practices among members of speech communities, including conventions and ritualized linguistic practices.

This section focuses on discussing the importance of recognising the cultural conceptualization of words such as *wakimae* from an emic perspective in linguistic research.[5] The word *wakimae* entails specific semantic components from emic perspectives. Haugh (2012: 116) reiterates the difficulties of using English as an analytical language.

> [T]he use of English as a scientific metalanguage may unduly restrict the scope of what we as analysts treat as worthy of interest, because words and concepts inevitably encapsulate a worldview, including ways of perceiving, categorizing and evaluating our social world. [...] [T]he use of English for some concepts may mask important differences as well as underlying assumptions about those concepts in different languages and cultures.

Recall that at the start of this chapter, I quoted from Hill et al. (1986), "no single English word translates *wakimae* adequately", and provided a long English explanation of *wakimae* by Ide (2012), which expressed the difficulties of conveying the semantically and pragmatically loaded meaning of the word.

One of the most prominent Japanese dictionaries, *Daijirin* (2010), defines *wakimae* 弁え as follows.

> 物事の区別や善悪の区別をする
> *Monogoto no kubetsu ya zenaku no kubetsu o suru.*
> 'To discern something as being good from evil.'
> 人としての道理を承知している
> *Hito to shite no doori o shoochi shiteiru.*
> 'To be aware of (one's) sensibility as a human being.' (Super Daijirin Japanese Dictionary 2010)

As we can see, *wakimae* is connected to moral value as a person. Looking at the verb form *wakimaeru* 弁える in a large corpus, from which the noun *wakimae* 弁え is derived, the most typically co-occurring object nouns reveal the sorts of things that have to be discerned in Japanese society. The following table shows the twenty most typically co-occurring objects of the verb 弁える (20,898 tokens) existing in Sketch Engine Japanese

---

5. The distinction between emic and etic perspectives is related to first order politeness (politeness 1) and second order politeness (politeness 2). The former is regarded as the layperson's common notion of politeness and the latter refers to its scientific conceptualization (Watts, Ide, and Ehlich 1992). See also Eelen (2014) and Haugh (2012) for a discussion about first-second order politeness.

Web 2011 (jaTenTen11).[6] These nouns occur in a sentence, for example, *minohodo o wakimaeru* (one's place ACC discern) 'discern one's place'. The English translation is necessarily rough (Super Daijirin Japanese Dictionary 2010).

Table 1. The most frequently co-occurring object nouns with the verb *wakimaeru*

The most typically co-occurring objects with *wakimaeru*.	Rough English translation	Frequency	Typicality score
身の程 *minohodo*	one's place or limitations	1,113	11.0
礼儀 *reigi*	courtesy, manners, etiquette	649	10.0
TPO *tiipiioo*	Time-Place-Occasion	245	9.1
礼節 *reisetsu*	manners	267	9.0
道理 *doori*	logic, sense	278	8.9
立場 *tachiba*	one's position	1,398	8.8
身分 *mibun*	one's position, social status/class	326	8.5
節度 *setsudo*	moderation, temperance	200	8.3
常識 *jooshiki*	common sense	550	8.1
マナー *manna*	manner	252	7.7
限度 *gendo*	limitation	142	7.6
分際 *bunzai*	one's place	77	7.5
分 *bun*	one's place, ability, degree, state, nature, duty	1,278	7.4
引き際 *hikigiwa*	appropriate time to quit	79	7.4
身の丈 *minotake*	one's place or limitations	66	7.2
場 *ba*	place	590	6.6
本分 *honbun*	one's nature	46	6.6
作法 *sahoo*	manners, etiquette	53	6.4
良識 *ryooshiki*	sensibility, good sense	46	6.4
領分 *ryoobun*	one's territory, one's domain	37	6.4

---

6. The jaTenTen11 is available in the Sketch Engine online corpus. It comprises texts from Japanese websites in 2011, built with more than eight billion words. 'Typicality' is different from 'frequency' in the sense that the frequency shows how often certain expressions appear with the target words. Among these frequent expressions, some of them also tend to co-occur with many other very general words, which means that they are very flexible in their use. Thus, 'frequency' is said to show weak collocations. On the other hand, expressions that only co-occur with a particular group of nouns, i.e., they 'specialize' in combining with certain words only, are regarded as strong collocations. Algorithms judge the most important or strongest collocates of the target word. This is shown as the 'typicality' score in the corpus.

Looking at the typically co-occurring objects with the verb *wakimaeru* (Table 1), it is apparent that the observation of one's place, manners, etiquette, and situations is very important. Recall Ide's (1992: 299) explanation of *wakimae* from Section 1: "[w]akimae is sets of social norms of appropriate behavior people have to observe in order to be considered polite in the society they live. One is polite only if he or she behaves in congruence with the expected norms in a certain situation, in a certain culture and society". The corpus shows that appropriate behaviours have to be judged by observing individuals' positions in relation to other people, contexts, and situations. Further, when people use phrases such as *ano hito wa ___ o wakimaeteiru* 'that person discerns/observes/knows ___', this has a positive evaluative connotation in Japanese and is linked to polite behaviours. Such a cultural conceptualization cannot easily be conveyed when translated into English.

While some scholars have recognised the dilemma or inappropriateness of analysing different languages with concepts from Anglo culture and with English as the metalanguage since the time of pioneering research about politeness (Lakoff 1973; Leech 1983; Brown and Levinson 1987), their ideas have tended to be regarded as peripheral or even, as Wierzbicka (2003: vi) puts it, 'heretical'. Wierzbicka has challenged this mindset by proposing an NSM *Natural Semantic Metalanguage*, which attempts to clarify meanings of items under discussion in terms of simple sentences in natural language.

Other approaches include recognising the importance of native speakers' metalinguistic activities as a crucial aspect of their conceptualization of certain notions and values, which in turn influences their language use through reflexive processes (Silverstein 1985; Agha 2007). Agha (2007: 17) states:

> The study of language as a social phenomenon must include the study of metalinguistic activity for a simple reason: language users employ language to categorize or classify aspects of language use, including forms of utterance, the situations in which they are used, and the persons who use them. Such reflexive classifications shape the construal of speech (and accompanying signs) for persons acquainted with them.

Importantly, metalinguistic activities are not restricted to language users' explicit acknowledgement of a certain concept. As Mertz and Yovel (2009: 252) note, metalanguage has a function of "constituting and framing ongoing discourse. In other words, metalinguistic features can be performatives whose domain is discourse". In this sense, the understood emic conception of *wakimae* is not only relevant at a form-meaning linkage level, such as the use of honorifics in a narrow sense, but to discourse level or broader cultural underpinnings in communication, where the concept of *wakimae* is 'enacted' dialogically through interactions. For example, an entire dialogue achieving certain speech acts may indirectly generate the moral underpinning of *wakimae*. The driving force of the increasing frequency of certain expressions, which are on the verge of the grammaticalization process, may involve broader cultural concepts such as *wakimae*.

As Haugh (2012: 116) suggests, "rather than treating the metalanguage which we use to describe and analyze interpersonal or relational phenomena simply as a given, and masking complex semantic issues behind 'operational' definitions, we need to make more serious attempts to tease out the worldviews that are inevitably intertwined with our analytical metalanguage".

6. Conclusion

This chapter has discussed the notion of *wakimae*/discernment. The chapter dealt with discernment/*wakimae* in its own right, holding the dichotomized view of discernment and volition to be irrelevant. Discernment – one's observation of social norms and adherence to the rules – was viewed here as being close to what are generally regarded as default communicative practices, including conventions, among members of speech communities, which has cross-cultural relevance. The chapter also discussed the importance of examining cultural concepts in discursive interaction, the dynamics of discourse.

Further, the chapter included a discussion of the term *wakimae* as a Japanese emic notion, referencing a growing discussion about the challenges of analysing diverse languages using English as a metalanguage. I acknowledge that this type of discussion must be conducted carefully because analysts do not wish to fall into the trap of cultural essentialism, and it is certainly not my intention to advocate some sort of uniqueness of Japanese culture when discussing *wakimae* as a Japanese emic notion. Scholars who perceive that the study of pragmatics has been dominated by views of language derived from Euro-American languages would also not wish to take the simplistic view of a Western vs. non-Western division. Rather, it is productive to consider that various conceptual frameworks derived from different languages provide additional powerful analytical tools for viewing language and communication. Hanks, Ide and Katagiri (2009: 2) state:

> We do not wish to reify the division between Western and non-Western languages or societies, for that division is a product of precisely the ideological posture from which we seek emancipation. Indeed, there is every reason to believe that pragmatics that is emancipatory in this sense would reveal overlooked features of Indo-European languages at the same time that it sheds light on other languages and cultures.

In the field of pragmatics there is an increasing amount of research which proposes different frameworks derived from different languages, taking a different approach from the pioneering research traditions of politeness (e.g., Gu 1990; Nwoye 1992; Okamoto and Shibamoto-Smith 2004; Anchimbe 2011; Anchimbe and Janney 2011; Hanks 2014; Ameka and Terkourafi 2019). Studies in linguistic typology have shown an enormous range of diverse languages from which generalizations are considered extremely hard to extract. Evans and Levinson (2009: 429) state that "languages differ so fundamentally from one another at every level of description (sound, grammar, lexicon, meaning) that it is very hard to find any single structural property they share". Findings arising from the diversity of languages offer an increased understanding of diverse ways of social cognition. Scholars using the NSM framework (e.g., Wierzbicka 2003), advocates of Postcolonial Pragmatics (e.g., Anchimbe and Janney 2011), and proponents of Emancipatory Pragmatics (e.g., Hanks, Ide, and Katagiri 2009), suggest drawing analytical concepts from various languages and working across languages "without necessarily passing through the filter of Euro-American theory" (ibid). The discussion of the concept of *wakimae*/discernment represents an other attempt to add new perspective to pragmatics research.

Abbreviations

2SG	second person singular	PST	past
ACC	accusative	Q	question marker
COP	copula	RESP	respectful honorific
GEN	genitive	TOP	topic
HON	honorific form	=	clitic boundary
INF	infinitive	-	morpheme boundary
NPST	non-past	:	lengthened syllable
POL	addressee honorific		

References

Agha, Asif. 2007. *Language and Social Relations*. Cambridge: Cambridge University Press.

Ameka, Felix K., and Marina Terkourafi. 2019. "What if…? Imagining non-Western perspectives on pragmatic theory and practice." *Journal of Pragmatics* 145: 72–82.

Anchimbe, Eric A. 2011. "On not calling people by their names: Pragmatic undertones of sociocultural relationships in a postcolony." *Journal of Pragmatics* 43: 1472–1483.

Anchimbe, Eric A., and Richard W. Janney. 2011. "Postcolonial pragmatics: An introduction." *Journal of Pragmatics* 43 (6): 1451–1459.

Backhouse, Anthony E. 1993. *The Japanese Language: An Introduction*. Melbourne: Oxford University Press.

Barke, Andrew. 2010. "Manipulating honorifics in the construction of social identities in Japanese television drama." *Journal of Sociolinguistics* 14 (1): 456–476.

Blum-Kulka, Shoshana. 1987. "Indirectness and politeness in requests: Same or different?" *Journal of Pragmatics* 11 (2): 131–146.

Brown, Penelope, and Stephen C. Levinson. 1987. *Politeness: Some Universals in Language Usage*. Cambridge: Cambridge University Press.

Brown, Roger W., and Albert Gilman. 1960. "The pronouns of power and solidarity." In *Style in Language*, ed. by Thomas A. Sebeok, 253–276. Cambridge, Mass: MIT Press.

Cook, Haruko Minegishi. 1996. "The use of addressee honorifics in Japanese elementary school classrooms." *Japanese/Korean Linguistics* 5: 67–81.

Cook, Haruko Minegishi. 1998. "Situational meanings of Japanese social deixis: The mixed use of the *masu* and plain forms." *Journal of Linguistic Anthropology* 8 (1): 87–110.

Cook, Haruko Minegishi. 2006. "Japanese politeness as an interactional achievement: Academic consultation sessions in Japanese universities." *Multilingua* 25 (3): 269–291.

Cook, Haruko Minegishi. 2008. "Style shifts in Japanese academic consultations." In *Style Shifting in Japanese*, ed. by Kimberly Jones and Ono Tsuyoshi, 9–38. Amsterdam: John Benjamins.

Cook, Haruko Minegishi. 2011. "Are honorifics polite? Uses of referent honorifics in a Japanese committee meeting." *Journal of Pragmatics* 43 (15): 3655–3672.

Dixon, R. M. W. 2021. "The semantics of the Dyirbal avoidance style." In *The Integration of Language and Society: A Cross-linguistic Typology*, ed. by Alexandra Y. Aikhenvald, R. M. W. Dixon and Nerida Jarkey, 144–174. Oxford: Oxford University Press.

Dunn, Cynthia Dickel. 2011. "Formal forms or verbal strategies? Politeness theory and Japanese business etiquette training." *Journal of Pragmatics* 43 (15): 3643–3654.

Eckert, Penelope, and Sally McConnell-Ginet. 1992. "Think practically and look locally: Language and gender as community-based practice." *Annual Review of Anthropology* 21 (1): 461–488.

Eelen, Gino. 2014. *A Critique of Politeness Theory*. London: Routledge.

Enfield, N. J. 2004. "Ethnosyntax: Introduction." In *Ethnosyntax: Explorations in Grammar and Culture*, ed. by N. J. Enfield, 1–32. New York: Oxford University Press.

Enfield, N. J. 2022. *Language vs. Reality: Why Language is Good for Lawyers and Bad for Scientists*. Cambridge, Mass: MIT Press.

Enfield, N. J., and Bernard Comrie. 2015. "Mainland Southeast Asian languages." In *Languages of Mainland Southeast Asia: The State of the Art*, ed. by N. J. Enfield and Bernard Comrie, 1–27. Berlin: De Gruyter.

Evans, Nicholas. 2010. *Dying Words: Endangered Languages and What They Have to Tell Us*. Chichester: Wiley-Blackwell.

Evans, Nicholas, and Stephen C. Levinson. 2009. "The myth of language universals: Language diversity and its importance for cognitive science." *Behavioural and Brain Sciences* 32: 429–492.

Fêng, Han-yi. 1967. *The Chinese Kinship System*. Cambridge, MA: Harvard University Press.

Foley, William A. 1997. *Anthropological Linguistics: An Introduction*. Oxford: Blackwell.

Green, Georgia M. 1995. "Ambiguity resolution and discourse interpretation." In *Semantic Ambiguity and Underspecification*, ed. by Kees van Deemter and Peters Stanley, 1–26. Stanford: CSLI Publications.

Gu, Yueguo. 1990. "Politeness phenomena in modern Chinese." *Journal of Pragmatics* 14 (2): 237–257.

Hanks, William F. 2014. "Introduction to emancipatory pragmatics, Special issue part 3: From practice theory to *ba* theory." *Journal of Pragmatics* 69:1–3.

Hanks, William F., Sachiko Ide and Yasuhiro Katagiri. 2009. "Towards an emancipatory pragmatics." *Journal of Pragmatics* 41: 1–9.

Hasegawa, Yoko. 2012. "Against the social constructionist account of Japanese politeness." *Journal of Politeness Research* 8 (2): 245–268.

Haugh, Michael. 2012. "Epilogue: The first-second order distinction in face and politeness research." *Journal of Politeness Research* 8 (1): 111–134.

Haugh, Michael. 2013. "Im/politeness, social practice and the participation order." *Journal of Pragmatics* 58: 52–72.

Haugh, Michael. 2018. "Linguistic politeness." In *The Cambridge Handbook of Japanese Linguistics*, ed. by Yoko Hasegawa. Cambridge: Cambridge University Press.

Haviland, John B. 1979. "Guugu Yimidhirr brother-in-law language." *Language in Society* 8 (3): 365–393.

Heritage, John. 1984. *Garfinkel and Ethnomethodology*. Cambridge: Polity Press.

Hill, Beverly, Sachiko Ide, Shoko Ikuta, Akiko Kawasaki and Tsunao Ogino. 1986. "Universals of linguistic politeness: Quantitative evidence from Japanese and American English." *Journal of Pragmatics* 10 (3): 347–371.

Holmes, Janet, and Miriam Meyerhoff. 1999. "The community of practice: Theories and methodologies in language and gender research." *Language in Society* 28 (2): 173–183.

Holtgraves, Thomas, and Yang Joong-Nam. 1990. "Politeness as universal: Cross-cultural perceptions of request strategies and inferences based on their use." *Journal of Personality and Social Psychology* 59 (4): 719–729.

Ide, Sachiko. 1982. "Japanese sociolinguistics politeness and women's language." *Lingua* 57: 357–385.

Ide, Sachiko. 1989. "Formal forms and discernment: Two neglected aspects of universals of linguistic politeness." *Multilingua* 8 (2/3): 223–248.

Ide, Sachiko. 1990. "Person references of Japanese and American children." In *Aspects of Japanese Women's Language*, ed. by Sachiko Ide and Naomi Hanaoka McGloin, 43–61. Tokyo: Kuroshio Shuppan.

Ide, Sachiko. 1992. "On the notion of *wakimae*: Toward an integrated framework of linguistic politeness." *Mosaic of Language: Essays in Honour of Professor Natsuko Okuda, Mejiro Linguistic Society*: 298–305.

Ide, Sachiko. 2005. "How and why honorifics can signify dignity and elegance: The indexicality and reflexivity of linguistic rituals." In *Broadening the Horizon of Linguistic Politeness*, ed. by Robin T. Lakoff and Sachiko Ide, 45–64. Amsterdam: John Benjamins.

Ide, Sachiko. 2006. *Wakimae no Goyooron* [Pragmatics of Wakimae]. Tokyo: Sanseido.

Ide, Sachiko. 2012. "Roots of the *wakimae* aspect of linguistic politeness: Modal expressions and Japanese sense of self." In *Pragmaticizing Understanding: Studies for Jef Verschueren*, ed. by Michel Meeuwis and Jan-Ola Östman, 121–138. Amsterdam: John Benjamins.

Ide, Sachiko, and Kishiko Ueno. 2011. "Honorifics and address terms." In *Pragmatics of Society*, ed. by Gisle Andersen and Karin Aijmer, 439–470. Berlin: De Gruyter.

Jakobson, Roman. 1971 [1957]. "Shifters, verbal categories and the Russian verb." In *Selected Writings*, ed. by Roman Jakobson, 130–147. The Hague: Mouton.

Jakobson, Roman. 1992 [1959]. "On Linguistic Aspects of Translation." In *Theories of Translation: An Anthology of Essays from Dryden to Derrida*, ed. by Rainer Schulte and John Biguenet, 144–51. Chicago: University of Chicago Press. Originally in *On Translation*, ed. by Reuben A. Brower, 232–239. Cambridge, MA: Harvard University Press.

Janney, Richard W., and Horst Arndt. 1993. "Universality and relativity in cross-cultural politeness research: A historical perspective." *Multilingua* 12 (1): 13–50.

Jarkey, Nerida. 2021. "The grammatical expression of social relations in Japanese." In *The Integration of Language and Society: A Cross-linguistic Typology*, ed. by Alexandra Y. Aikhenvald, R. M. W. Dixon and Nerida Jarkey, 58–84. Oxford: Oxford University Press.

Kádár, Dániel Z., and Sara Mills. 2013. "Rethinking discernment." *Journal of Politeness Research* 9 (2): 133–158.

Kasper, Gabriele. 1990. "Linguistic politeness: Current research issues." *Journal of Pragmatics* 14 (2): 193–218.

Lakoff, Robin. 1973. "The logic of politeness: Minding your p's and q's." *Chicago Linguistics Society (CLS)*: 292–395.

Lakoff, Robin T., and Sachiko Ide. 2005. "Introduction: Broadening the horizon of linguistic politeness." In *Broadening the Horizon of Linguistic Politeness*, ed. by Robin T. Lakoff and Sachiko Ide, 1–20. Amsterdam: John Benjamins.

Leech, Geoffrey. 1983. *Principles of Pragmatics*. London: Longman.

Levinson, Stephen C. 2000. *Presumptive Meanings: The Theory of Generalized Conversational Implicature*. Cambridge, Mass: MIT Press.

Liu, Xiangdong. 2021. "'I'll never call them by their names, because it's rude.': Kinship terms used by Chinese native speakers in daily interactions." Paper presented at the 17th International Pragmatics Conference, Winterthur, 27 June – 2 July 2021.

Matsumoto, Yoshiko. 1988. "Reexamination of the universality of face: Politeness phenomena in Japanese." *Journal of Pragmatics* 12 (4): 403–426.

Maynard, Senko K. 2001a. "Expressivity in discourse: Vocatives and themes in Japanese." *Language Sciences* 23: 679–705.

Maynard, Senko K. 2001b. "Falling in love with style: Expressive functions of stylistic shifts in a Japanese television drama series." *Functions of Language* 8 (1): 1–39.

Mertz, Elizabeth, and Jonathan Yovel. 2009. "Metalinguistic awareness." In *Cognition and Pragmatics*, ed. by Dominiek Sandra, Jan-Ola Östman and Jef Verschueren, 250–271. Amsterdam: John Benjamins.

Nwoye, Onuigbo G. 1992. "Linguistic politeness and socio-cultural variations of the notion of face." *Journal of Pragmatics* 18 (4): 309–328.

Obana, Yasuko, and Michael Haugh. 2021. "(Non-)propositional irony in Japanese: Impoliteness behind honorifics." *Lingua* 260: 103–119.

Okamoto, Shigeko. 2011. "The use and interpretation of addressee honorifics and plain forms in Japanese: Diversity, multiplicity, and ambiguity." *Journal of Pragmatics* 43 (15): 3673–3688.

Okamoto, Shigeko, and Janet S. Shibamoto Smith. 2004. *Japanese Language, Gender, and Ideology: Cultural Models and Real People*. New York: Oxford University Press.

Putnam, Hilary. 1975. *Mind, Language, and Reality*. Cambridge: Cambridge University Press.

Silverstein, Michael. 1985. "Language and the culture of gender: At the intersection of structure, usage, and ideology." In *Semiotic Mediation: Sociocultural and Psychological Perspectives*, ed. by Elizabeth Mertz and Richard J. Parmentier, 219–259. Orlando: Academic Press.

Suzuki, Takao. 1973. *Kotoba to Bunka* [Language and Culture]. Tokyo: Iwanami Shoten.

Terkourafi, Marina. 2015. "Conventionalization: A new agenda for im/politeness research." *Journal of Pragmatics* 86: 11–18.

Terkourafi, Marina, and Dániel Z. Kádár. 2017. "Convention and ritual (im)politeness." In *The Palgrave Handbook of Linguistic (Im)politeness*, 171–195. London: Springer.

Tomasello, Michael. 2008. *Origins of Human Communication*. Cambridge, Mass: MIT Press.

Traugott, Elizabeth Closs, and Richard B. Dasher. 2002. *Regularity in Semantic Change*. Cambridge: Cambridge University Press.

Usmanova, Shoira Rustamovna, and Nargiza Rasuljanovna Ismatullayeva. 2020. "Expression of lacunas in comparative study of kinship terms in Chinese and Uzbek languages." *Solid State Technology* 63 (6): 4974–4985.

Watts, Richard J., Sachiko Ide, and Konrad Ehlich. 1992. *Politeness in Language: Studies in its History, Theory and Practice*. Berlin: Mouton de Gruyter.

Wierzbicka, Anna. 2003. *Cross-cultural Pragmatics: The Semantics of Human Interaction*. Berlin: Mouton de Gruyter.

Yonezawa, Yoko. 2019. "Constructing fluid relationships through language: A study of address terms in a Japanese drama and its pedagogical implications." *Journal of Japanese Linguistics* 35 (2): 189–211.

Yonezawa, Yoko. 2021. *The Mysterious Address Term Anata 'you' in Japanese*. Amsterdam: John Benjamins.

Dictionary

Super Daijirin Japanese Dictionary. 2010. Tokyo: Sanseido.

Corpus

Sketch Engine (jaTenTen11). 2011. https://www.sketchengine.eu/

Cumulative index

This index refers to the whole of the *Handbook of Pragmatics*, its **Manual** as well as the 26 installments (the present one included), and it lists:

i. all labels used as entry headings in some part of the Handbook, with an indication of the part in which the entry is to be found, and with cross-references to other relevant entries;
ii. labels for traditions, methods, and topics for which separate entries have not (yet) been provided, indicating the entry-labels under which information can be found and the part of the Handbook where this is to be found.

The following abbreviations are used:

(MT)   the Traditions section of the Manual
(MM)   the Methods section of the Manual
(MN)   the Notational Systems section of the Manual
(H)   the thematic main body of the loose-leaf Handbook or (from the 21st installment onwards) of the specific annual installment (marked as H21, H22, etc.)
(T)   the Traditions update/addenda of the printed Handbook (further specified for the bound volumes as T21, T22, etc.)
(M)   the Methods update/addenda of the printed Handbook (further specified for the bound volumes as M21, M22, etc.)
(N)   the Notational Systems update/addenda of the printed Handbook (further specified for the bound volumes as N21, N22, etc.)

References in the index may take the following forms:

"**Label (section reference)** (abbreviated as above)" — for labels which occur only as headings of an autonomous article
"**Label (section reference)**; label(s)" — for labels which occur as article headings and for which it is relevant to refer to other articles as well
"**Label** label(s)" — for labels which do not (yet) occur as article headings, but which stand for topics dealt with under the label(s) indicated
"**Label** → label(s)" — for labels that are considered, for the time being and for the purposes of the Handbook, as (near)equivalents of the label(s) following the arrow; a further search must start from the label(s) following the arrow

A

Abduction see Grounded theory (M); Language change (H)
Abuse see Obscenity, slurs, and taboo (H24)
Academic concept see Vygotsky (H)
Academic language see Applied linguistics (MT); Postcolonial pragmatics (T)
Acceptability see Generative semantics (MT)
Accessibility see Anaphora (H)
Accommodation see Contact (H); Presupposition (H)
Accommodation theory (MT); *see also* Adaptability (H); Age and language use (H); Bilingualism and multilingualism (H); Context and contextualization (H); Social psychology (MT)
Accounting see Collaboration in dialogues (H); Social psychology (MT)
Acoustics see Sound symbolism (H)
Action see Action theory (MT); Agency and language (H); Austin (H); Bühler (H); Cognitive psychology (MT); Ethnomethodology (MT); Intentionality (H); Nexus analysis (T); Perception and language (H); Philosophy of action (MT); Speech act theory (MT)
Action theory (MT); *see also* Agency and language (H); Grounded theory (M); Philosophy of action (MT)
Activation see Relational ritual (H)
Activity see Action theory (MT)
Activity types and pragmatic acts (H26); *see also* Pragmemes (H22)
Adaptability (H); *see also* Activity types and pragmatic acts (H26); Evolutionary pragmatics (T); Methods in language-attitudes research (M); (The) pragmatic perspective (M)
Adjacency pair see Prosody (H); Sequence (H)

Adjective see Experimental pragmatics (M)
Adjunct control see Control phenomena (H)
Adolescent see Youth language (H25)
Adorno, T. see Critical theory (MT)
Affect see Appraisal (H); Complaining (H25); Computational pragmatics (T); Emotion display (H); Emotions (H21); Emphasis (H); Interpreter-mediated interaction (H); Laughter (H); Overlap (H); Stance (H21); Text and discourse linguistics (T); Think-aloud protocols (M)
Affiliation/disaffiliation → see Affect
Affirmation see Negation (H)
Affordance see Pragmatics of script (H22); Social media research (T)
Age and language use (H); *see also* 'Other' representation (H); Swearing (H25); Youth language (H25)
Ageism see Age and language use (H)
Agency and language (H); *see also* Action theory (MT); Case and semantic roles (H); Computational pragmatics (T); Intentionality (H); Metapragmatics (MT); Motivation and language (H)
Agreement see Social media research (T); Therapeutic conversation (H)
Aisatsu (H)
Aktionsart see Tense and aspect (H)
Alignment see Nigerian hospital setting discourse (H24); Pragmatics of script (H22); Stance (H21)
Allegory see Conceptual integration (H)
Allopract see Activity types and pragmatic acts (H26)
Ambiguity see Indeterminacy and negotiation (H); Mental spaces (H); Obscenity, slurs, and taboo (H24);

Polysemy (H); Sound symbolism (H); Truthfulness (H)
Amerindian languages see Anthropological linguistics (MT); Boas (H)
Analysis see Analytical philosophy (MT)
Analytical philosophy (MT); *see also* Austin (H); Conversational implicature (H); Hermeneutics (M); Philosophy of language (MT); Speech act theory (MT); Truth-conditional semantics (MT); Wittgenstein (H)
Anaphora (H); *see also* Grounding (H); Indexicals and demonstratives (H); Lexically triggered veridicality inferences (H22); Tense and aspect (H)
Anderson, Benedict (H21)
Animal communication see Adaptability (H); Communication (H); Primate communication (H)
Annotation see Corpus analysis (MM); Corpus pragmatics (M)
Antecedent see Anaphora (H)
Anthropological linguistics (MT); *see also* Anderson (H21); Bilingualism and multilingualism (H); Chronotope (H25); Cognitive anthropology (MT); Componential analysis (MT); Context and contextualization (H); Ethnography of speaking (MT); Fieldwork (MM); Gesture research (T); Gumperz (H); Hermeneutics (M); Hymes (H26); Intercultural communication (H); Language ideologies (H); Malinowski (H); Metalinguistic awareness (H); Metapragmatics (MT); Nexus analysis (T); Phatic communion (H); (The) pragmatic perspective (M); Pragmatics of script (H22); Sapir (H); Sociolinguistics (MT);

Ta'ārof (**H22**);
Taxonomy (**MM**);
Transience (**H22**);
Truthfulness (**H**); Whorf (**H**)
Anthropology see Hymes (**H26**)
Anti-language see Jargon (**H**)
Apel, K. O. see Universal and transcendental pragmatics (**MT**)
Aphasia see Adaptability (**H**); Cerebral representation of language; Clinical pragmatics (**T**); Jakobson (**H21**); Neurolinguistics (**MT**)
Apology see Corpus pragmatics (**M**); Mediated performatives (**H**)
Appeal → see Functions of language
Applied linguistics (**MT**); *see also* Forensic linguistics (**T**); Intercultural communication (**H**); Language policy, language planning and standardization (**H**); Sociolinguistics (**MT**)
Appraisal (**H**); *see also* Emphasis (**H**); Halliday (**H26**); Heteroglossia (**H26**)
Appreciation see Appraisal (**H**); Ọmọlúàbí (**H**)
Appropriateness see Creativity in language use (**H**); Workplace interaction (**H25**)
Approval and disapproval see Ta'ārof (**H22**)
Arbitrariness see Adaptability (**H**); Iconicity (**H**); Sound symbolism (**H**); Structuralism (**MT**)
Archive see Postcolonial pragmatics (**T**)
Archiving see Working with language data (**M25**)
Areal linguistics see Contact linguistics (**MT**); Language change (**H**)
Argument structure (**H23**); *see also* Dependency
Argumentation see Argumentation in discourse and grammar (**H**); Argumentation theory (**MT**); Rhetoric (**MT**)

Argumentation in discourse and grammar (**H**); *see also* Argumentation theory (**MT**)
Argumentation theory (**MT**); *see also* Argumentation in discourse and grammar (**H**); Rhetoric (**MT**)
Articulation see Humboldt (**H**); Sound symbolism (**H**)
Artificial intelligence (**MT**); *see also* Cognitive psychology (**MT**); Cognitive science (**MT**); Communication (**H**); Computational linguistics (**MT**); Connectionism (**MT**); Context and contextualization (**H**); Frame analysis (**M**); Frame semantics (**T**); Speech act theory (**MT**)
Artificial life see Language acquisition (**H**)
Ascription see Functional discourse grammar (**T**)
Aspect see Event representation (**H22**); Markedness (**H**); Tense and aspect (**H**)
Assertion see Austin (**H**); Speech act theory (**MT**)
Assimilation see Language rights (**H**)
Asymmetric interaction see Applied linguistics (**MT**); Communicative success vs. failure (**H**); Computer-mediated communication (**H**); Conversation types (**H**); Frame analysis (**M**); Mass media (**H**); Nigerian hospital setting discourse (**H24**)
Attention and language (**H**)
Attitude see Appraisal (**H**); Dialectology (**MT**); Methods in language-attitudes research (**M**); Pluricentric languages (**H23**); Social psychology (**MT**); Stance (**H21**)
Attribution theory see Social psychology (**MT**)
Audience → see Hearer
Audience design → see Recipient design
Audience effect see Primate communication (**H**)
Augmentative see Morphopragmatics (**T**)

Austin, J. L. (**H**); *see also* Analytical philosophy (**MT**); Communicative success vs. failure (**H**); Contextualism (**T**); Grice (**H**); Speech act theory (**MT**)
Authenticity (**H**); *see also* Identity (**H24**); Reported speech (**H**)
Authier-Revuz, J. see Énonciation (**H**)
Authority (**H**); *see also* Evidentiality (**H22**); Honorifics (**H**)
Authorship see Experimental pragmatics (**M**); Forensic linguistics (**T**)
Autism see Clinical pragmatics (**T**); Conceptual integration (**H**)
Auto-ethnography see Postcolonial pragmatics (**T**)
Automata theory see Computational linguistics (**MT**)
Automated communication see Globalization (**H25**)
Automaticity see Think-aloud protocols (**M**)
Autonomous vs. non-autonomous syntax (**MT**); *see also* Chomskyan linguistics (**MT**); Functionalism vs. formalism (**MT**); Structuralism (**MT**)
Autonomy see Legitimation Code Theory (**T25**)
Avoidance see Obscenity, slurs, and taboo (**H24**); Wakimae (**H26**)
Awareness see Metalinguistic awareness (**H**); Orthography and cognition (**H22**)
Axiology see Morris (**H**)

B

Baby talk → see Motherese
Back channel cue see Listener response (**H**)
Background information see Cognitive science (**MT**); Collaboration in dialogues (**H**); Common ground (**H**); Communication (**H**); Context and contextualization (**H**); Text and discourse linguistics (**T**)

Backgrounding see Argument structure (H23); Grounding (H)
Bakhtin, M.M. (H); *see also* Chronotope (H25); Collaboration in dialogues (H); Crossing (H26); Dialogical analysis (MM); Genre (H); Heteroglossia (H26); Ideology (H); Intertextuality (H); Polyphony (H); Reported speech (H)
Bally, C. see Énonciation (H)
Basilect see Creole linguistics (MT)
Bateson, G. (H); *see also* Communication (H)
Behaviorism (MT); *see also* Cognitive psychology (MT); Grice (H); Morris (H); Objectivism vs. subjectivism (MT)
Benveniste, E. (H); *see also* Énonciation (H)
Bernstein, B. see Applied linguistics (MT); Communicative success vs. failure (H); Legitimation Code Theory (T25)
Bilingual interactive activation (BIA) see The multilingual lexicon (H)
Bilingualism and multilingualism (H); *see also* Accommodation theory (MT); Anderson (H21); Anthropological linguistics (MT); Borrowing (H); Code-switching (H); Code-switching and translanguaging (H22); Contact (H); Contact linguistics (MT); Developmental psychology (MT); Ervin-Tripp, S. (H24); Intercultural communication (H); Language contact (H); Language dominance and minorization (H); Language maintenance and shift (H21); Language policy, language planning and standardization (H); The multilingual lexicon (H); Pragmatics of script (H22); Social psychology (MT);

Sociolinguistics (MT); Transience (H22); Translanguaging pedagogy (T)
Binding see Anaphora (H)
Biodiversity see Language ecology (T)
Biology see Morris (H)
Biosemiotics see Communication (H)
Blended data see Social media research (T)
Blog see Social media research (T)
Boas, F. (H); *see also* Anthropological linguistics (MT); Culture (H); Fieldwork (MM); Sapir (H); Typology (MT); Whorf (H)
Body see Ta'ārof (H22); Tactile sign languages (H21)
Bootstrapping see Language acquisition (H)
Borrowing (H); *see also* Contact (H); Interjections (H); Language contact (H)
Bourdieu, P. (H); *see also* Anderson (H21); Ideology (H); Legitimation Code Theory (T25); Power and the role of language (H25); Social institutions (H)
Brain see Clinical pragmatics (T); Developmental dyslexia (H); Emotions (H21); Neurolinguistics (MT); Neuropragmatics (T)
Brain imaging → see Cerebral representation of language; Cognitive science (MT); Language acquisition (H); Neurolinguistics (MT); Neuropragmatics (T); Perception and language (H); Psycholinguistics (MT)
Bureaucratic language see Applied linguistics (MT)
Business communication see Communication (H)
Bühler, K. (H); *see also* Language psychology (T); Phatic communion (H)

C

Caretaker discourse see Age and language use (H)

Carnap, R. see Analytical philosophy (MT); Intensional logic (MT)
Carnival(esque) see Bakhtin (H); Intertextuality (H)
Cartesian philosophy see Chomskyan linguistics (MT)
Case and semantic roles (H); *see also* Agency and language (H); Case grammar (MT); Cognitive grammar (MT); Cognitive linguistics (MT); Dependency and valency grammar (MT); Functional grammar (MT); Role and reference grammar (MT)
Case grammar (MT); *see also* Case and semantic roles (H); Construction grammar (MT); Dependency and valency grammar (MT); Frame semantics (T); Functional grammar (MT); Role and reference grammar (MT)
Caste and language (H23)
Catastrophe theory (MT)
Categorial imperative see Truthfulness (H)
Categorization (H); *see also* Adaptability (H); Cognitive grammar (MT); Cognitive linguistics (MT); Language dominance and minorization (H); Membership categorization analysis (T); Polysemy (H)
Causality (H)
Census see Caste and language (H23)
Centering theory see Tense and aspect (H)
Cerebral division of labour in verbal communication (H)
Cerebral representation of language see Cerebral division of labour in verbal communication (H); Neurolinguistics (MT)
Channel (H); *see also* Computer-mediated communication (H); Conversation types (H); Literacy (H); Mass media (H); Non-verbal communication (H); Politeness (H); Social media research (T); Text and discourse linguistics (T)

Chaos theory see Catastrophe theory (MT)
Chat see Computer-mediated communication (H)
Child language see Ellipsis (H); Ervin-Tripp, S. (H24); Language acquisition (H)
'CHILDES' see Language acquisition (H)
Choice-making see Adaptability (H)
Chomskyan linguistics (MT); *see also* Autonomous vs. non-autonomous syntax (MT); Interpretive semantics (MT); Language acquisition (H); Mentalism (MT)
Chronometric studies see Psycholinguistics (MT)
Chronotope (H25); *see also* Bakhtin (H)
Chunking see Linear Unit Grammar (T)
Cicourel, A. V. see Cognitive sociology (MT)
Citation see Working with language data (M25)
Class see Social class and language (H)
Classification1 see Typology (MT)
Classification2 see Taxonomy (MM)
Classroom interaction see Applied linguistics (MT); Communicative success vs. failure (H); Language learning in immersion and CLIL classrooms (H)
Clause structure see Attention and language (H); Control phenomena (H); Role and reference grammar (MT)
Clinical pragmatics (T); *see also* Cerebral representation of language; Nigerian hospital setting discourse (H24); Perception and language (H)
Co-ordination see Cognitive psychology (MT); Ellipsis (H)
Code see Code-switching (H); Code-switching and translanguaging (H22); Metalinguistic awareness (H); Pragmatics of script (H22); Register (H); Semiotics (MT)

Code-autonomy see Code-switching and translanguaging (H22)
Code-switching (H); *see also* Bilingualism and multilingualism (H); Borrowing (H); Code-switching and translanguaging (H22); Contact linguistics (MT); Crossing (H26); Heteroglossia (H26); Language contact (H); Language learning in immersion and CLIL classrooms (H); Language maintenance and shift (H21); Pragmatics of script (H22)
Code-switching and translanguaging (H22); *see also* Crossing (H26); Heteroglossia (H26)
Codemixing see Code-switching (H); Crossing (H26)
Coding see Bateson (H); Evidentiality (H22)
Cognate see The multilingual lexicon (H)
Cognition see Adaptability (H); Caste and language (H23); Language acquisition (H); Orthography and cognition (H22)
Cognitive anthropology (MT); *see also* Anthropological linguistics (MT)
Cognitive grammar (MT); *see also* Case and semantic roles (H); Cognitive linguistics (MT); Metaphor (H)
Cognitive linguistics (MT); *see also* Attention and language (H); Case and semantic roles (H); Cognitive grammar (MT); Cognitive science (MT); Directive (H26); Embodiment (H); Emotions (H21); Event representation (H22); Gesture research (T); Hermeneutics (M); Humor (H23); Language psychology (T); Mental spaces (H); (The) pragmatic perspective (M)

Cognitive pragmatics see Clinical pragmatics (T); Philosophy of mind (MT)
Cognitive psychology (MT); *see also* Artificial intelligence (MT); Behaviorism (MT); Clinical pragmatics (T); Cognitive science (MT); Comprehension vs. production (H); Connectionism (MT); Developmental psychology (MT); Experimentation (MM); Frame semantics (T); Gesture research (T); Intentionality (H); Perception and language (H); Psycholinguistics (MT)
Cognitive science (MT); *see also* Artificial intelligence (MT); Cognitive linguistics (MT); Cognitive psychology (MT); Connectionism (MT); Context and contextualization (H); Experimentation (MM); Grice (H); Mentalism (MT); Perception and language (H); Philosophy of mind (MT)
Cognitive semantics see Cognitive science (MT); Componential analysis (MT); Conceptual semantics (T); Frame semantics (T); Lexical semantics (T)
Cognitive sociology (MT); *see also* Emphasis (H); Ethnomethodology (MT); Sociolinguistics (MT); Symbolic interactionism (MT); Text and discourse linguistics (T)
Cohesion and coherence (H); *see also* Communicative success vs. failure (H); Computational pragmatics (T); Ellipsis (H); Frame analysis (M); Systemic functional grammar (MT); Tense and aspect (H); Text and discourse linguistics (T)
Collaboration in dialogues (H); *see also* Common ground (H); Conversational implicature (H); Conversational logic (MT); Listener response (H)
Colligation see Collocation and colligation (H); Metaphor (H)

Collocation and colligation (H)
Colonization see Caste and language (H23); Language dominance and minorization (H)
Color terms see Anthropological linguistics (MT); Lexical semantics (T); Perception and language (H)
Commodification see Ideology (H)
Common ground (H); *see also* Cognitive science (MT); Collaboration in dialogues (H); Communication (H); Context and contextualization (H); Lexically triggered veridicality inferences (H22); Text and discourse linguistics (T)
Common sense see Ethnomethodology (MT)
Communication (H); *see also* Common ground (H)
Communication disorders → see Language disorders
Communication failure see Applied linguistics (MT)
Communicational dialectology see Dialectology (MT)
Communicative competence see Ethnography of speaking (MT); Gumperz (H); Hymes (H26); Linguistic explanation (MM); Motivation (H)
Communicative dynamism (H); *see also* Functional sentence perspective (H); Ọmọlúàbí (H); Word order (H)
Communicative effect see Interlanguage pragmatics (T)
Communicative style (H); *see also* Cultural scripts (H); Ervin-Tripp, S. (H24); Non-verbal communication (H); Register (H)
Communicative success vs. failure (H)
Community see Pragmatics of script (H22)
Community of practice see Social class and language (H); Workplace interaction (H25)
Comparative method see Contrastive analysis (MM)

Competence vs. performance → see Cerebral representation of language; Chomskyan linguistics (MT)
Complaining (H25)
Complement control see Control phenomena (H)
Complexity see Workplace interaction (H25); Youth language (H25)
Compliment see Corpus pragmatics (M)
Componential analysis (MT); *see also* Anthropological linguistics (MT); Cultural scripts (H); Generative semantics (MT); Lexical field analysis (MT); Lexical semantics (T); Structuralism (MT)
Comprehension vs. production (H); *see also* Cohesion and coherence (H); Communication (H); Irony (H); Mediated performatives (H); Psycholinguistics (MT); Speech act theory (MT); Text comprehension (H)
Compression see Conceptual integration (H)
Computational linguistics (MT); *see also* Artificial intelligence (MT); Lexical functional grammar (MT); Text and discourse linguistics (T)
Computational pragmatics (T)
Computer communication see Artificial intelligence (MT); Computational pragmatics (T); Computer-mediated communication (H)
Computer corpora see Notation Systems in Spoken Language Corpora (N)
Computer modeling see Cognitive science (MT)
Computer programming see Artificial intelligence (MT)
Computer-mediated communication (H); *see also* Chronotope (H25); Complaining (H25); Computational pragmatics (T); Literacy (H); Social media research (T)

Conceptual blending see Conceptual integration (H); Metaphor (H)
Conceptual dependency theory see Artificial intelligence (MT)
Conceptual integration (H)
Conceptual metaphor theory see Metaphor (H)
Conceptual semantics (T); *see also* Interpretive semantics (MT)
Conceptual vs. linguistic representation see Cognitive anthropology (MT); Cognitive psychology (MT); Event representation (H22)
Conceptualization see Cognitive grammar (MT); Cognitive linguistics (MT); Event representation (H22)
Condition of satisfaction see Intentionality (H)
Conditional see Lexically triggered veridicality inferences (H22)
Conflict talk see Applied linguistics (MT)
Connectionism (MT); *see also* Artificial intelligence (MT); Cognitive psychology (MT); Cognitive science (MT); Language acquisition (H); Psycholinguistics (MT)
Connectivity see Cohesion and coherence (H)
Connotation → see Cerebral representation of language; Obscenity, slurs, and taboo (H24)
Consciousness and language (H); *see also* Attention and language (H); Folk pragmatics (T); Metapragmatics (MT); Participation (H); Perception and language (H)
Considerateness → see Tact
Consistency-checking device see Manipulation (H)
Construction grammar (MT); *see also* Case grammar (MT); Emergent grammar (T); Frame semantics (T); Word order (H)
Constructional analysis (T); *see also* Collocation and colligation (H); Construction

grammar (**MT**);
Constructional analysis (**T**)
Constructionism see Applied
linguistics (**MT**);
Argumentation theory (**MT**);
Cognitive anthropology (**MT**);
Critical Linguistics and Critical
Discourse Analysis (**MT**);
Developmental
psychology (**MT**); Intercultural
communication (**H**);
Narrative (**H**); Social
institutions (**H**)
Constructivism →
see Constructionism
Contact (**H**); *see also* Bilingualism
and multilingualism (**H**);
Bilingualism and
multilingualism (**H**); Contact
linguistics (**MT**); Creole
linguistics (**MT**); Creoles and
creolization (**H**);
Crossing (**H26**); Language
change (**H**); Language
contact (**H**); Language
maintenance and shift (**H21**)
Contact linguistics (**MT**); *see also*
Bilingualism and
multilingualism (**H**);
Contact (**H**); Creole
linguistics (**MT**); Creoles and
creolization (**H**);
Dialectology (**MT**);
Intercultural
communication (**H**);
Interjections (**H**); Language
policy, language planning and
standardization (**H**);
Sociolinguistics (**MT**); Speech
community (**H**);
Typology (**MT**); Variational
pragmatics (**T**)
Context and contextualization
(**H**); *see also* Accommodation
theory (**MT**); Activity types
and pragmatic acts (**H26**);
Aisatsu (**H**); Anthropological
linguistics (**MT**); Argument
structure (**H23**); Artificial
intelligence (**MT**);
Bateson (**H**); Cerebral
representation of language;
Cognitive science (**MT**);
Cohesion and coherence (**H**);
Common ground (**H**);
Communication (**H**);
Communicative style (**H**);
Computational

pragmatics (**T**);
Contextualism (**T**);
Conversation analysis (**MT**);
Conversation types (**H**);
Conversational
implicature (**H**);
Conversational logic (**MT**);
Crossing (**H26**); Dialogical
analysis (**MM**); Discourse
markers (**H**); Ellipsis (**H**);
Emphasis (**H**);
Énonciation (**H**); Ervin-Tripp,
S. (**H24**); Ethnography of
speaking (**MT**);
Ethnomethodology (**MT**);
Evolutionary pragmatics (**T**);
Experimental pragmatics (**M**);
Firthian linguistics (**MT**);
Frame analysis (**M**);
Generative semantics (**MT**);
Goffman (**H**); Gumperz (**H**);
Halliday (**H26**);
Hymes (**H26**);
Impoliteness (**H**); Indexicals
and demonstratives (**H**);
Integrational linguistics (**T**);
Intensional logic (**MT**);
Interactional
sociolinguistics (**MT**);
Intercultural
communication (**H**);
Intertextuality (**H**); Language
psychology (**T**); Laughter (**H**);
Literary pragmatics (**MT**);
Metalinguistic awareness (**H**);
Model-theoretic
semantics (**MT**); Motivation
and language (**H**);
Narrative (**H**); Notation in
formal semantics (**MN**);
Politeness (**H**); Polysemy (**H**);
Presupposition (**H**);
Prosody (**H**); Rhetoric (**MT**);
Social media research (**T**);
Stance (**H21**); Style and
styling (**H21**); Symbolic
interactionism (**MT**); Tactile
sign languages (**H21**); Text
comprehension (**H**);
Truthfulness (**H**); Workplace
interaction (**H25**)
Context change see Context and
contextualization (**H**)
Context modelling see Formal
pragmatics (**MT**)
Context-of-situation see Context
and contextualization (**H**);
Firthian linguistics (**MT**);

Malinowski (**H**); Register (**H**);
Systemic functional
grammar (**MT**)
Context-sensitive vs. context-free
grammar see Computational
linguistics (**MT**); Functional
sentence perspective (**H**)
Context-sensitiveness
see Context and
contextualization (**H**)
Contextualism (**T**); *see also*
Context and
contextualization (**H**)
Contextualization cue
see Gumperz (**H**); Style and
styling (**H21**)
Continuity see Historical
politeness (**T**)
Continuity hypothesis
see Language acquisition (**H**)
Contrast see Functional discourse
grammar (**T**)
Contrastive analysis (**MM**); *see*
also Developmental
psychology (**MT**); Error
analysis (**MM**); Historical
politeness (**T**); Intercultural
communication (**H**);
Interlanguage pragmatics (**T**);
Language change (**H**);
Pragmatic markers (**H**)
Contrastive pragmatics (**T**); *see*
also Contrastive
pragmatics (**T**); Ethnography
of speaking (**MT**);
Intercultural
communication (**H**);
Interlanguage pragmatics (**T**);
Mianzi / lian (**H21**);
Translation studies (**T**);
Typology (**MT**); Variational
pragmatics (**T**)
Control see Public discourse (**H**);
Social institutions (**H**)
Control phenomena (**H**)
Conventional implicature
see Grice (**H**); Implicitness (**H**);
Truth-conditional
pragmatics (**T**)
Conventionalism see Lexically
triggered veridicality
inferences (**H22**)
Conventionality
see Adaptability (**H**);
Conventions of language (**H**);
Gesture research (**T**);
Metaphor (**H**); Nigerian
hospital setting

discourse (H24); Primate communication (H); Speech act theory (MT); Wakimae (H26)
Conventions of language (H); *see also* Austin (H); Conversational implicature (H); Conversational logic (MT); Grice (H); Speech act
Convergence see Accommodation theory (MT); Contact (H)
Conversation see Collaboration in dialogues (H); Conversation analysis (MT); Gesture research (T); Humor (H23); Indeterminacy and negotiation (H); Institutional interaction (H23); Mass media (H); Narrative (H)
Conversation analysis (MT); *see also* Age and language use (H); Communication (H); Communicative success vs. failure (H); Computational pragmatics (T); Context and contextualization (H); Conversation types (H); Conversational storytelling (H24); Discourse markers (H); Embodied interaction (H23); Emphasis (H); Ethnography of speaking (MT); Ethnomethodology (MT); Forensic linguistics (T); Goffman (H); Gumperz (H); Hermeneutics (M); Humor (H23); Institutional interaction (H23); Interactional linguistics (T); Interactional sociolinguistics (MT); Intertextuality (H); Language psychology (T); Laughter (H); Linear Unit Grammar (T); Listener response (H); Mass media (H); Membership categorization analysis (T); Notation Systems in Spoken Language Corpora (N); Overlap (H); (The) pragmatic perspective (M); Prosody (H); Repair (H); Sacks (H); Sequence (H); Social psychology (MT); Text and discourse linguistics (T); Therapeutic conversation (H); Transcription systems for spoken discourse (MN); Workplace interaction (H25)
Conversation types (H)
Conversational implicature (H); *see also* Analytical philosophy (MT); Clinical pragmatics (T); Context and contextualization (H); Conversational logic (MT); Ellipsis (H); Experimental pragmatics (M); Grice (H); Implicature and language change (H); Implicitness (H); Interlanguage pragmatics (T); Language and the law (H); Politeness (H); Relevance theory (MT); Speech act theory (MT); Truth-conditional pragmatics (T); Truthfulness (H)
Conversational logic (MT); *see also* Context and contextualization (H); Conversational implicature (H); Generative semantics (MT); Grice (H); Philosophy of language (MT); Relevance theory (MT); Speech act theory (MT)
Conversational move → see Move
Conversational storytelling (H24); *see also* Conversation analysis (MT); Life stories (H); Narrative (H)
Conversationalism see Lexically triggered veridicality inferences (H22)
Cooperative principle see Computational pragmatics (T); Conversational implicature (H); Conversational logic (MT); Creativity in language use (H); Grice (H); Humor (H23); Implicature and language change (H); Implicitness (H); Irony (H); Politeness (H); Silence (H); Truthfulness (H); Universals (H23)
Copenhagen circle see Structuralism (MT)
Coreference see Anaphora (H)
Corpus analysis (MM); *see also* Collocation and colligation (H); Corpus pragmatics (M); Language acquisition (H); Leech (H); Postcolonial pragmatics (T); Pragmatic markers (H); Psycholinguistics (MT); Statistics (MM); Structuralism (MT); Text and discourse linguistics (T); Translation studies (T); Variational pragmatics (T)
Corpus pragmatics (M); *see also* Corpus analysis (MM)
Correlational sociolinguistics (T); *see also* Dialectology (MT); Methods in language-attitudes research (M); Pluricentric languages (H23); Sociolinguistics (MT); Statistics (MM)
Coseriu see Structuralism (MT)
Cosmology see Legitimation Code Theory (T25)
Courtroom conversation see Forensic linguistics (T); Interpreter-mediated interaction (H); Language and the law (H)
Creativity in language use (H); *see also* Authenticity (H); Bühler (H); Code-switching and translanguaging (H22); Cognitive science (MT); Euphemism (H24); Humboldt (H); Language acquisition (H); Think-aloud protocols (M)
Creature construction see Grice (H)
Creole linguistics (MT); *see also* Contact (H); Contact linguistics (MT); Creoles and creolization (H); Historical linguistics (MT); Sociolinguistics (MT)
Creoles and creolization (H); *see also* Contact (H); Contact linguistics (MT); Creole linguistics (MT); Historical linguistics (MT); Intercultural communication (H); Language contact (H); Sociolinguistics (MT)
Critical Linguistics and Critical Discourse Analysis (MT); *see also* Emphasis (H); General semantics (MT); Ideology (H); Intercultural communication (H); Intertextuality (H); Language ideologies (H);

Manipulation (H); Marxist linguistics (MT); Mass media (H); Nexus analysis (T); Polyphony (H); Postcolonial pragmatics (T); Text and discourse linguistics (T); Text linguistics (MT); Truthfulness (H)

Critical theory (MT); *see also* Intercultural communication (H); Universal and transcendental pragmatics (MT)

Cross-cultural communication see Intercultural communication (H)

Cross-cultural pragmatics see Directive (H26); Listener response (H); Overlap (H); Text and discourse linguistics (T); Wakimae (H26)

Cross-cultural psychology see Cognitive anthropology (MT); Developmental psychology (MT)

Cross-sectional method see Developmental psychology (MT)

Crossing (H26); *see also* Code-switching and translanguaging (H22); Heteroglossia (H26); Style and styling (H21)

Crying see Emotion display (H)

Culioli, A. see Énonciation (H)

Cultural anthropology see Anthropological linguistics (MT); Cognitive anthropology (MT)

Cultural model see Cognitive science (MT)

Cultural scripts (H); *see also* Communicative style (H); Componential analysis (MT); Culture (H)

Cultural studies see Ethnography of speaking (MT); Literary pragmatics (MT); Translation studies (T)

Culture (H); *see also* Anthropological linguistics (MT); Behaviorism (MT); Boas (H); Context and contextualization (H); Contrastive analysis (MM);

Cultural scripts (H); Default interpretations (H); Ethnography (MM); Evolutionary pragmatics (T); Fieldwork (MM); Gumperz (H); Humboldt (H); Ideology (H); Intercultural communication (H); Interjections (H); Mentalism (MT); Mianzi / lian (H21); Morphopragmatics (T); Objectivism vs. subjectivism (MT); Ọmọlúàbí (H); Politeness (H); Repair (H); Sapir (H); Semiotics (MT); Sociolinguistics (MT); Style and styling (H21); Whorf (H)

Curse see Impoliteness (H)

Cynicism see Irony (H)

D

Data collection/coding/analysis see Working with language data (M25)

Davidson, D. see Analytical philosophy (MT)

Deception see Truthfulness (H)

Decolonizing see Postcolonial pragmatics (T)

Deconstruction (MM); *see also* Literary pragmatics (MT)

Deduction see Grounded theory (M)

Default interpretations (H)

Default semantics see Default interpretations (H)

Deference see Ọmọlúàbí (H); Ta'arof (H22)

Definite articles see Definiteness (H)

Definite description see Game-theoretical semantics (MT); Reference and descriptions (H)

Definiteness (H)

Degree see Communicative dynamism (H)

Deixis (H); *see also* Bühler (H); Context and contextualization (H); Énonciation (H); Honorifics (H); Mental spaces (H); Non-verbal communication (H); Peirce (H); Politeness (H); Universals (H23)

Deletion see Ellipsis (H)

Dementia see Clinical pragmatics (T)

Demonstrative see Indexicals and demonstratives (H)

Denotation → see Cerebral representation of language; Polysemy (H)

Deontic logic (MT); *see also* Epistemic logic (MT); Logical semantics (MT); Modal logic (MT); Modality (H)

Dependency see Argument structure (H23); Dependency and valency grammar (MT); Frame semantics (T); Polysemy (H); Predicates and predication (H); Role and reference grammar (MT)

Dependency and valency grammar (MT); *see also* Case and semantic roles (H); Case grammar (MT); Role and reference grammar (MT)

Depiction see Gesture research (T)

Derogatory language see Feminism and language (H24); Obscenity, slurs, and taboo (H24)

Derrida, J. see Deconstruction (MM)

Detention hearing → see Police interrogation

Deutero-learning see Bateson (H)

Developmental dyslexia (H); *see also* Clinical pragmatics (T); Developmental psychology (MT); Language acquisition (H); Literacy (H); Pragmatic acquisition (H); Psycholinguistics (MT)

Developmental pragmatics see Developmental psychology (MT); Ervin-Tripp, S. (H24); Language acquisition (H); Second language acquisition

Developmental psychology (MT); *see also* Bilingualism and multilingualism (H); Cognitive psychology (MT); Ervin-Tripp, S. (H24); Psycholinguistics (MT); Vygotsky (H)

Dewey, J. see Morris (H); Pragmatism (MT)

Diachrony see Language change (H)
Diacritic see Phonetic notation systems (N)
Dialect (H); *see also* Anderson (**H21**); Argument structure (**H23**); Dialectology (**MT**); Dialectology and geolinguistic dynamics (T); Folk pragmatics (T); Heteroglossia (**H26**); Integrational linguistics (T)
Dialect formation see Dialectology and geolinguistic dynamics (T)
Dialect geography see Dialectology (MT)
Dialect leveling/loss see Dialectology and geolinguistic dynamics (T)
Dialectology (**MT**); *see also* Contact linguistics (**MT**); Correlational sociolinguistics (T); Dialect (H); Dialectology and geolinguistic dynamics (T); Historical linguistics (**MT**); Reconstruction (**MM**); Sociolinguistics (**MT**); Youth language (**H25**)
Dialectology and geolinguistic dynamics (T)
Dialog modeling see Artificial intelligence (**MT**); Computational pragmatics (T)
Dialog system see Artificial intelligence (**MT**); Computational pragmatics (T)
Dialogical analysis (**MM**); *see also* Collaboration in dialogues (H); Context and contextualization (H); Foucault (H); Humboldt (H); Interactional linguistics (T); Peirce (H)
Dialogism see Appraisal (H); Heteroglossia (**H26**); Intertextuality (H); Stance (**H21**)
Dialogue see Bakhtin (H); Collaboration in dialogues (H); Interpreter-mediated interaction (H); Polyphony (H)
Diaphor see Metaphor (H)
Digital world see Chronotope (**H25**); Complaining (**H25**); Computer-mediated communication (H); Youth language (**H25**)
Digitization see Working with language data (**M25**)
Diglossia see Language contact (H)
Dik, S. see Functional grammar (MT)
Diminutive see Morphopragmatics (T)
Direct vs. indirect speech see Reported speech (H)
Directive (**H26**); *see also* Ervin-Tripp, S. (**H24**); Speech act; Speech act theory (MT)
Discourse see Argumentation in discourse and grammar (H); Bakhtin (H); Cognitive sociology (MT); Critical Linguistics and Critical Discourse Analysis (**MT**); Discourse markers (H); Ethnography (MM); Foucault (H); Grounding (H); Intertextuality (H); Language psychology (T); Mental spaces (H); Narrative (H); Neuropragmatics (T); Nexus analysis (T); Polyphony (H); Public discourse (H); Social institutions (H); Systemic functional grammar (MT); Text and discourse linguistics (T); Text structure (H)
Discourse act see Functional discourse grammar (T)
Discourse analysis see Channel (H); Cognitive sociology (MT); Common ground (H); Conversation analysis (MT); Corpus analysis (MM); Creole linguistics (MT); Critical Linguistics and Critical Discourse Analysis (MT); Geneva school (MT); Grounding (H); Historical pragmatics (T); Ideology (H); Mass media (H); Multimodality (H); Nigerian hospital setting discourse (**H24**); Prague school (MT); Rhetoric (MT); Social psychology (MT); Structuralism (MT); Stylistics (MT); Text and discourse linguistics (T); Text linguistics (MT); Truthfulness (H)
Discourse attuning see Accommodation theory (MT)
Discourse completion test see Intercultural communication (H)
Discourse focus see Anaphora (H)
Discourse genre see Genre (H)
Discourse linking see Discourse representation theory (MT)
Discourse markers (H); *see also* Historical pragmatics (T); Interjections (H); Polyphony (H); Pragmatic markers (H); Pragmatic particles (H)
Discourse mode see Register (H)
Discourse representation theory (**MT**); *see also* Default interpretations (H); Game-theoretical semantics (**MT**); Logical semantics (**MT**); Montague and categorial grammar (**MT**); Situation semantics (**MT**); Tense and aspect (H)
Discourse sociolinguistics see Critical Linguistics and Critical Discourse Analysis (MT)
Discourse topic see Consciousness and language (H)
Discursive ethics see Universal and transcendental pragmatics (MT)
Discursive formation see Foucault (H)
Discursive order see Foucault (H)
Discursive psychology see Authority (H); Language psychology (T); Motivation (H)
Discursive relation see Legitimation Code Theory (**T25**)
Dismissal see Impoliteness (H)
Displacement see Adaptability (H)
Distinctive feature see Jakobson (**H21**)
Divergence see Accommodation theory (MT)

Diversity see Anderson (H21); Language maintenance and shift (H21); Superdiversity (H21)
Doctor-patient interaction → see Medical interaction
Document design see Applied linguistics (MT)
Donnellan, K. see Reference and descriptions (H)
Double bind see Bateson (H)
Double object construction see Argument structure (H23)
Drift see Language change (H)
Ducrot, O. see Argumentation theory (MT); Énonciation (H); Polyphony (H)
Dummett, M. see Analytical philosophy (MT)
Durkheim, Emile see Sociology of language (T)
Dyadic interaction see Conversation types (H); Statistics (MM)
Dynamic semantic functions see Communicative dynamism (H)
Dynamic semantics see Presupposition (H)
Dyslexia see Orthography and cognition (H22)
Dysphasia see Cerebral division of labour in verbal communication (H)
Dysphemism see Obscenity, slurs, and taboo (H24)

E
E-mail communication see Computer-mediated communication (H)
Ebonics see 'Other' representation (H)
Education see Applied linguistics (MT); Code-switching and translanguaging (H22); Ideology (H); Language learning in immersion and CLIL classrooms (H); Language rights (H); Linguistic landscape studies (T); Literacy (H); Translanguaging pedagogy (T)
Effectiveness see Communicative success vs. failure (H); Swearing (H25)

Egocentric speech see Vygotsky (H)
Elicitation (MM); *see also* Fieldwork (MM); Interview (MM); Methods in language-attitudes research (M)
Ellipsis (H); *see also* Argument structure (H23)
Emancipation see Feminism and language (H24); Postcolonial pragmatics (T)
Emancipatory pragmatics see Postcolonial pragmatics (T)
Embedding see Frame analysis (M)
Embodied interaction (H23)
Embodiment (H); *see also* Embodied interaction (H23); Gesture research (T); Humor (H23); Pragmatics of script (H22)
Emergence see Adaptability (H)
Emergent grammar (T)
Emotion display (H); *see also* Laughter (H); Silence (H)
Emotions (H21); *see also* Appraisal (H); Emotion display (H); Impoliteness (H); Obscenity, slurs, and taboo (H24); Swearing (H25)
Emphasis (H)
Encoding see Orthography and cognition (H22)
Endangered languages see Language ecology (H)
Engagement see Appraisal (H); Evidentiality (H22); Nexus analysis (T)
Engels, Friedrich see Ideology (H)
English (as a global language) see Linguistic landscape studies (T); Postcolonial pragmatics (T)
Énonciation (H); *see also* Benveniste (H)
Enregisterment see Crossing (H26)
Entailment see Implicitness (H); Lexically triggered veridicality inferences (H22)
Entrenchment see Conceptual integration (H)
Enunciation see Benveniste (H); Polyphony (H)
Environment see Context and contextualization (H); Gesture

research (T); Tactile sign languages (H21)
Epiphor see Metaphor (H)
Epistemic authority see Conversational storytelling (H24); Evidentiality (H22)
Epistemic dynamics see Epistemic logic (MT)
Epistemic logic (MT); *see also* Deontic logic (MT); Logical semantics (MT); Modal logic (MT); Modality (H); Possible worlds semantics (MT)
Epistemic relation see Legitimation Code Theory (T25)
Epistemology (MT); *see also* Austin (H); Foucault (H); Objectivism vs. subjectivism (MT); Ontology (MT); Perception and language (H)
Epistemology of testimony (T)
Erklären vs. Verstehen see Grounded theory (M)
Error analysis (MM); *see also* Contrastive analysis (MM)
Ervin-Tripp, S. (H24); *see also* Developmental psychology (MT); Language acquisition (H); Sociolinguistics (MT)
Ethnicity see Crossing (H26); Culture (H); Humor (H23); Intercultural communication (H); Language dominance and minorization (H); Language policy, language planning and standardization (H)
Ethnographic semantics see Anthropological linguistics (MT); Taxonomy (MM)
Ethnography (MM); *see also* Anderson (H21); Anthropological linguistics (MT); Bourdieu (H); Developmental psychology (MT); Ethnography of speaking (MT); Fieldwork (MM); Hymes (H26); Linguistic landscape studies (T); Social media research (T)

Ethnography of communication see Ethnography of speaking (MT); Hymes (H26)
Ethnography of speaking (MT); *see also* Anthropological linguistics (MT); Context and contextualization (H); Conversation analysis (MT); Ervin-Tripp, S. (H24); Gumperz (H); Hymes (H26); Interactional sociolinguistics (MT); Intercultural communication (H); Nexus analysis (T); Phatic communion (H); Style and styling (H21)
Ethnomethodology (MT); *see also* Cognitive sociology (MT); Context and contextualization (H); Conversation analysis (MT); Humor (H23); Interactional sociolinguistics (MT); Language psychology (T); Membership categorization analysis (T); Phenomenology (MT); (The) pragmatic perspective (M); Sacks (H); Social psychology (MT); Symbolic interactionism (MT)
Ethnopoetics see Hymes (H26)
Ethnoscience see Anthropological linguistics (MT)
Ethogenics see Social psychology (MT)
Euphemism (H24); *see also* Morphopragmatics (T); Obscenity, slurs, and taboo (H24)
Evaluation see Appraisal (H); Chronotope (H25); Emphasis (H); Stance (H21)
Evaluation task see Methods in language-attitudes research (M)
Event representation (H22)
Event types see Event representation (H22)
Event-related potential see Cognitive science (MT); Language acquisition (H)
Evidence see Evidentiality (H22)
Evidentiality (H22); *see also* Appraisal (H); Authority (H); Modality (H); Stance (H21)

Evolution (theory) see Adaptability (H); Evolutionary pragmatics (T)
Evolutionary pragmatics (T)
Executive function see Clinical pragmatics (T)
Exemplar model see Psycholinguistics (MT)
Expectation see Frame analysis (M); Mediated performatives (H)
Experimental pragmatics (M); *see also* Experimentation (MM)
Experimentation (MM); *see also* Cognitive psychology (MT); Cognitive science (MT); Ethnomethodology (MT); Experimental pragmatics (M); Methods in language-attitudes research (M); Orthography and cognition (H22); Psycholinguistics (MT); Sound symbolism (H); Statistics (MM); Think-aloud protocols (M); Variational pragmatics (T)
Expertise see Cognitive sociology (MT); Forensic linguistics (T)
Explaining vs. understanding → see Erklären vs. Verstehen
Explanation see Linguistic explanation (MM)
Explicature see Implicitness (H); Truth-conditional pragmatics (T)
Expression → see Functions of language
Extension → see Intension vs. extension

F
Face see Directive (H26); Goffman (H); Impoliteness (H); Mianzi / lian (H21); Politeness (H); Silence (H); Ta'ārof (H22); Wakimae (H26)
Face-to-face interaction see Accommodation theory (MT); Cognitive sociology (MT); Computer-mediated communication (H); Conversation analysis (MT); Intercultural communication (H); Prosody (H)

Facebook see Social media research (T)
Factivity see Lexically triggered veridicality inferences (H22)
False friends see The multilingual lexicon (H)
Familiarity see Information structure (H)
Feedback see Adaptability (H); Tactile sign languages (H21)
Feeling(s) see Appraisal (H)
Felicity condition see Speech act theory (MT)
Feminism and language (H24)
Ferguson, C. see Register (H)
Field see Register (H)
Fieldwork (MM); *see also* Anthropological linguistics (MT); Boas (H); Elicitation (MM); Ethnography (MM); Ethnography of speaking (MT); Interview (MM); Malinowski (H)
Figure vs. ground see Grounding (H)
Figures of speech (H); *see also* Cultural scripts (H); Emphasis (H)
File change semantics see Computational linguistics (MT); Discourse representation theory (MT)
Fillmore, C. J. see Case grammar (MT); Frame semantics (T)
Firth, J. R. (H); *see also* Firthian linguistics (MT); Halliday (H26); Register (H); Systemic functional grammar (MT)
Firthian linguistics (MT); *see also* Context and contextualization (H); Firth (H); Phatic communion (H); Systemic functional grammar (MT)
Flexibility see Primate communication (H)
Focalisation see Tense and aspect (H)
Focalizer see Functional sentence perspective (H)
Focus → see Topic vs. focus
Focus domain see Argument structure (H23)

Focus structure see Role and reference grammar (MT)
Folk classification see Anthropological linguistics (MT); Cognitive anthropology (MT); Language ideologies (H); Metalinguistic awareness (H); Taxonomy (MM)
Folk linguistics see Socio-onomastics (T)
Folk pragmatics (T); *see also* Methods in language-attitudes research (M)
Folk psychology see Philosophy of mind (MT)
Footing see Frame analysis (M); Goffman (H); Participation (H)
Foregrounding see Grounding (H)
Foreigner talk see Intercultural communication (H); Register (H)
Forensic linguistics (T); *see also* Applied linguistics (MT)
Form vs. function see Corpus pragmatics (M); Sapir (H)
Form-function mapping → see Form vs. function
Formal dialectics see Argumentation theory (MT)
Formal linguistics see Linguistic explanation (MM)
Formal pragmatics (MT); *see also* Analytical philosophy (MT); Logical semantics (MT); Montague and categorial grammar (MT)
Formality see Conversation types (H); Register (H)
Formulaic language → see Routine formula
Formulation see Rhetoric (MT)
Foucault, M. (H); *see also* Critical theory (MT); Ideology (H); Jargon (H); Power and the role of language (H25)
Frame (analysis) (M); *see also* Artificial intelligence (MT); Bateson (H); Cognitive science (MT); Emphasis (H); Frame semantics (T); Gesture research (T); Goffman (H); Humor (H23); Mental spaces (H); Metalinguistic awareness (H); Non-verbal communication (H); (The) pragmatic perspective (M)

Frame semantics (T); *see also* Collocation and colligation (H); Context and contextualization (H); Dependency and valency grammar (MT); Event representation (H22); Lexical field analysis (MT); Lexical semantics (T)
Frankfurt school → see Adorno; Habermas
Frege, G. see Analytical philosophy (MT); Intensional logic (MT); Reference and descriptions (H); Semantics vs. pragmatics (T); Speech act theory (MT)
Fremdverstehen see Grounded theory (M)
Frequency see Markedness (H); Statistics (MM); Swearing (H25)
Functional discourse grammar (T)
Functional explanation see Linguistic explanation (MM)
Functional grammar (MT); *see also* Case and semantic roles (H); Case grammar (MT); Mathesius (H); Prague school (MT); Predicates and predication (H); Systemic functional grammar (MT); Word order (H)
Functional sentence perspective (H); *see also* Communicative dynamism (H); Mathesius (H); Prague school (MT); Word order (H)
Functionalism vs. formalism (MT); *see also* Autonomous vs. non-autonomous syntax (MT); Cognitive science (MT); Communicative dynamism (H); Emergent grammar (T); Linguistic explanation (MM); Mathesius (H); (The) pragmatic perspective (M); Translation studies (T)
Functions of language see Bühler (H); Emotion display (H); Evolutionary pragmatics (T); Functional

discourse grammar (T); Functionalism vs. formalism (MT); Historical politeness (T); Impoliteness (H); Jakobson (H21); Participation (H); Prague school (MT); Relational ritual (H); Silence (H); Systemic functional grammar (MT)
Fund see Predicates and predication (H)
Fuzziness → see Vagueness
Fuzzy set theory see Categorization (H); Lexical semantics (T)

G
Game-theoretical semantics (MT); *see also* Discourse representation theory (MT); Logical semantics (MT); Model-theoretic semantics (MT)
Gapping see Ellipsis (H)
Garfinkel, H. see Ethnomethodology (MT)
GDPR see Working with language data (M25)
Gender (H); *see also* Authority (H); Caste and language (H23); Computer-mediated communication (H); Critical Linguistics and Critical Discourse Analysis (MT); Feminism and language (H24); Humor (H23); Identity (H24); Interjections (H); Laughter (H); Listener response (H); Overlap (H); Silence (H); Swearing (H25); Workplace interaction (H25)
General rhetoric see Rhetoric (MT)
General semantics (MT); *see also* Critical Linguistics and Critical Discourse Analysis (MT)
Generalized catastrophe see Catastrophe theory (MT)
Generalized phrase structure grammar see Computational linguistics (MT); Construction grammar (MT); Interpretive semantics (MT)
Generative semantics (MT); *see also* Componential

analysis (**MT**); Conceptual semantics (**T**); Conversational logic (**MT**); Interpretive semantics (**MT**); (The) pragmatic perspective (**M**)
Generative(-transformational) linguistics see Attention and language (**H**); Chomskyan linguistics (**MT**); Cognitive linguistics (**MT**); Computational linguistics (**MT**); Creativity in language use (**H**); Historical linguistics (**MT**); Interpretive semantics (**MT**); Language acquisition (**H**); Language change (**H**); Lexical semantics (**T**)
Genetic linguistics see Historical linguistics (**MT**); Language change (**H**); Reconstruction (**MM**)
Geneva school (**MT**); *see also* Structuralism (**MT**); Text and discourse linguistics (**T**)
Genre (**H**); *see also* Bakhtin (**H**); Channel (**H**); Conversation types (**H**); Conversational logic (**MT**); Narrative (**H**); Tense and aspect (**H**); Text and discourse linguistics (**T**); Text type (**H**)
Geographical origin see Laughter (**H**)
Geolinguistics see Contact linguistics (**MT**); Dialectology and geolinguistic dynamics (**T**); Linguistic landscape studies (**T**)
Gestalt psychology see Behaviorism (**MT**); Cognitive psychology (**MT**); Metaphor (**H**)
Gesticulation see Gesture research (**T**)
Gesture see Communication (**H**); Gesture research (**T**); Non-verbal communication (**H**); Primate communication (**H**); Prosody (**H**)
Gesture research (**T**); *see also* Non-verbal communication (**H**)
Given vs. new see Argument structure (**H23**); Argumentation in discourse and grammar (**H**); Computational pragmatics (**T**); Definiteness (**H**); Functional sentence perspective (**H**);

Information structure (**H**); Word order (**H**)
Globalization (**H25**); *see also* Code-switching and translanguaging (**H22**); Dialectology and geolinguistic dynamics (**T**); Language dominance and minorization (**H**); Power and the role of language (**H25**); Translanguaging pedagogy (**T**); Youth language (**H25**)
Glossematics see Semiotics (**MT**); Structuralism (**MT**)
Glottochronology see Historical linguistics (**MT**)
Goffman, E. (**H**); *see also* Conversation analysis (**MT**); Frame analysis (**M**); Participation (**H**); Politeness (**H**); Public discourse (**H**); Reported speech (**H**); Symbolic interactionism (**MT**)
Government and binding theory see Chomskyan linguistics (**MT**); Construction grammar (**MT**); Interpretive semantics (**MT**)
Gradience see Categorization (**H**)
Grammar see Argumentation in discourse and grammar (**H**); Leech (**H**); Nigerian hospital setting discourse (**H24**)
Grammatical constraints see Code-switching (**H**)
Grammatical metaphor see Metaphor (**H**)
Grammatical relations see Agency and language (**H**); Polysemy (**H**); Role and reference grammar (**MT**)
Grammatical status see Grammaticalization and pragmatics (**T**)
Grammaticalization see Constructional analysis (**T**); Emergent grammar (**T**); Implicature and language change (**H**); Language change (**H**); Metaphor (**H**); Modality (**H**); Negation (**H**); Pragmatic markers (**H**); Predicates and predication (**H**)
Grammaticalization and pragmatics (**T**)

Grammatization see Emergent grammar (**T**)
Gramsci, A. see Hegemony (**H23**); Marxist linguistics (**MT**)
Greeting see Ọmọlúàbí (**H**); Ta'ārof (**H22**)
Grice, H. P. (**H**); *see also* Analytical philosophy (**MT**); Clinical pragmatics (**T**); Conversational implicature (**H**); Conversational logic (**MT**); Default interpretations (**H**); Humor (**H23**); Semantics vs. pragmatics (**T**); Silence (**H**); Speech act theory (**MT**); Truth-conditional pragmatics (**T**); Truthfulness (**H**); Universals (**H23**)
Grounded theory (**M**)
Grounding (**H**); *see also* Anaphora (**H**); Computational pragmatics (**T**); Text and discourse linguistics (**T**)
Guillaume, G. see Énonciation (**H**)
Gumperz, J. J. (**H**); *see also* Anthropological linguistics (**MT**); Communicative success vs. failure (**H**); Culture (**H**); Ethnography of speaking (**MT**); Interactional sociolinguistics (**MT**); Intercultural communication (**H**); Prosody (**H**); Register (**H**)

H
Habermas, J. see Critical theory (**MT**); Ideology (**H**); Public discourse (**H**); Universal and transcendental pragmatics (**MT**)
Habitus see Anderson (**H21**); Bourdieu (**H**); Communication (**H**); Lifestyle (**H**)
Half-truth see Truthfulness (**H**)
Halliday, M. A. K. (**H26**); *see also* Critical Linguistics and Critical Discourse Analysis (**MT**); Firthian linguistics (**MT**); Genre (**H**); Jargon (**H**); Phatic communion (**H**); Register (**H**); Social

semiotics (T); Systemic functional grammar (MT)
Harold Garfinkel and pragmatics (H); *see also* Conversation analysis (MT); Ethnomethodology (MT); Metapragmatics (MT); Sacks (H)
Head-driven phrase structure grammar see Computational linguistics (MT); Construction grammar (MT); Formal pragmatics (MT); Interpretive semantics (MT)
Hearer see Appraisal (H); Mass media (H)
Hegemony (H23); *see also* Ideology (H); Intertextuality (H); Language ecology (H); Metalinguistic awareness (H); Postcolonial pragmatics (T)
Hemisphere dominance see Neurolinguistics (MT)
Heritage language see Language maintenance and shift (H21)
Hermeneutics (M); *see also* Analytical philosophy (MT); Anthropological linguistics (MT); Cognitive linguistics (MT); Cohesion and coherence (H); Conversation analysis (MT); Language psychology (T); Literary pragmatics (MT); Structuralism (MT); Truthfulness (H); Universal and transcendental pragmatics (MT)
Heterogeneity see Language dominance and minorization (H)
Heteroglossia (H26); *see also* Appraisal (H); Bakhtin (H); Dialogism; Ideology (H); Intertextuality (H); Polyphony (H)
Heterosemy see Polysemy (H)
Hierarchy see Nigerian hospital setting discourse (H24); Power and the role of language (H25)
Historical linguistics (MT); *see also* Borrowing (H); Creole linguistics (MT); Creoles and creolization (H); Dialectology (MT); Historical pragmatics (T); Language change (H);

Reconstruction (MM); de Saussure (H); Typology (MT)
Historical politeness (T)
Historical pragmatics (T); *see also* Historical linguistics (MT); Interjections (H); Mass media (H); Text and discourse linguistics (T)
Historical sociolinguistics (T); *see also* Correlational sociolinguistics (T); Dialectology and geolinguistic dynamics (T); Historical linguistics (MT); Historical pragmatics (T); Interactional sociolinguistics (MT); Language change (H); Sociolinguistics (MT)
History see Critical Linguistics and Critical Discourse Analysis (MT); Dialectology (MT); Hegemony (H23)
Homogeneity see Anderson (H21); Metalinguistic awareness (H)
Homogenisation see 'Other' representation (H)
Homonymy see Indeterminacy and negotiation (H); Obscenity, slurs, and taboo (H24); Polysemy (H)
Honorifics (H); *see also* Politeness (H); Terms of address (H); Universals (H23); Wakimae (H26)
Humboldt, W. von (H)
Humor (H23); *see also* Computer-mediated communication (H); Emotion display (H); Ervin-Tripp, S. (H24); Irony (H); Laughter (H); 'Other' representation (H); Truthfulness (H)
Hybridity see Genre (H); Intensional logic (MT); Intertextuality (H); 'Other' representation (H); Presupposition (H)
Hymes, D. (H26); *see also* Anthropological linguistics (MT); Culture (H); Ethnography of speaking (MT)
Hyperlink see Social media research (T)
Hyponymy see Polysemy (H)

I
I-principle see Anaphora (H); Semantics vs. pragmatics (T)
Iconicity (H); *see also* Jakobson (H21); Language change (H); Sound symbolism (H)
Identifiability see Definiteness (H)
Identity (H24); *see also* Age and language use (H); Anderson (H21); Chronotope (H25); Dialectology and geolinguistic dynamics (T); Feminism and language (H24); Gumperz (H); Ideology (H); Language maintenance and shift (H21); Laughter (H); Life stories (H); Membership categorization analysis (T); Motivation and language (H); Pluricentric languages (H23); Postcolonial pragmatics (T); Pragmatics of script (H22); Social class and language (H); Social media research (T); Superdiversity (H21); Swearing (H25); Teasing (H25); Translanguaging pedagogy (T); Variational pragmatics (T); Youth language (H25)
Ideology (H); *see also* Critical Linguistics and Critical Discourse Analysis (MT); Culture (H); Hegemony (H23); Honorifics (H); Manipulation (H); Marxist linguistics (MT); Mass media (H); Nigerian hospital setting discourse (H24); Postcolonial pragmatics (T); Public discourse (H); Social psychology (MT); Social semiotics (T); Workplace interaction (H25)
Idiolect see Forensic linguistics (T); Integrational linguistics (T)
Idéologues see Humboldt (H)
Illiteracy see Literacy (H)
Illocution see Directive (H26); Functional discourse grammar (T); Functional

discourse grammar (T);
Functional grammar (MT);
Indeterminacy and
negotiation (H);
Intentionality (H);
Modality (H); Non-verbal
communication (H); Speech act
theory (MT)

Illocutionary force see Speech act
theory (MT)

**Illocutionary force-indicating
device** see Corpus
pragmatics (M); Speech act
theory (MT)

Imagined community
see Anderson (H21)

Immersion see Language learning
in immersion and CLIL
classrooms (H)

Implication see Lexically
triggered veridicality
inferences (H22)

Implicature → see Conventional
implicature; Conversational
implicature (H); Implicature
and language change (H)

Implicature and language change
(H); *see also* Conventional
implicature; Conversational
implicature (H)

Implicitness (H); *see also*
Argument structure (H23);
Cerebral representation of
language; Discourse
markers (H); Emphasis (H);
Lexically triggered veridicality
inferences (H22); Methods in
language-attitudes
research (M); Truth-
conditional pragmatics (T)

Implicitée see Implicitness (H)

Impoliteness (H); *see also*
Euphemism (H24); Historical
politeness (T); Obscenity,
slurs, and taboo (H24);
Politeness (H);
Swearing (H25);
Teasing (H25);
Wakimae (H26)

Incongruity resolution
see Humor (H23)

Indeterminacy and negotiation
(H); *see also* Ellipsis (H);
Integrational linguistics (T);
Truthfulness (H)

Indexicalism
see Contextualism (T)

Indexicality
see Ethnomethodology (MT);
Gesture research (T);
Jakobson (H21); Language
change (H); Language
psychology (T); Metalinguistic
awareness (H); Prosody (H);
Stance (H21); Truth-conditional
semantics (MT)

Indexicals and demonstratives
(H); *see also* Anaphora (H);
Context and
contextualization (H)

Indifference see Postcolonial
pragmatics (T)

Indirect speech act see Activity
types and pragmatic acts (H26)

Indirectness
see Complaining (H25);
Conversational logic (MT);
Discourse representation
theory (MT); Leech (H)

Individualism see Sociology of
language (T)

Individuality
see Intentionality (H)

Induction see Grounded
theory (M)

Industrialization see Sociology of
language (T); Workplace
interaction (H25)

Inequality see Power and the role
of language (H25)

(In)felicity see Communicative
success vs. failure (H)

Inferencing → see Cerebral
representation of language;
Clinical pragmatics (T);
Cognitive psychology (MT);
Cognitive sociology (MT);
Computational pragmatics (T);
Conceptual semantics (T);
Default interpretations (H);
Discourse representation
theory (MT); Ellipsis (H);
Emphasis (H);
Evidentiality (H22);
Experimental pragmatics (M);
Figures of speech (H);
Grice (H); Gumperz (H);
Implicature and language
change (H); Irony (H);
Language psychology (T);
Lexically triggered veridicality
inferences (H22); Prosody (H);
Speech act theory (MT)

Informal logic see Argumentation
theory (MT)

Information processing
see Attention and language (H);
Cognitive psychology (MT);
Cognitive science (MT);
Comprehension vs.
production (H);
Evidentiality (H22); Text
comprehension (H)

Information source
see Evidentiality (H22)

Information structure (H); *see
also* Argument structure (H23);
Argumentation in discourse
and grammar (H);
Computational
pragmatics (T); Discourse
markers (H); Emphasis (H);
Narrative (H); Signed language
pragmatics (T); Tense and
aspect (H); Text and discourse
linguistics (T); Text
structure (H); Word order (H)

Informativeness
see Definiteness (H);
Humor (H23); Information
structure (H);
Presupposition (H)

Informing see Mediated
performatives (H)

Innateness see Language
acquisition (H)

Inner speech see Vygotsky (H)

Instagram see Social media
research (T)

Institutional interaction (H23);
see also Social institutions (H)

Institutional role
see Laughter (H)

Institutional setting
see Complaining (H25);
Nigerian hospital setting
discourse (H24); Social
institutions (H)

Instructional science see Applied
linguistics (MT)

Instrumentality see Evolutionary
pragmatics (T)

Insult see Impoliteness (H);
Obscenity, slurs, and
taboo (H24)

Integration see Language
rights (H)

Integrational linguistics (T); *see
also* Pragmatics of script (H22)

Integrity see Truthfulness (H)

Intension vs. extension
see Intensional logic (MT);

Notation in formal semantics (MN)
Intensional logic (MT); *see also* Logical semantics (MT)
Intensional semantics
see Analytical philosophy (MT)
Intention see Artificial intelligence (MT); Computational pragmatics (T); Directive (H26); Grice (H); Intentionality (H); Irony (H); Mediated performatives (H); Neuropragmatics (T); Philosophy of action (MT); Philosophy of mind (MT); Primate communication (H); Speech act theory (MT); Truthfulness (H)
Intentionality (H); *see also* Agency and language (H); Communication (H); Impoliteness (H); Philosophy of mind (MT)
Interaction-organization theory
see Metaphor (H)
Interactional analysis
see Multimodality (H)
Interactional linguistics (T); *see also* Emergent grammar (T); Linear Unit Grammar (T)
Interactional relation
see Legitimation Code Theory (T25)
Interactional sense-making →
see Meaning construction
Interactional sociolinguistics (MT); *see also* Code-switching (H); Communicative style (H); Context and contextualization (H); Conversation analysis (MT); Ethnography of speaking (MT); Ethnomethodology (MT); Gumperz (H); Intercultural communication (H); Metapragmatics (MT); Mianzi / lian (H21); Nexus analysis (T); (The) pragmatic perspective (M); Sociolinguistics (MT); Workplace interaction (H25)
Interactive failure →
see Communication failure
Interactive-activation model
see Psycholinguistics (MT)
Interactivity see Computer-mediated communication (H);

Conversational storytelling (H24); Deixis (H); Functional discourse grammar (T); Psycholinguistics (MT); Reported speech (H)
Intercultural communication (H); *see also* Aisatsu (H); Anthropological linguistics (MT); Applied linguistics (MT); Bilingualism and multilingualism (H); Code-switching (H); Communication (H); Communicative success vs. failure (H); Contact linguistics (MT); Context and contextualization (H); Contrastive analysis (MM); Creoles and creolization (H); Critical Linguistics and Critical Discourse Analysis (MT); Critical theory (MT); Crossing (H26); Culture (H); Ethnography of speaking (MT); Gumperz (H); Interactional sociolinguistics (MT); Interlanguage pragmatics (T); Language and the law (H); Language policy, language planning and standardization (H); Non-verbal communication (H); Text and discourse linguistics (T); Truthfulness (H)
Intercultural politeness research →
Interference see Contact linguistics (MT); Language contact (H); Psycholinguistics (MT)
Interjections (H)
Interlanguage pragmatics (T); *see also* Contrastive analysis (MM); Conversational implicature (H); Intercultural communication (H); Politeness (H)
Internalization see Foucault (H)
Internet see Chronotope (H25); Computer-mediated communication (H); Social media research (T)
Interpersonal relation
see Complaining (H25);

Intentionality (H); Mianzi / lian (H21); Swearing (H25)
Interpreter-mediated interaction (H)
Interpretive processes →
see Inferencing
Interpretive semantics (MT); *see also* Chomskyan linguistics (MT); Conceptual semantics (T); Generative semantics (MT)
Interpretive sociolinguistics
see Interactional sociolinguistics (MT)
Interrogative see Lexically triggered veridicality inferences (H22)
Interruption see Overlap (H)
Intersubjectivity
see Appraisal (H); Bourdieu (H); Bühler (H); Collaboration in dialogues (H); Communication (H); Language psychology (T); Peirce (H)
Intertextuality (H); *see also* Bakhtin (H); Computer-mediated communication (H); Heteroglossia (H26); Polyphony (H)
Interview (MM); *see also* Elicitation (MM); Fieldwork (MM); Methods in language-attitudes research (M)
Intimacy see Laughter (H)
Intonation see Communicative dynamism (H); Information structure (H); Markedness (H); Prosody (H)
Intonation unit
see Consciousness and language (H)
Intuition and introspection (MM); *see also* Cognitive science (MT)
Involvement → see Affect
Irony (H); *see also* Experimental pragmatics (M); Frame analysis (M); Humor (H23); Polyphony (H)
Isomorphism see Iconicity (H)
Isotopy see Humor (H23)

J
Jakobson, R. (H21); *see also* Emotions (H21); Hymes (H26);

Participation (H); Phatic communion (H); Prague school (MT); Structuralism (MT)
James, W. see Morris (H); Pragmatism (MT)
Jargon (H); *see also* Nigerian hospital setting discourse (H24)
Joke see Humor (H23); Irony (H)
Journalism see Mass media (H); Mediated performatives (H)
Judgement see Appraisal (H)
Jury instruction see Forensic linguistics (T)

K
Kilivila see Malinowski (H)
Kinesics see Non-verbal communication (H)
Knowledge see Artificial intelligence (MT); Austin (H); Authority (H); Epistemology of testimony (T); Foucault (H); Power and the role of language (H25)
Knowledge representation see Artificial intelligence (MT); Cognitive psychology (MT); Cognitive science (MT); Connectionism (MT)
Koineization see Dialectology and geolinguistic dynamics (T)
Kripke, S. see Reference and descriptions (H)
Kristeva, J. see Intertextuality (H)

L
L2 → see Second language acquisition
Labov, W. see Correlational sociolinguistics (T); Creole linguistics (MT); Sociolinguistics (MT)
Language acquisition (H); *see also* Developmental psychology (MT); Discourse markers (H); Ervin-Tripp, S. (H24); Interjections (H); Irony (H); Jakobson (H21); Literacy (H); Metalinguistic awareness (H); Morphopragmatics (T); Pragmatic particles (H); Psycholinguistics (MT); Repair (H); Text and discourse

linguistics (T); Text structure (H); Vygotsky (H)
Language acquisition device see Language acquisition (H)
Language and the law (H)
Language and thought see Boas (H); Consciousness and language (H); Developmental psychology (MT); Embodiment (H); Humboldt (H); Perception and language (H); Sapir (H); Vygotsky (H); Whorf (H)
Language attitudes → see Attitude; Methods in language-attitudes research (M); Pluricentric languages (H23)
Language change (H); *see also* Borrowing (H); Contact linguistics (MT); Correlational sociolinguistics (T); Creativity in language use (H); Creoles and creolization (H); Dialectology (MT); Dialectology and geolinguistic dynamics (T); Genre (H); Historical linguistics (MT); Historical politeness (T); Historical pragmatics (T); Implicature and language change (H); Language maintenance and shift (H21); Morphopragmatics (T); Obscenity, slurs, and taboo (H24); Polysemy (H); Pragmatic markers (H); de Saussure (H); Structuralism (MT); Superdiversity (H21); Text and discourse linguistics (T); Text structure (H); Youth language (H25)
Language choice see Bilingualism and multilingualism (H); Ervin-Tripp, S. (H24); Intercultural communication (H); Language policy, language planning and standardization (H)
Language comprehension see Comprehension vs. production (H)
Language conflict see Identity (H24); Language contact (H); Language dominance and minorization (H)

Language contact (H); *see also* Borrowing (H); Contact (H); Language change (H); Literacy (H)
Language death see Language contact (H); Language ecology (H); Language rights (H)
Language disorders → see Cerebral representation of language; Clinical pragmatics (T); Neurolinguistics (MT)
Language dominance and minorization (H); *see also* Language ecology (H); Pluricentric languages (H23)
Language ecology (H)
Language for special purposes (LSP) see Applied linguistics (MT); Genre (H)
Language game see Game-theoretical semantics (MT); Wittgenstein (H)
Language generation and interpretation → see Natural language generation and interpretation
Language ideologies (H); *see also* Bilingualism and multilingualism (H); Bourdieu (H); Feminism and language (H24); Identity (H24); Ideology (H); Language dominance and minorization (H); Literacy (H); Metalinguistic awareness (H); Wakimae (H26)
Language impairment → see Cerebral representation of language; Clinical pragmatics (T); Neurolinguistics (MT); Perception and language (H)
Language learning in immersion and CLIL classrooms (H)
Language maintenance and shift (H21); *see also* Contact (H); Interjections (H); Language ecology (H); Language policy, language planning and standardization (H); Translanguaging pedagogy (T)
Language pathology → see Cerebral representation of language; Clinical pragmatics (T); Language

acquisition (H); Perception and language (H)
Language planning see Language policy, language planning and standardization (H)
Language policy, language planning and standardization (H); *see also* Applied linguistics (**MT**); Authority (H); Bilingualism and multilingualism (H); Contact linguistics (**MT**); Feminism and language (**H24**); Intercultural communication (H); Language ideologies (H); Language maintenance and shift (**H21**); Linguistic landscape studies (**T**); Literacy (H); Sociolinguistics (**MT**)
Language processing → see Natural language processing
Language psychology (**T**)
Language rights (H)
Language shift see Language maintenance and shift (**H21**)
Language teaching see Applied linguistics (**MT**); Code-switching and translanguaging (**H22**); Error analysis (**MM**); Ideology (H); Interlanguage pragmatics (**T**); Language learning in immersion and CLIL classrooms (H); Motivation and language (H); Orthography and cognition (**H22**); Pragmatic particles (H); Register (H); Translanguaging pedagogy (**T**)
Language technology see Artificial intelligence (**MT**)
Language universals see Universals (**H23**)
Language variation see Dialect (H); Dialectology (**MT**); Variational pragmatics (**T**)
Languaging see Code-switching and translanguaging (**H22**); Translanguaging pedagogy (**T**)
Langue vs. parole see de Saussure (H); Structuralism (**MT**)
Lateralization see Neurolinguistics (**MT**)
Laughable see Laughter (H)
Laughter (H); *see also* Emotion display (H)

Learnability see Language acquisition (H)
Least-effort hypothesis see Semantics vs. pragmatics (**T**)
Lect see Dialect (H)
Leech, G. (H)
Left vs. right hemisphere → see Cerebral representation of language; Clinical pragmatics (**T**); Neurolinguistics (**MT**)
Legal aspects of research see Working with language data (**M25**)
Legal language see Applied linguistics (**MT**); Authority (H); Forensic linguistics (**T**); Language and the law (H); Sequence (H); Silence (H)
Legal settings see Forensic linguistics (**T**)
Legitimation see Foucault (H)
Legitimation Code Theory (**T25**)
Lesion syndrome see Neurolinguistics (**MT**)
Lexical bundle/cluster/string see Collocation and colligation (H)
Lexical decomposition see Componential analysis (**MT**)
Lexical field analysis (**MT**); *see also* Componential analysis (**MT**); Lexical semantics (**T**); Structuralism (**MT**)
Lexical functional grammar (**MT**); *see also* Computational linguistics (**MT**)
Lexical primitive → see Semantic primitive
Lexical semantics (**T**); *see also* Componential analysis (**MT**); Frame semantics (**T**); Lexical field analysis (**MT**); Markedness (H); Metonymy (H); Polysemy (H); Vygotsky (H)
Lexicalist hypothesis see Interpretive semantics (**MT**)
Lexically triggered veridicality inferences (**H22**)
Lexicase see Case grammar (**MT**)
Lexico-grammar see Metaphor (H)

Lexicography see Discourse markers (H); Frame semantics (**T**); Pragmatic particles (H)
Lexicology see Caste and language (**H23**)
Lexicometry see Critical Linguistics and Critical Discourse Analysis (**MT**)
Lexicon see Collocation and colligation (H); Comprehension vs. production (H); Default interpretations (H); Discourse representation theory (**MT**); Euphemism (**H24**); Feminism and language (**H24**); Interactional linguistics (**T**); Language acquisition (H); Lexically triggered veridicality inferences (**H22**); The multilingual lexicon (H); Obscenity, slurs, and taboo (**H24**); Predicates and predication (H); Word (H)
Lexicostatistics see Historical linguistics (**MT**)
Life stories (H); *see also* Conversational storytelling (**H24**); Narrative (H)
Lifestyle (H)
Linear modification see Communicative dynamism (H)
Linear Unit Grammar (**T**)
Linearization see Word order (H)
Lingua franca see Pragmatics of script (**H22**)
Linguicide see Language ecology (H); Language rights (H)
Linguistic action verb → see Metapragmatic term
Linguistic activism see Feminism and language (**H24**)
Linguistic anthropology see Hymes (**H26**)
Linguistic atlas see Dialectology (**MT**)
Linguistic determinism see Manipulation (H); Perception and language (H)
Linguistic diversity see Heteroglossia (**H26**); Language ecology (H)

Linguistic dominance
see Language ecology (H); Language rights (H)
Linguistic engineering
see Artificial intelligence (MT)
Linguistic explanation (MM); *see also* Functionalism vs. formalism (MT)
Linguistic genocide →
see Linguicide
Linguistic hierarchy see Language dominance and minorization (H)
Linguistic human rights
see Language dominance and minorization (H); Language ecology (H); Language rights (H)
Linguistic imperialism
see Language ecology (H)
Linguistic landscape studies (T)
Linguistic relativity (principle)
see Anthropological linguistics (MT); Boas (H); Cognitive anthropology (MT); Culture (H); Lexical semantics (T); Manipulation (H); 'Other' representation (H); Perception and language (H); Sapir (H); Speech act theory (MT); Taxonomy (MM); Whorf (H)
Linguistic repertoire
see Gumperz (H)
Linguistic turn see Analytical philosophy (MT)
Linking see Conceptual semantics (T)
Listener response (H); *see also* Conversational storytelling (H24)
Literacy (H); *see also* Anderson (H21); Applied linguistics (MT); Channel (H); Computer-mediated communication (H); Identity (H24); Language acquisition (H); Language ideologies (H); Language policy, language planning and standardization (H); Metalinguistic awareness (H); Multilingualism; Orthography and cognition (H22); Social media research (T)
Literary criticism see Figures of speech (H)

Literary pragmatics (MT); *see also* Bakhtin (H); Caste and language (H23); Context and contextualization (H); Creativity in language use (H); Deconstruction (MM); Figures of speech (H); Hermeneutics (M); Narrative (H); Rhetoric (MT); Structuralism (MT); Stylistics (MT)
Localization problem
see Neurolinguistics (MT)
Location see Contact linguistics (MT)
Logic see Generative semantics (MT); Grice (H); Modality (H); Semiotics (MT); Truth-conditional pragmatics (T); Wittgenstein (H)
Logic-based formalism
see Artificial intelligence (MT)
Logical analysis (MM)
Logical atomism see Analytical philosophy (MT)
Logical empiricism/Logical positivism see Analytical philosophy (MT); Grice (H); Morris (H)
Logical notation see Notation in formal semantics (MN)
Logical semantics (MT); *see also* Deontic logic (MT); Discourse representation theory (MT); Epistemic logic (MT); Formal pragmatics (MT); Game-theoretical semantics (MT); Intensional logic (MT); Modal logic (MT); Model-theoretic semantics (MT); Montague and categorial grammar (MT); Ontology (MT); Possible worlds semantics (MT); Situation semantics (MT); Truth-conditional semantics (MT)
Logical typing of communication
see Bateson (H); Communication (H)
Longitudinal method
see Developmental psychology (MT)
Loudness see Prosody (H)
Lying see Truthfulness (H)

M
M-principle see Anaphora (H); Semantics vs. pragmatics (T)
Machine translation
see Translation studies (T)
Macro-sociolinguistics
see Sociolinguistics (MT)
Malinowski, B. K. (H); *see also* Anthropological linguistics (MT); Culture (H); Firthian linguistics (MT); Participation (H); Phatic communion (H)
Manipulation (H); *see also* Truthfulness (H)
Mapping see Cognitive science (MT)
Markedness (H); *see also* Emphasis (H); Language change (H); Negation (H)
Marrism see Marxist linguistics (MT)
Marx, Karl see Bourdieu (H); Ideology (H); Sociology of language (T)
Marxist linguistics (MT); *see also* Critical Linguistics and Critical Discourse Analysis (MT); Halliday (H26)
Mass media (H); *see also* Argumentation in discourse and grammar (H); Channel (H); Communication (H); Conversation analysis (MT); Critical Linguistics and Critical Discourse Analysis (MT); Ideology (H); Manipulation (H); Membership categorization analysis (T); Public discourse (H); Silence (H); Text and discourse linguistics (T)
Matched guise see Methods in language-attitudes research (M)
Materialism see Cognitive science (MT)
Mathematical linguistics
see Communication (H)
Mathesius, V. (H); *see also* Prague school (MT)
Maxims of conversation →
see Cooperative principle
Mead, G. H. see Morris (H); Symbolic interactionism (MT)
Mead, M. see Culture (H)

Meaning see Analytical philosophy (MT); Austin (H); Cohesion and coherence (H); Deixis (H); Emotions (H21); Firth (H); Grice (H); Integrational linguistics (T); Linear Unit Grammar (T); Model-theoretic semantics (MT); Phatic communion (H); Semiotics (MT); Situation semantics (MT); Sound symbolism (H); Truth-conditional pragmatics (T); Wittgenstein (H)
Meaning construction see Cognitive science (MT); Cognitive sociology (MT); Critical Linguistics and Critical Discourse Analysis (MT); Grounded theory (M)
Meaning definition see Predicates and predication (H)
Meaning postulate see Lexical semantics (T)
Meaning potential see Social class and language (H)
Media see Mass media (H)
Media panic see Youth language (H25)
Mediated communication see Globalization (H25); Youth language (H25)
Mediated performatives (H)
Medical interaction see Institutional interaction (H23); Interpreter-mediated interaction (H); Nigerian hospital setting discourse (H24); Therapeutic conversation (H)
Medical language see Applied linguistics (MT); Authority (H)
Medium see Channel (H); Computer-mediated communication (H); Mass media (H); Mediated performatives (H); Multimodality (H); Social media research (T)
Medvedev, P. N. see Bakhtin (H)
Membership categorization see Age and language use (H); Conversational storytelling (H24); Membership categorization analysis (T); Sacks (H)

Membership categorization analysis (T)
Memory see Attention and language (H); Consciousness and language (H); Perception and language (H)
Mental map see Methods in language-attitudes research (M)
Mental spaces (H); *see also* Conceptual integration (H)
Mental states see Experimental pragmatics (M); Language psychology (T)
Mentalism (MT); *see also* Chomskyan linguistics (MT); Cognitive science (MT); Objectivism vs. subjectivism (MT); Philosophy of mind (MT)
Mesolect see Creole linguistics (MT)
Metacommunication see Bateson (H); Gesture research (T)
Metadata see Working with language data (M25)
Metalanguage see Corpus pragmatics (M); Feminism and language (H24); Feminism and language (H24); Impoliteness (H); Methods in language-attitudes research (M); Reported speech (H)
Metalinguistic awareness (H); *see also* Adaptability (H); Collaboration in dialogues (H); Computer-mediated communication (H); Consciousness and language (H); Evolutionary pragmatics (T); Folk pragmatics (T); Language acquisition (H); Language ideologies (H); Literacy (H); Metapragmatics (MT)
Metalinguistic negation see Negation (H)
Metalinguistics see Bakhtin (H)
Metaphor (H); *see also* Cerebral representation of language; Cognitive linguistics (MT); Embodiment (H); Emphasis (H); Euphemism (H24); Experimental pragmatics (M); Figures of speech (H); Gesture research (T); Iconicity (H);

Implicature and language change (H); Language change (H); Metonymy (H); Polysemy (H); Silence (H); Truthfulness (H)
Metaphysics see Grice (H)
Metapragmatic term see Metapragmatics (MT)
Metapragmatics (MT); *see also* Agency and language (H); Aisatsu (H); Anthropological linguistics (MT); Cerebral representation of language; Folk pragmatics (T); Halliday (H26); Humor (H23); Interactional sociolinguistics (MT); Language ideologies (H); Metalinguistic awareness (H); Teasing (H25); Wakimae (H26)
Methods in language-attitudes research (M)
Metonymy (H); *see also* Euphemism (H24); Figures of speech (H); Implicature and language change (H); Lexical semantics (T); Metaphor (H); Polysemy (H); Speech act
Metrolingualism see Heteroglossia (H26); Transience (H22)
Mey, J. see Activity types and pragmatic acts (H26)
Mianzi / lian (H21)
Micro-sociolinguistics see Sociolinguistics (MT)
Micro-sociology see Social psychology (MT)
Mind-body problem see Philosophy of mind (MT)
Minority see Language dominance and minorization (H); Language ecology (H); Language rights (H); Linguistic landscape studies (T); 'Other' representation (H)
Misunderstanding see Communicative success vs. failure (H); Truthfulness (H)
Mitigation see Laughter (H)
Mixed languages see Language contact (H)
Mixed methods see Social media research (T)
Mobility see Globalization (H25); Transience (H22)

Modal logic (MT); *see also* Deontic logic (MT); Epistemic logic (MT); Logical semantics (MT)
Modal particle see Pragmatic particles (H)
Modality (H); *see also* Appraisal (H); Authority (H); Énonciation (H); Event representation (H22); Evidentiality (H22); Implicature and language change (H); Lexically triggered veridicality inferences (H22); Modal logic (MT); Signed language pragmatics (T)
Mode see Firth (H); Multimodality (H); Social semiotics (T)
Model-theoretic semantics (MT); *see also* Game-theoretical semantics (MT); Logical semantics (MT); Montague and categorial grammar (MT); Notation in formal semantics (MN); Possible worlds semantics (MT); Situation semantics (MT)
Modeling see Regression analysis (M)
Modularity → see Cerebral representation of language; Clinical pragmatics (T); Cognitive psychology (MT); Cognitive science (MT); Conceptual semantics (T); Irony (H); Language acquisition (H); Psycholinguistics (MT)
Monolingualism see Language dominance and minorization (H)
Monologizing see Interpreter-mediated interaction (H)
Monologue see Think-aloud protocols (M)
Monosemy see Polysemy (H)
Montague and categorial grammar (MT); *see also* Discourse representation theory (MT); Formal pragmatics (MT); Intensional logic (MT); Logical semantics (MT); Model-theoretic semantics (MT)
Moore, G. E. see Analytical philosophy (MT)

Morpheme see Orthography and cognition (H22)
Morphology see Deixis (H); Discourse markers (H); Euphemism (H24); Jakobson (H21); Language change (H); Morphopragmatics (T); Word (H)
Morphopragmatics (T)
Morris, C. (H)
Motherese see Register (H)
Motivation (H)
Motivation and language (H)
Move see Predicates and predication (H); Therapeutic conversation (H)
MTA see Tense and aspect (H)
Multi-party talk see Collaboration in dialogues (H); Conversation types (H)
Multiculturalism see Culture (H)
Multifunctionality see Pragmatic markers (H)
Multilingual lexicon (The) (H)
Multilingualism see Bilingualism and multilingualism (H); Code-switching (H); Code-switching and translanguaging (H22); Creativity in language use (H); Language contact (H); Language ecology (H); Linguistic landscape studies (T); Literacy (H); The multilingual lexicon (H); Power and the role of language (H25); Translanguaging pedagogy (T)
Multimodality (H); *see also* Computational pragmatics (T); Computer-mediated communication (H); Embodied interaction (H23); Embodiment (H); Emphasis (H); Genre (H); Historical politeness (T); Metaphor (H); Social semiotics (T); Translation studies (T)
Multiscriptality see Pragmatics of script (H22)
Multisensoriality see Embodied interaction (H23)
Multivoicedness see Heteroglossia (H26)
Mutual knowledge see Common ground (H)

N
Name see Linguistic landscape studies (T); Reference and descriptions (H); Socio-onomastics (T)
Narrative (H); *see also* Appraisal (H); Collaboration in dialogues (H); Conversational storytelling (H24); Emotion display (H); Ervin-Tripp, S. (H24); Grounded theory (M); Grounding (H); Metalinguistic awareness (H); Reported speech (H); Sequence (H); Text and discourse linguistics (T); Text type (H)
Narratology see Semiotics (MT); Text and discourse linguistics (T)
Nationalism see Anderson (H21); Identity (H24); Language dominance and minorization (H)
Native-nonnative interaction see Discourse markers (H); Intercultural communication (H)
Nativism see Authenticity (H); Language acquisition (H)
Natural history of discourse see Metalinguistic awareness (H)
Natural language generation and interpretation → see Natural language processing
Natural language processing see Artificial intelligence (MT); Borrowing (H); Cognitive psychology (MT); Computational linguistics (MT); Connectionism (MT); The multilingual lexicon (H); Psycholinguistics (MT)
Natural logic see Argumentation theory (MT)
Natural semantic metalanguage see Componential analysis (MT)
Naturalness see Authenticity (H); Language change (H)
Nature vs. nurture see Cognitive science (MT)
Negation (H); *see also* Indeterminacy and

negotiation (**H**); Lexically triggered veridicality inferences (**H22**); Modality (**H**); Polyphony (**H**); Truthfulness (**H**)
Negotiation see Activity types and pragmatic acts (H26); Adaptability (**H**); Applied linguistics (**MT**); Indeterminacy and negotiation (**H**); Prosody (**H**); Truthfulness (**H**)
Neo-Gricean pragmatics see Anaphora (**H**); Grice (**H**); Implicature and language change (**H**); Semantics vs. pragmatics (**T**)
Neo-Kaplanean semantics see Semantics vs. pragmatics (**T**)
Neogrammarians see Historical linguistics (**MT**); Lexical field analysis (**MT**); Prague school (**MT**); Reconstruction (**MM**); de Saussure (**H**)
Neoliberalism see Ideology (**H**)
Network (social) see Computer-mediated communication (**H**); Language change (**H**); Social media research (**T**)
Neuroimaging → see Brain imaging
Neurolinguistic programming see General semantics (**MT**)
Neurolinguistics (**MT**); *see also* Adaptability (**H**); Bilingualism and multilingualism (**H**); Cerebral representation of language; Clinical pragmatics (**T**); Emotions (**H21**); Language acquisition (**H**); Perception and language (**H**)
Neurophysiology see Connectionism (**MT**); Irony (**H**); Neurolinguistics (**MT**); Neuropragmatics (**T**)
Neuropragmatics (**T**); *see also* Clinical pragmatics (**T**)
Neuropsychology see Cognitive science (**MT**); Perception and language (**H**)
New Left see Bourdieu (**H**)
New rhetoric see Argumentation theory (**MT**); Genre (**H**); Rhetoric (**MT**)

News interview see Mass media (**H**)
Newspaper see Mass media (**H**)
Nexus analysis (**T**); *see also* Bourdieu (**H**)
Nigerian hospital setting discourse (**H24**); *see also* Clinical pragmatics (**T**); Institutional interaction (**H23**); Social institutions (**H**); Therapeutic conversation (**H**)
Nominalization see Predicates and predication (**H**)
Non-literal meaning see Neuropragmatics (**T**); Swearing (**H25**)
Non-modular grammar see Construction grammar (**MT**)
Non-seriousness see Laughter (**H**)
Non-verbal communication (**H**); *see also* Channel (**H**); Cultural scripts (**H**); Frame analysis (**M**); Gesture research (**T**)
Normality see Ethnomethodology (**MT**)
Norms see Creativity in language use (**H**); Ethnomethodology (**MT**); Methods in language-attitudes research (**M**); Power and the role of language (**H25**); Workplace interaction (**H25**)
Notation in formal semantics (**MN**)
Notation Systems in Spoken Language Corpora (**N**); *see also* Transcription systems for spoken discourse (**MN**)
Noun phrase see Situation semantics (**MT**)
Novelty see Creativity in language use (**H**)

O

Object language see Metalinguistic awareness (**H**)
Objectivism vs. subjectivism (**MT**); *see also* Behaviorism (**MT**); Epistemology (**MT**); Foucault (**H**); Mentalism (**MT**)

Obscenity, slurs, and taboo (**H24**); *see also* Euphemism (**H24**); Swearing (**H25**)
Observation see Cognitive science (**MT**); Culture (**H**); Fieldwork (**MM**); Regression analysis (**M**)
Offence see Obscenity, slurs, and taboo (**H24**); Swearing (**H25**)
Omolúàbí (**H**)
Online communication see Chronotope (**H25**); Complaining (**H25**); Computer-mediated communication (**H**); Youth language (**H25**)
Onomastics see Socio-onomastics (**T**)
Ontic relation see Legitimation Code Theory (**T25**)
Ontology (**MT**); *see also* Epistemology (**MT**); Logical semantics (**MT**)
Opacity see Mental spaces (**H**)
Open science see Working with language data (**M25**)
Operationism see Behaviorism (**MT**)
Optimality theory see Default interpretations (**H**)
Orality see Channel (**H**)
Orders (of discourse) see Critical Linguistics and Critical Discourse Analysis (**MT**); Ideology (**H**); Workplace interaction (**H25**)
Ordinary language philosophy see Analytical philosophy (**MT**); Conversational logic (**MT**); Grice (**H**); Indeterminacy and negotiation (**H**); Metalinguistic awareness (**H**); Metapragmatics (**MT**); (The) pragmatic perspective (**M**); Pragmatism (**MT**); Speech act theory (**MT**); Wittgenstein (**H**)
Organizational setting see Social institutions (**H**)
Organon model see Bühler (**H**)
Orientalism see Postcolonial pragmatics (**T**)
Origins of language see Cognitive anthropology (**MT**); Evolutionary pragmatics (**T**); Humboldt (**H**)
Orthography see Developmental dyslexia (**H**); Orthography and

cognition (H22); Pragmatics of script (H22)
Orthography and cognition (H22); *see also* Pragmatics of script (H22)
'Other' representation (H); *see also* Age and language use (H)
Other(ing) see Authority (H); Crossing (H26); Mianzi / lian (H21); 'Other' representation (H)
Other-repair see Repair (H)
Overhearer → see Audience
Overlap (H)

P

Paralanguage → see Cerebral representation of language; Non-verbal communication (H)
Paraphrase semantics see Componential analysis (MT)
Parole → see Langue vs. parole
Parsing see Computational linguistics (MT)
Participant observation → see Observation
Participation (H); *see also* Frame analysis (M); Goffman (H)
Participation framework see Participation (H)
Pêcheux, M. see Marxist linguistics (MT)
Peirce, C. S. (H); *see also* Iconicity (H); Morris (H); Pragmatism (MT); Semiotics (MT); Sign (H)
Pejorative see Morphopragmatics (T); 'Other' representation (H)
Perception and language (H); *see also* Austin (H); Embodiment (H); Iconicity (H); Language acquisition (H)
Perceptron see Connectionism (MT); Psycholinguistics (MT)
Performance see Computer-mediated communication (H)
Performativity see Austin (H); Benveniste (H); Mediated performatives (H); Metalinguistic awareness (H); Speech act theory (MT)

Perlocution see Intentionality (H); Speech act theory (MT)
Persian see Ta'ārof (H22)
Persistence see Obscenity, slurs, and taboo (H24)
Person reference see Wakimae (H26)
Personality see Sapir (H)
Perspectives on language and cognition (H)
Persuasion see Manipulation (H)
Phatic communion (H); *see also* Anthropological linguistics (MT); Ethnography of speaking (MT); Evolutionary pragmatics (T); Firthian linguistics (MT); Malinowski (H); Participation (H)
Phenomenology (MT); *see also* Austin (H); Embodiment (H); Ethnomethodology (MT); Semiotics (MT)
Philosophy of action (MT); *see also* Action theory (MT); Austin (H)
Philosophy of language (MT); *see also* Analytical philosophy (MT); Austin (H); Conversational logic (MT); Emotions (H21); Humboldt (H); (The) pragmatic perspective (M); Speech act theory (MT); Wittgenstein (H)
Philosophy of mind (MT); *see also* Cognitive science (MT); Grice (H); Mentalism (MT)
Phoneme see Orthography and cognition (H22)
Phonetic notation systems (N)
Phonetics see Boas (H); Discourse markers (H); de Saussure (H)
Phonology see Developmental dyslexia (H); Euphemism (H24); Jakobson (H21); Structuralism (MT)
Phrase-structure grammar see Chomskyan linguistics (MT); Computational linguistics (MT)
Physical symbol system see Artificial intelligence (MT); Cognitive psychology (MT); Cognitive science (MT)

Picture-theory of meaning see Wittgenstein (H)
Pidgins and pidginization see Contact (H); Contact linguistics (MT); Creole linguistics (MT); Creoles and creolization (H); Intercultural communication (H)
Pitch see Prosody (H)
Plagiarism → see Authorship
Planning see Computational pragmatics (T)
Pluricentric languages (H23)
Poetic language see Figures of speech (H); Grounding (H)
Poetics see Bakhtin (H)
Point of view see Grounding (H)
Polarity see Negation (H)
Police interrogation see Applied linguistics (MT); Forensic linguistics (T); Interpreter-mediated interaction (H)
Politeness (H); *see also* Aisatsu (H); Conversational implicature (H); Conversational logic (MT); Directive (H26); Goffman (H); Historical politeness (T); Historical pragmatics (T); Honorifics (H); Implicitness (H); Impoliteness (H); Interlanguage pragmatics (T); Leech (H); Mianzi / lian (H21); Morphopragmatics (T); Obscenity, slurs, and taboo (H24); Silence (H); Social media research (T); Swearing (H25); Ta'ārof (H22); Teasing (H25); Terms of address (H); Truthfulness (H); Universals (H23); Wakimae (H26)
Political correctness see Euphemism (H24); 'Other' representation (H)
Political language see Authority (H)
Political linguistics see Critical Linguistics and Critical Discourse Analysis (MT)
Polylanguaging see Transience (H22)
Polylingualism see Heteroglossia (H26)

Polyphony (H); *see also* Appraisal (H); Bakhtin (H); Collaboration in dialogues (H); Dialogical analysis (MM); Heteroglossia (H26)
Polysemy (H); *see also* Implicature and language change (H); Indeterminacy and negotiation (H)
Polysystemic analysis see Firth (H)
Positioning see Evidentiality (H22); Social media research (T); Stance (H21)
Positivism see Sociology of language (T)
Possible worlds semantics (MT); *see also* Epistemic logic (MT); Logical semantics (MT); Model-theoretic semantics (MT); Truth-conditional semantics (MT)
Postcolonial pragmatics (T); *see also* Caste and language (H23); Critical Linguistics and Critical Discourse Analysis (MT); Hegemony (H23); Ideology (H)
Postcolonial studies see Caste and language (H23); Postcolonial pragmatics (T)
Postcolonialism →
Postmodernism see Postcolonial pragmatics (T)
Poststructuralism see Critical Linguistics and Critical Discourse Analysis (MT); Deconstruction (MM)
Posture see Non-verbal communication (H); Ta'ārof (H22)
Power and the role of language (H25); *see also* Authority (H); Cognitive sociology (MT); Critical Linguistics and Critical Discourse Analysis (MT); Foucault (H); Gumperz (H); Honorifics (H); Ideology (H); Manipulation (H); Metalinguistic awareness (H); Nigerian hospital setting discourse (H24); Politeness (H); Postcolonial pragmatics (T); Silence (H); Social institutions (H)

Pract see Activity types and pragmatic acts (H26)
Practice (theory) see Agency and language (H); Nexus analysis (T); Social class and language (H)
Pragma-dialectics see Argumentation theory (MT)
Pragmalinguistics see Leech (H)
Pragmastylistics see Stylistics (MT)
Pragmatic acquisition (H); *see also* Cognitive psychology (MT); Developmental dyslexia (H); Developmental psychology (MT); Experimental pragmatics (M); Experimentation (MM); Language acquisition (H); Psycholinguistics (MT)
Pragmatic enrichment see Truth-conditional pragmatics (T)
Pragmatic explanation see Linguistic explanation (MM)
Pragmatic function see Functional grammar (MT)
Pragmatic impairment see Clinical pragmatics (T)
Pragmatic intrusion see Semantics vs. pragmatics (T)
Pragmatic markers (H); *see also* Discourse markers (H); Pragmatic particles (H)
Pragmatic norm see Interlanguage pragmatics (T)
Pragmatic particles (H); *see also* Discourse markers (H); Interjections (H)
Pragmatic perspective (The) (M)
Pragmatic scale → see Scalarity
Pragmatic transfer see Interlanguage pragmatics (T)
Pragmaticalization see Pragmatic markers (H)
Pragmaticism see Evolutionary pragmatics (T); Morris (H); Objectivism vs. subjectivism (MT); Pragmatism (MT)
Pragmatics → see Cognitive pragmatics; Corpus pragmatics (M); Experimental

pragmatics (M); Folk pragmatics (T); Formal pragmatics (MT); Historical pragmatics (T); Interlanguage pragmatics (T); Literary pragmatics (MT); Metapragmatics (MT); Neo-Gricean pragmatics; Neuropragmatics (T); Postcolonial pragmatics (T); (The) pragmatic perspective (M); Pragmatics of script (H22); Semantics vs. pragmatics (T); Truth-conditional pragmatics (T); Variational pragmatics (T)
Pragmatics of script (H22)
Pragmatism (MT); *see also* Morris (H); Peirce (H); Semiotics (MT)
Pragmemes (H22); *see also* Activity types and pragmatic acts (H26)
Prague school (MT); *see also* Communicative dynamism (H); Functional grammar (MT); Functional sentence perspective (H); Halliday (H26); Markedness (H); Mathesius (H); Structuralism (MT); Text and discourse linguistics (T); Text linguistics (MT); Word order (H)
Pre-request see Directive (H26)
Precisification principle see Indeterminacy and negotiation (H)
Predicate logic see Artificial intelligence (MT); Notation in formal semantics (MN)
Predicates and predication (H); *see also* Event representation (H22); Lexically triggered veridicality inferences (H22)
Preference organization see Complaining (H25); Repair (H); Sequence (H)
Prejudice see 'Other' representation (H)
Prestige see Language dominance and minorization (H)
Presumptive meaning see Default interpretations (H)
Presupposition (H); *see also* Argumentation in discourse

and grammar (**H**); Context and contextualization (**H**); Discourse representation theory (**MT**); Formal pragmatics (**MT**); Implicitness (**H**); Mental spaces (**H**); Truthfulness (**H**)
Primate communication (**H**)
Priming
see Psycholinguistics (**MT**)
Print see Channel (**H**)
Private language
see Wittgenstein (**H**)
Probabilistic technique
see Statistics (**MM**)
Problematization
see Foucault (**H**)
Problematology
see Argumentation theory (**MT**); Rhetoric (**MT**)
Procedural semantics
see Cognitive psychology (**MT**)
Processing see Comprehension vs. production (**H**); Inferencing; Information processing; Production; Text comprehension (**H**)
Production see Conceptual semantics (**T**); Psycholinguistics (**MT**)
Productivity see Creativity in language use (**H**)
Projection problem
see Presupposition (**H**)
Pronoun see Anaphora (**H**); Creole linguistics (**MT**); Humboldt (**H**); Negation (**H**); Ta'ārof (H22)
Proper name → see Name
Property theory see Intensional logic (**MT**)
Propositional attitude
see Discourse representation theory (**MT**); Intensional logic (**MT**)
Propositional semantics
see Evolutionary pragmatics (**T**)
Prosody (**H**); *see also* Cerebral representation of language; Emphasis (**H**); Firth (**H**); Gumperz (**H**); Information structure (**H**); Interactional linguistics (**T**); Language acquisition (**H**)
Proto-grammar see Iconicity (**H**)
Prototype (theory)
see Categorization (**H**);

Cognitive linguistics (**MT**); Dependency and valency grammar (**MT**); Language acquisition (**H**); Lexical semantics (**T**); Polysemy (**H**); Taxonomy (**MM**)
Proxemics see Non-verbal communication (**H**)
Psychiatry see Bateson (**H**); Therapeutic conversation (**H**)
Psycholinguistics (**MT**); *see also* Bilingualism and multilingualism (**H**); Borrowing (**H**); Bühler (**H**); Cognitive psychology (**MT**); Comprehension vs. production (**H**); Connectionism (**MT**); Developmental psychology (**MT**); Ervin-Tripp, S. (**H24**); Experimental pragmatics (**M**); Experimentation (**MM**); Gesture research (**T**); Language psychology (**T**); The multilingual lexicon (**H**); Non-verbal communication (**H**); Perception and language (**H**); (The) pragmatic perspective (**M**); Text comprehension (**H**); Translation studies (**T**); Vygotsky (**H**)
Psychological anthropology
see Cognitive anthropology (**MT**)
Psychosemantics see Philosophy of mind (**MT**)
Psychotherapy → see Psychiatry
Public discourse (**H**); *see also* Goffman (**H**); Mediated performatives (**H**); Social institutions (**H**)
Putnam, H. see Analytical philosophy (**MT**)

Q
Q-principle see Anaphora (**H**); Semantics vs. pragmatics (**T**)
Qualitative methods
see Grounded theory (**M**)
Quantifier see Model-theoretic semantics (**MT**); Notation in formal semantics (**MN**)
Quantitative method
see Regression analysis (**M**); Statistics (**MM**)

Question answering
see Computational pragmatics (**T**); Tactile sign languages (H21)
Question word see Repair (**H**)
Questionnaire
see Interview (**MM**)
Quine, W.v.O. see Reported speech (**H**)
Quotation see Analytical philosophy (**MT**); Evidentiality (H22)

R
Race see Caste and language (H23)
Racism see Ideology (**H**); Obscenity, slurs, and taboo (H24); 'Other' representation (**H**)
Radical argumentativism
see Argumentation theory (**MT**)
Radical pragmatics see Grice (**H**)
Radio see Mass media (**H**)
Rampton, B. see Crossing (H26)
Ranking task see Methods in language-attitudes research (**M**)
Rationality see Default interpretations (**H**); Emotions (H21); Ethnomethodology (**MT**); Foucault (**H**); Grice (**H**); Ideology (**H**)
Reading analysis see Critical Linguistics and Critical Discourse Analysis (**MT**); Text comprehension (**H**)
Recall see Collaboration in dialogues (**H**)
Reception theory see Literary pragmatics (**MT**)
Recipient design
see Collaboration in dialogues (**H**); Communicative style (**H**)
Reconstruction (**MM**); *see also* Dialectology (**MT**); Historical linguistics (**MT**); Language change (**H**)
Recording see Working with language data (M25)
Recoverability see Ellipsis (**H**)
Reference see Anaphora (**H**); Definiteness (**H**); Experimental pragmatics (**M**); Functional discourse grammar (**T**);

Functional grammar (MT); Information structure (H); Mental spaces (H); Metalinguistic awareness (H); Model-theoretic semantics (MT); Polysemy (H); Pragmemes (H22); Predicates and predication (H); Reference and descriptions (H); Tagmemics (MT); Universals (H23)
Reference and descriptions (H)
Referential choice see Definiteness (H)
Referring → see Reference; Reference and descriptions (H)
Reflection see Communicative success vs. failure (H); Humboldt (H)
Reflexive see Anaphora (H)
Reflexivity see Adaptability (H); Ethnomethodology (MT); Foucault (H); Metalinguistic awareness (H); 'Other' representation (H); Style and styling (H21)
Reflexology see Behaviorism (MT)
Refusal see Ta'ārof (H22)
Register (H); *see also* Applied linguistics (MT); Channel (H); Context and contextualization (H); Correlational sociolinguistics (T); Error analysis (MM); Firthian linguistics (MT); Frame analysis (M); Gumperz (H); Halliday (**H26**); Honorifics (H); Intercultural communication (H); Regression analysis (M); Rhetoric (MT); Sociolinguistics (MT); Stylistics (MT); Systemic functional grammar (MT)
Regression analysis (M); *see also* Statistics (MM)
Regularity see Relational ritual (H)
Reinforcement see Emphasis (H)
Relational grammar see Lexical functional grammar (MT)
Relational ritual (H)
Relevance see Computational pragmatics (T); Conversation analysis (MT); Conversational logic (MT); Irony (H); Relevance theory (MT)
Relevance theory (MT); *see also* Anaphora (H); Clinical pragmatics (T); Communication (H); Conversational implicature (H); Conversational logic (MT); Emotions (**H21**); Experimental pragmatics (M); Humor (**H23**); Manipulation (H); Semantics vs. pragmatics (T); Tense and aspect (H); Truth-conditional pragmatics (T); Truth-conditional semantics (MT); Truthfulness (H)
Religion see Authority (H); Caste and language (H23)
Repair (H); *see also* Communicative success vs. failure (H); Conversation analysis (MT); Conversational storytelling (**H24**); Prosody (H); Sequence (H)
Repertoire → see Linguistic repertoire
Repetition see Emergent grammar (T)
Reported speech (H); *see also* Énonciation (H); Evidentiality (**H22**); Intertextuality (H)
Representation see Adaptability (H); Conceptual semantics (T); Event representation (H22); Evolutionary pragmatics (T); Foucault (H); Iconicity (H); Indeterminacy and negotiation (H); Intentionality (H); Metalinguistic awareness (H); 'Other' representation (H); Psycholinguistics (MT); Social psychology (MT); Truthfulness (H); Wittgenstein (H)
Request see Directive (H26)
Requests see Directive (H26)
Research ethics see Working with language data (M25)
Resistance see Power and the role of language (H25); Therapeutic conversation (H)
Resource see Multimodality (H)
Respect → see Deference
Response see Complaining (H25); Conversational storytelling (H24); Listener response (H); Obscenity, slurs, and taboo (H24); Ọmọlúàbí (H); Teasing (H25)
Response cry see Emotion display (H); Goffman (H)
Responsibility see Austin (H); Membership categorization analysis (T)
Responsiveness see Social media research (T)
Rheme → see Theme vs. rheme
Rhetoric (MT); *see also* Argumentation theory (MT); Figures of speech (H); Functional discourse grammar (T); Genre (H); Gesture research (T); Literary pragmatics (MT); Manipulation (H); Metalinguistic awareness (H); Narrative (H); Social psychology (MT); Stylistics (MT); Text and discourse linguistics (T)
Rhetorical relations see Discourse representation theory (MT)
Rhetorical structure theory see Artificial intelligence (MT); Computational pragmatics (T); Text and discourse linguistics (T)
Ritual see Goffman (H); Relational ritual (H)
Role and reference grammar (MT); *see also* Case and semantic roles (H); Case grammar (MT); Dependency and valency grammar (MT)
Role vs. value see Mental spaces (H)
Rossi-Landi, F. see Morris (H)
Routine (formula) see Aisatsu (H); Impoliteness (H); Ọmọlúàbí (H); Relational ritual (H); Swearing (H25)
Routinization see Emergent grammar (T); Nigerian hospital setting discourse (H24)
Rule see Ethnomethodology (MT); Psycholinguistics (MT); Speech act theory (MT); Wittgenstein (H)

Rule-based formalism
see Artificial intelligence (MT)
Russell, B. see Analytical philosophy (MT); Definiteness (H); Reference and descriptions (H)
Russian formalism
see Deconstruction (MM); Literary pragmatics (MT); Prague school (MT); Semiotics (MT); Stylistics (MT); Text and discourse linguistics (T)

S
Sacks, H. (H); *see also* Conversation analysis (**MT**)
Sales encounter see Institutional interaction (H23)
Salience see Anaphora (H); Emphasis (H); Experimental pragmatics (M); Grounding (H); Irony (H); Word order (H)
Sameness see Youth language (H25)
Sampling → see Data collection
Sapir, E. (H); *see also* Anthropological linguistics (**MT**); Boas (H); Culture (H); Whorf (H)
Sapir-Whorf hypothesis → see Linguistic relativity principle
Sarcasm see Irony (H)
Saturation see Truth-conditional pragmatics (T)
Saussure, F. de (H); *see also* Geneva school (**MT**); Participation (H); Sign (H); Structuralism (**MT**)
Scalarity see Conceptual integration (H); Experimental pragmatics (M); Implicitness (H); Negation (H)
Scale see Chronotope (H25)
Scale and category grammar see Systemic functional grammar (MT)
Scaling see Pragmatics of script (H22)
Scenario see Frame semantics (T); Lexical semantics (T)
Scene see Frame semantics (T); Lexical semantics (T)

Scene-and-frame semantics see Frame semantics (T)
Schema see Cognitive science (MT); Frame analysis (M)
Schizophrenia see Clinical pragmatics (T)
Schooling see Aisatsu (H); Language acquisition (H)
Scientific language see Analytical philosophy (MT); Applied linguistics (MT); Text comprehension (H)
Script1 see Orthography and cognition (H22); Pragmatics of script (H22)
Script2 see Cognitive science (MT); Frame analysis (M); Frame semantics (T); Humor (H23)
Searle, J. R. see Analytical philosophy (MT); Contextualism (T); Intentionality (H); Reference and descriptions (H); Speech act theory (MT)
Second language acquisition see Applied linguistics (MT); Contact linguistics (MT); Conversational storytelling (H24); Ervin-Tripp, S. (H24); Intercultural communication (H); Interlanguage pragmatics (T); Language learning in immersion and CLIL classrooms (H); Motivation (H); The multilingual lexicon (H); Silence (H); Text comprehension (H)
Securitization see Power and the role of language (H25)
Selection restrictions see Predicates and predication (H)
Self see Authenticity (H); Authority (H); Goffman (H); Laughter (H); Life stories (H); Mianzi / lian (H21)
Self-discipline see Power and the role of language (H25)
Self-repair see Repair (H)
Self-report see Methods in language-attitudes research (M)
Semantic density
see Legitimation Code Theory (T25)

Semantic differential see Social psychology (MT)
Semantic field analysis
see Lexical field analysis (MT)
Semantic gravity see Legitimation Code Theory (T25)
Semantic minimalism
see Contextualism (T)
Semantic network see Artificial intelligence (MT)
Semantic primitive
see Componential analysis (MT); Cultural scripts (H)
Semantic structure see Role and reference grammar (MT)
Semantics vs. pragmatics (T); *see also* Anaphora (H); Cerebral representation of language; Discourse representation theory (**MT**); Emotions (**H21**); Generative semantics (**MT**); Grice (H); Implicitness (**H**); Indeterminacy and negotiation (H); Leech (H); Metalinguistic awareness (H); Metaphor (H); Montague and categorial grammar (**MT**); Reference and descriptions (H); Semiotics (**MT**); Structuralism (**MT**); Truth-conditional pragmatics (T)
Semiology see Integrational linguistics (T); de Saussure (H); Semiotics (MT)
Semiophysics see Catastrophe theory (MT)
Semiotic resource see Social semiotics (T)
Semiotics (**MT**); *see also* Bakhtin (H); Benveniste (H); Iconicity (**H**); Morris (H); Peirce (**H**); (The) pragmatic perspective (**M**); Pragmatism (**MT**); Sign (H); Social semiotics (T); Speech community (H)
Sense see Analytical philosophy (MT); Polysemy (H)
Sensorimotor dysfunction
see Clinical pragmatics (T)
Sensuous theory →
Sentence fragment
see Ellipsis (H)

Sentence grammar → see Cerebral representation of language
Sentence linearity see Communicative dynamism (H)
Sentence processing see The multilingual lexicon (H)
Sentence type see Markedness (H)
Sequence (H); *see also* Chronotope (H25); Conversation analysis (MT); Embodied interaction (H23); Grounding (H); Language and the law (H); Notation Systems in Spoken Language Corpora (N); Prosody (H); Relational ritual (H); Repair (H); Stance (H21); Therapeutic conversation (H)
Sequencing see Sequence (H)
Sequentiality see Iconicity (H)
Sexism see Feminism and language (H24); Obscenity, slurs, and taboo (H24)
Sexual orientation see Silence (H)
Shared knowledge see Common ground (H)
Shibboleth see Anderson (H21)
Sign (H); *see also* Evolutionary pragmatics (T); Iconicity (H); Integrational linguistics (T); Morris (H); de Saussure (H); Semiotics (MT); Signed language pragmatics (T); Social semiotics (T); Speech community (H)
Sign language(s) see Language ecology (H); Non-verbal communication (H); Tactile sign languages (H21)
Signed language pragmatics (T)
Silence (H)
Silencing see 'Other' representation (H); Silence (H)
Simile see Metaphor (H)
Simmel, Georg see Sociology of language (T)
Sincerity see Authenticity (H); Truthfulness (H)
Singular term see Indexicals and demonstratives (H)
Situated action theory see Cognitive science (MT)
Situation semantics (MT); *see also* Communication (H); Discourse representation theory (MT); Logical semantics (MT); Model-theoretic semantics (MT)
Slang see Jargon (H)
Sluicing see Ellipsis (H)
Slur see Obscenity, slurs, and taboo (H24)
Smith, Adam see Sociology of language (T)
Social anthropology see Anthropological linguistics (MT); Cognitive anthropology (MT)
Social class and language (H); *see also* Caste and language (H23)
Social cognition see Bühler (H); Language psychology (T); Social psychology (MT); Style and styling (H21)
Social difference/inequality see Power and the role of language (H25)
Social distancing see 'Other' representation (H)
Social dynamics see Obscenity, slurs, and taboo (H24)
Social institutions (H); *see also* Applied linguistics (MT); Authority (H); Cognitive sociology (MT); Communication (H); Conversation types (H); Forensic linguistics (T); Frame analysis (M); Institutional interaction (H23); Intercultural communication (H); Narrative (H); Nigerian hospital setting discourse (H24); Politeness (H); Public discourse (H); Therapeutic conversation (H)
Social media research (T)
Social organization see Aisatsu (H); Authority (H); Cognitive sociology (MT)
Social psychology (MT); *see also* Accommodation theory (MT); Bilingualism and multilingualism (H); Conversation analysis (MT); Ethnomethodology (MT); Language psychology (T); Methods in language-attitudes research (M); Motivation (H); Nexus analysis (T); Overlap (H); Symbolic interactionism (MT); Terms of address (H)
Social relation see Legitimation Code Theory (T25)
Social relationship → see Social organization
Social science see Grounded theory (M)
Social semiotics (T); *see also* Appraisal (H); Critical Linguistics and Critical Discourse Analysis (MT); Critical theory (MT); Linguistic landscape studies (T); Literary pragmatics (MT); Multimodality (H); Semiotics (MT); Sign (H)
Socialization see Aisatsu (H); Developmental psychology (MT); Vygotsky (H)
Socio-onomastics (T)
Sociolect see Dialect (H); Heteroglossia (H26)
Sociolinguistics (MT); *see also* Anthropological linguistics (MT); Applied linguistics (MT); Bilingualism and multilingualism (H); Code-switching (H); Code-switching and translanguaging (H22); Cognitive sociology (MT); Contact linguistics (MT); Correlational sociolinguistics (T); Creole linguistics (MT); Creoles and creolization (H); Dialectology (MT); Ervin-Tripp, S. (H24); Gumperz (H); Hymes (H26); Interactional sociolinguistics (MT); Language contact (H); Language dominance and minorization (H); Language maintenance and shift (H21); Language policy, language planning and standardization (H); Lifestyle (H); Linguistic landscape studies (T); Metalinguistic awareness (H); Methods in language-attitudes research (M); Pragmatic markers (H); (The) pragmatic perspective (M); Social class and language (H); Social media research (T); Speech

community (**H**);
Superdiversity (**H21**);
Transience (**H22**);
Translanguaging pedagogy (**T**)
Sociology see Bourdieu (**H**);
Cognitive sociology (**MT**);
Goffman (**H**); Gumperz (**H**);
Sociology of language (**T**)
Sociology of language (**T**); *see also* Dialectology (**MT**);
Methods in language-attitudes research (**M**);
Sociolinguistics (**MT**)
Sociopragmatics see Leech (**H**)
Sociosemiotics see Social semiotics (**T**)
Sonority see Language change (**H**)
Sound symbolism (**H**); *see also* Iconicity (**H**)
Speaker vs. listener
see Comprehension vs. production (**H**); Dialogical analysis (**MM**);
Manipulation (**H**);
Participation (**H**); Terms of address (**H**); Truthfulness (**H**)
Speaker's meaning
see Evidentiality (**H22**); Speech act theory (**MT**)
Speaking vs. writing see Applied linguistics (**MT**); Channel (**H**);
Communicative style (**H**);
Computer-mediated communication (**H**);
Integrational linguistics (**T**);
Language acquisition (**H**);
Notation Systems in Spoken Language Corpora (**N**);
Pragmatics of script (**H22**);
Register (**H**); de Saussure (**H**);
Text and discourse linguistics (**T**)
Specialization see Legitimation Code Theory (**T25**)
Speech accommodation
see Accommodation theory (**MT**); Social psychology (**MT**)
Speech act see Adaptability (**H**);
Adaptability (**H**);
Argumentation theory (**MT**);
Austin (**H**); Cerebral representation of language;
Conventions of language (**H**);
Directive (**H26**); Formal pragmatics (**MT**); Grice (**H**);
Historical pragmatics (**T**);

Intercultural communication (**H**);
Interlanguage pragmatics (**T**);
Mediated performatives (**H**);
Metonymy (**H**); Modality (**H**);
Morphopragmatics (**T**);
Neuropragmatics (**T**); Non-verbal communication (**H**);
Politeness (**H**); Pragmatic particles (**H**); Speech act theory (**MT**); Truth-conditional pragmatics (**T**);
Universals (**H23**); Workplace interaction (**H25**)
Speech act classification
see Speech act theory (**MT**)
Speech act theory (**MT**); *see also* Analytical philosophy (**MT**);
Artificial intelligence (**MT**);
Austin (**H**); Benveniste (**H**);
Clinical pragmatics (**T**);
Conversational implicature (**H**);
Conversational logic (**MT**);
Directive (**H26**);
Indeterminacy and negotiation (**H**);
Intentionality (**H**); Language and the law (**H**); Philosophy of language (**MT**); (The) pragmatic perspective (**M**);
Truthfulness (**H**)
Speech circuit
see Participation (**H**)
Speech community (**H**); *see also* Anderson (**H21**); Computer-mediated communication (**H**);
Gumperz (**H**);
Superdiversity (**H21**)
Speech event see Directive (**H26**);
Pragmatic particles (**H**)
Speech genre see Bakhtin (**H**);
Metalinguistic awareness (**H**)
Spelling see Language acquisition (**H**); Orthography and cognition (**H22**);
Pragmatics of script (**H22**);
Psycholinguistics (**MT**); Social media research (**T**)
Spoken discourse → see Speaking vs. writing
Spoken language corpora
see Notation Systems in Spoken Language Corpora (**N**)
Sprachbund ('linguistic area')
see Contact linguistics (**MT**);
Language change (**H**);

Language contact (**H**);
Sociolinguistics (**MT**)
Stance (**H21**); *see also* Appraisal (**H**); Emotion display (**H**);
Evidentiality (**H22**)
Standard language
see Dialectology and geolinguistic dynamics (**T**)
Standardization
see Anderson (**H21**);
Authority (**H**); Integrational linguistics (**T**); Language dominance and minorization (**H**); Language policy, language planning and standardization (**H**);
Literacy (**H**)
State of Affairs see Predicates and predication (**H**)
State-space search see Artificial intelligence (**MT**)
Statistics (**MM**); *see also* Computational linguistics (**MT**); Corpus analysis (**MM**); Correlational sociolinguistics (**T**);
Experimentation (**MM**);
Regression analysis (**M**)
Stereotype see 'Other' representation (**H**)
Stigmatization see Caste and language (**H23**)
Story(-telling) see Conversational storytelling (**H24**);
Narrative (**H**)
Strategy see Impoliteness (**H**);
Nigerian hospital setting discourse (**H24**); Taʾārof (**H22**)
Strawson, P. F. see Analytical philosophy (**MT**);
Definiteness (**H**); Reference and descriptions (**H**)
Stress see Information structure (**H**); Prosody (**H**)
Stripping see Ellipsis (**H**)
Structuralism (**MT**); *see also* Autonomous vs. non-autonomous syntax (**MT**);
Benveniste (**H**);
Bourdieu (**H**); Componential analysis (**MT**); Corpus analysis (**MM**); Geneva school (**MT**);
Hermeneutics (**M**); Language change (**H**); Lexical field analysis (**MT**); Lexical semantics (**T**); Prague

school (**MT**); de Saussure (**H**); Semiotics (**MT**); Sign (**H**); Text and discourse linguistics (**T**)
Style see Communicative style (**H**); Creole linguistics (**MT**); Ellipsis (**H**); Ervin-Tripp, S. (**H24**); Figures of speech (**H**); Register (**H**)
Style and styling (**H21**); *see also* Crossing (**H26**)
Stylistic stratification see Social class and language (**H**)
Stylistics (**MT**); *see also* Communicative style (**H**); Emphasis (**H**); Figures of speech (**H**); Literary pragmatics (**MT**); Mathesius (**H**); Rhetoric (**MT**); Text and discourse linguistics (**T**); Text linguistics (**MT**)
Subject see Communicative dynamism (**H**)
Subjective relation see Legitimation Code Theory (**T25**)
Subjectivity see Benveniste (**H**); Énonciation (**H**); Foucault (**H**); Implicature and language change (**H**); Signed language pragmatics (**T**)
Substitution see Anaphora (**H**)
Superdiversity (**H21**); *see also* Code-switching and translanguaging (**H22**); Transience (**H22**); Translanguaging pedagogy (**T**)
Surveillance see Power and the role of language (**H25**)
Swearing (**H25**)
Syllable structure see Prosody (**H**)
Symbol see Jakobson (**H21**)
Symbolic behavior see Evolutionary pragmatics (**T**); Ta'ārof (**H22**)
Symbolic capital see Bourdieu (**H**); Social institutions (**H**)
Symbolic interactionism (**MT**); *see also* Bourdieu (**H**); Cognitive sociology (**MT**); Context and contextualization (**H**); Ethnomethodology (**MT**);

Goffman (**H**); Social psychology (**MT**)
Symbolic vs. subsymbolic architecture see Cognitive science (**MT**)
Symbolism see Morris (**H**)
Symbolization see Bühler (**H**); Cognitive grammar (**MT**)
Symmetry see Language change (**H**)
Synchrony see Iconicity (**H**); Non-verbal communication (**H**); Structuralism (**MT**)
Synergetics see Catastrophe theory (**MT**)
Synesthesia see Metaphor (**H**)
Syntax see Anaphora (**H**); Comprehension vs. production (**H**); Discourse markers (**H**); Ellipsis (**H**); Ervin-Tripp, S. (**H24**); Grice (**H**); Interactional linguistics (**T**); Language acquisition (**H**); Language change (**H**); Polysemy (**H**)
Systemic functional grammar (**MT**); *see also* Appraisal (**H**); Emphasis (**H**); Firth (**H**); Firthian linguistics (**MT**); Functional grammar (**MT**); Genre (**H**); Halliday (**H26**); Heteroglossia (**H26**); Metaphor (**H**); Multimodality (**H**)
systemic functional lingistics see Systemic functional grammar (**MT**)

T
Taboo see Obscenity, slurs, and taboo (**H24**); Swearing (**H25**)
Tact see Leech (**H**); Ọmọlúàbí (**H**); Politeness (**H**)
Tactile sign languages (**H21**)
Tagging see Corpus analysis (**MM**)
Tagmemics (**MT**)
Taxonomy (**MM**)
Ta'ārof (**H22**)
Teasing (**H25**)
Technology see Power and the role of language (**H25**)
Telephone conversation see Emotion display (**H**)

Television see Argumentation in discourse and grammar (**H**); Channel (**H**); Mass media (**H**)
Temporal reference see Narrative (**H**)
Tenor see Register (**H**)
Tense see Event representation (**H22**); Modality (**H**); Regression analysis (**M**); Tense and aspect (**H**)
Tense and aspect (**H**); *see also* Event representation (**H22**)
Tense logic see Modal logic (**MT**)
Terms of address (**H**); *see also* Honorifics (**H**)
Territoriality see Language rights (**H**)
Testimony see Epistemology of testimony (**T**); Interpreter-mediated interaction (**H**)
Testing see Text comprehension (**H**)
Text see Boas (**H**); Culture (**H**); Systemic functional grammar (**MT**)
Text analysis see Computational linguistics (**MT**); Text type (**H**)
Text and discourse linguistics (**T**); *see also* Common ground (**H**); Text linguistics (**MT**)
Text comprehension (**H**)
Text linguistics (**MT**); *see also* Critical Linguistics and Critical Discourse Analysis (**MT**); Prague school (**MT**); Stylistics (**MT**); Text and discourse linguistics (**T**); Translation studies (**T**)
Text structure (**H**); *see also* Narrative (**H**)
Text type (**H**); *see also* Genre (**H**); Pragmatic particles (**H**); Text and discourse linguistics (**T**); Think-aloud protocols (**M**)
Theme vs. rheme see Communicative dynamism (**H**); Functional grammar (**MT**); Word order (**H**)
Theory and theorizing see Firth (**H**); Grounded theory (**M**)
Theory of mind see Adaptability (**H**); Clinical

pragmatics (T);
Communication (H)
Therapeutic conversation (H)
Think-aloud protocols (M)
Thirdness see Morris (H)
Threat see Impoliteness (H)
Timing problem
see Neurolinguistics (MT); Neuropragmatics (T)
Topic management
see Laughter (H)
Topic vs. focus see Anaphora (H); Argumentation in discourse and grammar (H); Functional discourse grammar (T); Functional grammar (MT); Functional sentence perspective (H)
Topic-comment structure
see Computational pragmatics (T); Information structure (H); Signed language pragmatics (T); Word order (H)
Topicality see Argument structure (H23); Signed language pragmatics (T)
Toponym see Socio-onomastics (T)
Trajectory see Sequence (H)
Transcription see Grounded theory (M); Laughter (H); Phonetic notation systems (N)
Transcription systems for spoken discourse (MN); *see also* Conversation analysis (MT); Notation Systems in Spoken Language Corpora (N)
Transformational grammar →
see Generative(-transformational) linguistics
Transience (H22)
Transitivity see Event representation (H22); Grounding (H)
Translanguaging see Code-switching and translanguaging (H22); Crossing (H26); Heteroglossia (H26); Transience (H22);
Translanguaging pedagogy (T)
Translation see Interpreter-mediated interaction (H); Postcolonial pragmatics (T); Pragmatic particles (H); Think-aloud protocols (M); Translation studies (T)

Translation studies (T); *see also* Pragmatic markers (H)
Traumatic brain injury
see Clinical pragmatics (T)
Triangulation see Grounded theory (M)
Troubles talk
see Complaining (H25); Emotion display (H); Laughter (H)
Trust see Adaptability (H)
Truth see Austin (H); Euphemism (H24); Euphemism (H24); Grice (H); Ideology (H); Model-theoretic semantics (MT); Speech act theory (MT); Truthfulness (H)
Truth-conditional pragmatics (T); *see also* Default interpretations (H)
Truth-conditional semantics (MT); *see also* Analytical philosophy (MT); Logical semantics (MT); Possible worlds semantics (MT); Relevance theory (MT)
Truthfulness (H); *see also* Lexically triggered veridicality inferences (H22); Manipulation (H); Ọmọlúàbí (H)
Turing machine
see Computational linguistics (MT)
Turn(-taking) see Conversation analysis (MT); Embodied interaction (H23); Frame analysis (M); Intertextuality (H); Language and the law (H); Prosody (H); Silence (H); Tactile sign languages (H21)
Twitter see Social media research (T)
Typology (MT); *see also* Boas (H); Contact linguistics (MT); Deixis (H); Historical linguistics (MT); Language acquisition (H); Language change (H); Language contact (H); Negation (H); Sound symbolism (H); Universals (H23); Word order (H)

U
UN language system
see Language ecology (H)
Underspecification →
see Vagueness
Understanding
see Comprehension vs. production (H)
Unidirectionality see Language change (H)
Universal and transcendental pragmatics (MT); *see also* Critical theory (MT); Hermeneutics (M); Truthfulness (H)
Universal grammar see Language acquisition (H); Language change (H)
Universals (H23); *see also* Conversational logic (MT); Dialectology (MT); Humboldt (H); Jakobson (H21); Language acquisition (H); Sound symbolism (H); Speech act theory (MT); Typology (MT); Word order (H)
User modeling see Artificial intelligence (MT); Computational pragmatics (T)
Utterance see Predicates and predication (H); Speech act theory (MT)

V
Vagueness see Indeterminacy and negotiation (H); Polysemy (H); Tense and aspect (H); Truthfulness (H)
Valency → see Dependency
Variability → see Variation
Variable rule see Correlational sociolinguistics (T)
Variable, dependent/response vs independent/predicting
see Regression analysis (M)
Variable-rule analysis
see Statistics (MM)
Variation see Adaptability (H); Argument structure (H23); Bilingualism and multilingualism (H); Communicative style (H); Context and contextualization (H); Correlational sociolinguistics (T); Creole

linguistics (MT); Creoles and creolization (H); Dialectology (MT); Hegemony (H23); Honorifics (H); Humor (H23); Language acquisition (H); Language change (H); Language dominance and minorization (H); Language policy, language planning and standardization (H); Methods in language-attitudes research (M); Pluricentric languages (H23); Polysemy (H); Register (H); Regression analysis (M); Sociolinguistics (MT); Variational pragmatics (T)
Variational pragmatics (T); *see also* Contact linguistics (MT); Language change (H); Pluricentric languages (H23)
Variationist sociolinguistics see Correlational sociolinguistics (T); Youth language (H25)
Verb see Communicative dynamism (H); Taʾārof (H22)
Verba dicendi see Reported speech (H)
Verbal guise see Methods in language-attitudes research (M)
Veridicality see Lexically triggered veridicality inferences (H22)
Vernacular see Anderson (H21); Authenticity (H); Dialect (H)
Versioning see Working with language data (M25)
Verstehen → see Erklären vs. Verstehen

Vitality see Motivation (H)
Vocabulary see Borrowing (H); Language acquisition (H)
Voice see Polyphony (H)
Vološinov, V. N. see Bakhtin (H); Deconstruction (MM); Intertextuality (H); Marxist linguistics (MT); Reported speech (H)
Vygotsky, L. (H)

W
Wakimae (H26)
Web 2.0 see Social media research (T)
Weber, Max see Sociology of language (T)
WhatsApp see Social media research (T)
White-washing see Euphemism (H24)
Whorf, B. L. (H); *see also* Anthropological linguistics (MT); Boas (H); Culture (H); Iconicity (H); Sapir (H)
Whorfianism → see Linguistic relativity principle
Wittgenstein, L. (H); *see also* Analytical philosophy (MT); Austin (H); Contextualism (T); (The) pragmatic perspective (M); Speech act theory (MT)
Word (H)
Word order (H); *see also* Negation (H); Typology (MT)
Word recognition see The multilingual lexicon (H); Orthography and cognition (H22); Psycholinguistics (MT)
Word root see Orthography and cognition (H22)
Word-search see Gesture research (T)
Working with language data (M25); *see also* Conversation analysis (MT); Developmental psychology (MT); Grounded theory (M); Historical pragmatics (T); Linguistic landscape studies (T); Statistics (MM); Tactile sign languages (H21); Terms of address (H); Typology (MT)
Workplace interaction (H25); *see also* Aisatsu (H); Applied linguistics (MT)
Writing system see Identity (H24); Orthography and cognition (H22); Pragmatics of script (H22)
Written discourse → see Speaking vs. writing

X
X-bar syntax see Chomskyan linguistics (MT); Computational linguistics (MT); Role and reference grammar (MT)

Y
Youth language (H25); *see also* Crossing (H26)
Youtube see Social media research (T)